Inspiration, Perspiration, and Time

Operations and Achievement in Edison Schools

Brian P. Gill, Laura S. Hamilton, J.R. Lockwood,
Julie A. Marsh, Ron W. Zimmer, Deanna Hill,
Shana Pribesh

Prepared for Edison Schools, Inc.

RAND EDUCATION

The research described in this report was conducted by RAND Education for Edison Schools, Inc.

Library of Congress Cataloging-in-Publication Data

Inspiration, perspiration, and time : operations and achievement in Edison Schools / Brian P. Gill ... [et al.].
p. cm.
"MG-351."
Includes bibliographical references.
ISBN 0-8330-3824-9 (pbk. : alk. paper)
1. Edison Schools Inc. 2. Privatization in education—United States—Evaluation. 3. School management and organization—United States—Evaluation. I. Gill, Brian P., 1968–

LB2806.36.I575 2005
371.01'0973—dc22

2005018311

Cover Illustration by Nick Henderson

Published 2005 by the RAND Corporation
1776 Main Street, P.O. Box 2138, Santa Monica, CA 90407-2138
1200 South Hayes Street, Arlington, VA 22202-5050
201 North Craig Street, Suite 202, Pittsburgh, PA 15213-1516
RAND URL: http://www.rand.org/
To order RAND documents or to obtain additional information, contact
Distribution Services: Telephone: (310) 451-7002;
Fax: (310) 451-6915; Email: order@rand.org

Preface

Edison Schools, Inc., is the nation's largest educational management organization (EMO), operating 103 schools in 18 states and the District of Columbia in 2004–2005. Although EMOs are part of a growing trend toward alternative forms of governance of public schools, there is little empirical evidence about their effects to inform policy decisions.

In 2000, Edison contracted with the RAND Corporation to conduct a comprehensive evaluation of the performance of the schools it manages. This monograph is the final product of this multiyear evaluation. It examines Edison's strategies for improving schools, the implementation of these strategies in a sample of Edison schools across the United States, and the achievement trends attained by students in Edison schools.

This research has been conducted by RAND Education, a unit of the RAND Corporation, under a contract with Edison Schools, Inc. It is part of a larger body of RAND Education work addressing school reform, assessment and accountability, and teachers and teaching, and it fits into a recent body of work on school choice and charter schools.

Dedication

We dedicate this work to Tom Glennan, who was instrumental in launching the project and in helping to guide our theoretical framework. We wish he were here to see its conclusion. Tom was a nurturing mentor, an invaluable colleague, and a dear friend.

Contents

APPENDIX

Figures

Tables

Summary

New forms of governing and managing public schools have proliferated in recent years, spawning the establishment and growth of companies that operate public schools under contract. Among these education management organizations, or EMOs, the largest and most visible is Edison Schools, Inc., with a nationwide network in 2004–2005 of 103 managed schools, including preexisting schools contracted to Edison by districts and charter schools that Edison played a role in starting up. In 2004–2005, Edison served approximately 65,000 students in the schools it managed and tens of thousands of additional students through other initiatives. The entry of EMOs, many of which operate as for-profit companies, into the public education system has generated fierce debate, and Edison has been the focus of much of that debate. To date, however, there has been little empirical evidence regarding EMOs' effects on schools and students. In 2000, Edison asked the RAND Corporation to conduct a comprehensive analysis of its achievement outcomes and its design implementation. RAND designed an evaluation to address the following research questions:

- What are Edison's strategies for promoting student achievement in the schools it manages?
- How are Edison's strategies implemented in the schools it manages?
- How does Edison's management of schools affect student achievement?

- What factors explain differences in achievement trends among Edison schools?

Data Collection and Research Methods

We gathered data from multiple sources to address these research questions. Our examination of Edison's strategies relies on interviews with Edison staff at all levels of the organization, and on inspection of a variety of documents that Edison has produced over the years. To assess how Edison's design has been implemented in schools, we visited 23 Edison elementary schools across the United States. We selected schools that provide a range of school contexts and operating characteristics.

Our student achievement analysis was designed to be as comprehensive as possible and to examine achievement in currently operating as well as formerly operating Edison schools for which data were available. An ideal analysis would use longitudinal, student-level data, but those data were not available for most of the districts included in our analysis, so we relied on school-level data. We gathered school-level test scores in mathematics and reading from the state tests that serve as schools' primary measures of accountability. We obtained this information both for Edison schools and for matched comparison schools serving similar student populations in the districts and states in which the Edison schools are located.

Our first set of achievement analyses attempts to estimate the effect of Edison management on reading and mathematics achievement by examining longitudinal trends in average student proficiency levels. The second set of analyses uses both the school-level, systemwide achievement data and the case study data to identify factors that may explain differences in achievement among Edison schools.

Findings

Inspiration: Edison's Strategies for Promoting Student Achievement

Edison's strategies can be broadly classified into two categories: (1) providing resources in support of a coherent and comprehensive school design; and (2) implementing accountability systems that aim to ensure that the resources for the design are in place and used as intended. The resources that Edison seeks to provide to its schools begin with a curriculum that includes widely recognized programs in reading and math, along with science, social studies, foreign language, art, and music—a breadth that exemplifies Edison's aim of providing a "world-class" education to all students. Edison invests in a substantial amount of professional development for its principals and teachers, both centrally provided and school based. And it supports data-driven decisionmaking in schools with an online "Benchmark" system of monthly diagnostic tests in reading and math, which provides immediate feedback to teachers and principals.

In terms of accountability systems, Edison (like other EMOs) is distinct from other comprehensive reform models in having operational authority over the schools, including the power to hire and fire principals. At the same time, Edison is distinct from conventional school districts in its favored modes of accountability, relying more on outcomes-based and market-based systems and less on political and bureaucratic accountability. Edison seeks to insulate its schools from the negative aspects of bureaucracy and politics with the aim of focusing school staff attention on raising student achievement, managing budgets effectively, and implementing Edison curriculum and school design.

In sum, Edison distinguishes itself from most other school improvement strategies (e.g., school choice, high-stakes testing, comprehensive school reform, class-size reduction, teacher development) by addressing resources and accountability systems simultaneously, rather than focusing on one or the other. Together, the resources and accountability systems that constitute Edison's design represent a coherent, comprehensive, and ambitious strategy to address key elements relevant to providing high-quality education, including capacities, motivation, and opportunities for school staff. Edison's well-developed information systems and focus on achievement-based accountability should make it especially well suited to the high-stakes testing environment of No Child Left Behind (NCLB), the federal law that now demands improvement in student achievement in public schools across the country.

Perspiration: Implementation of Edison's Strategies in Schools

The comprehensive ambitions implicit in Edison's model suggest that successful implementation requires whole-hearted commitment—and hard work—from its clients and the staff in its schools. In fact, our case study analysis suggests that the best-functioning Edison schools demonstrate the promise inherent in Edison's model. They are schools with strong instructional leadership, motivated teachers, effective use of achievement data, high-fidelity implementation of the Edison curricula, and high levels of professional collaboration.

Nearly all of the Edison schools we visited across the country showed enough consistency of implementation to be clearly recognizable as Edison schools, but we observed considerable variation in the extent to which the schools realized the Edison ideal.

Among the 23 Edison schools we visited, several factors appear to be important in explaining some of the variation in implementation of the Edison model:

- Full implementation of the Edison design takes time—as might be expected in the implementation of a comprehensive, ambitious reform. Schools in the first year of operation had frequent challenges in implementing various elements of the design. Edison has been largely, but not entirely, successful in keeping its contracts long enough to ensure the opportunity for full implementation: Through spring 2005, 87 percent of Edison schools had remained under contract at least four years,[1] a record that appears to compare favorably to those of comprehensive reform

[1] This figure includes only schools that could have been under Edison management for at least four years, i.e., schools that initiated Edison management between 1995 and 2001.

models. Edison's charter schools have been somewhat more stable contractually than its district schools.
- Strong instructional leadership by principals is associated with stronger implementation of the curriculum, not only in high-stakes subjects (reading and math) but also in other areas of the curriculum such as science, social studies, art, and music.
- Among the case study schools, strong instructional leadership by principals appeared to be somewhat more prevalent in charter schools than in district schools. But charter status did not appear to affect curriculum implementation directly.
- Local constraints, sometimes resulting from compromises required by local contracts, undermine the implementation of Edison's preferred professional environment in some schools.

These findings bear out the importance of the sustained commitment of clients and school staff in promoting effective implementation of the Edison model.

Time: Effects of Edison Management on Student Achievement

Our analysis seeks to identify the effects of Edison management on student achievement by examining Edison's longitudinal trends in schoolwide test results. In absolute terms, Edison schools are showing gains in the proportion of their students achieving proficiency: From 2002 to 2004, average proficiency rates in currently operating Edison schools increased by 11 percentage points in reading and 17 percentage points in math. Meanwhile, average proficiency rates in a matched set of comparison schools serving similar student populations increased by lesser amounts, nine percentage points in reading and 13 percentage points in math (although the Edison advantage is statistically significant only in math).

The results for 2002–2004 provide incomplete information about Edison's effects because they do not include the full period of Edison management for most schools. Using spring of the first year under Edison management as a baseline for examining more complete achievement trends in Edison schools, both Edison schools and comparison schools show test-score gains, as indicated in Figures S.1

and S.2 (where results are indicated in standardized z-scores, because measures used to determine proficiency changed over time in many states). In the first three years of Edison management, gains for Edison schools in reading and math are similar to the gains of matched comparison schools. By their fourth year of operation, Edison schools demonstrate larger test-score gains than their comparison schools in both reading and mathematics, and they generally retain this relative advantage in later years.[2]

The improving trend is partly, but not entirely, attributable to the termination of the contracts of some low-performing Edison schools prior to Y4. A policy impact analysis that includes the terminated schools (during and after Edison management) alongside continuing Edison schools likewise shows an improving trend, with positive results in Y4 and beyond (although those results achieve statistical significance only in math). While the results of this analysis cannot be attributed entirely to Edison's management, they provide information that is useful for understanding what happens to all schools that are ever managed by Edison—a key question for clients and prospective clients, who need to consider effects on schools that discontinue their relationships with Edison as well as schools that remain under Edison management.

Because the tests used for baseline purposes are typically conducted in spring or late winter, trends from Y1 exclude most of the first year of operation of each Edison school and consequently might not accurately capture Edison's net long-term effects. We therefore also examine performance using a pre-Edison baseline (spring of the year before Edison began managing the school, which we label as year zero [Y0]). This baseline includes the entire period of Edison management, but its interpretation is complicated by the possibility that student populations may change when Edison takes over management. Moreover, it is not comprehensive in scope: Because a substan-

---

[2] As operation year increases, the number of Edison schools with data decreases (as indicated in the Edison sample sizes provided in the charts), so these figures should not be interpreted as depicting trends over time for a common set of schools.

Figure S.1
Z-Score Changes in Reading from Year-One (Y1) Baseline, Edison Schools and Matched Comparison Schools

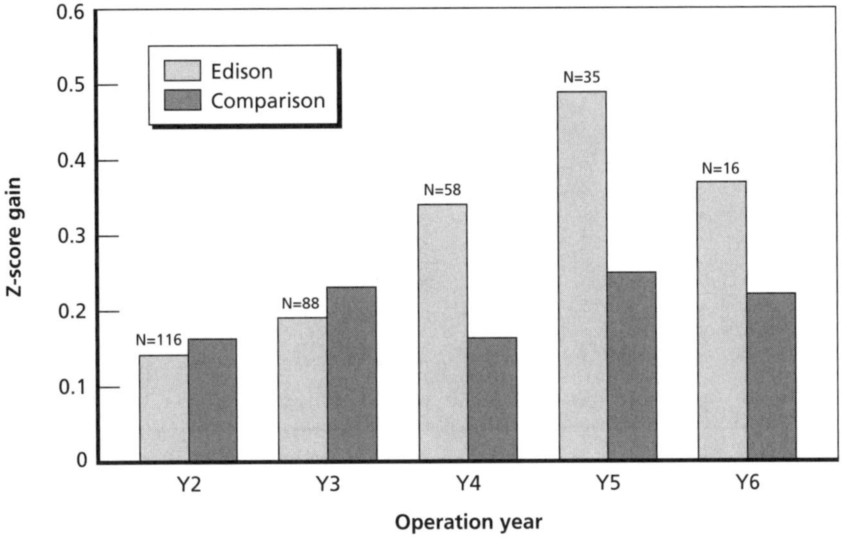

RAND *MG351-S.1*

tial number of Edison's schools (typically charter schools) were new start-ups that did not exist prior to Edison's management, this analysis includes only conversion schools (i.e., schools that existed prior to being managed by Edison), and in years one through three it is dominated by a large number of schools from only three districts (Chester, Pennsylvania; Philadelphia; and Dallas), so it does not accurately represent the range of Edison's clients.[3] Despite these limitations, the Y0 analysis provides the only available evidence on achievement results in the first year of Edison operation. Unlike the Y1 analysis, it is comprehensive in including the entire period of operation of each included Edison school.

---

[3] Sample sizes in the Y0 analysis are typically about half as large as sample sizes in the Y1 analysis; details are in Chapter Six.

Figure S.2
Z-Score Changes in Mathematics from Y1 Baseline, Edison Schools and Matched Comparison Schools

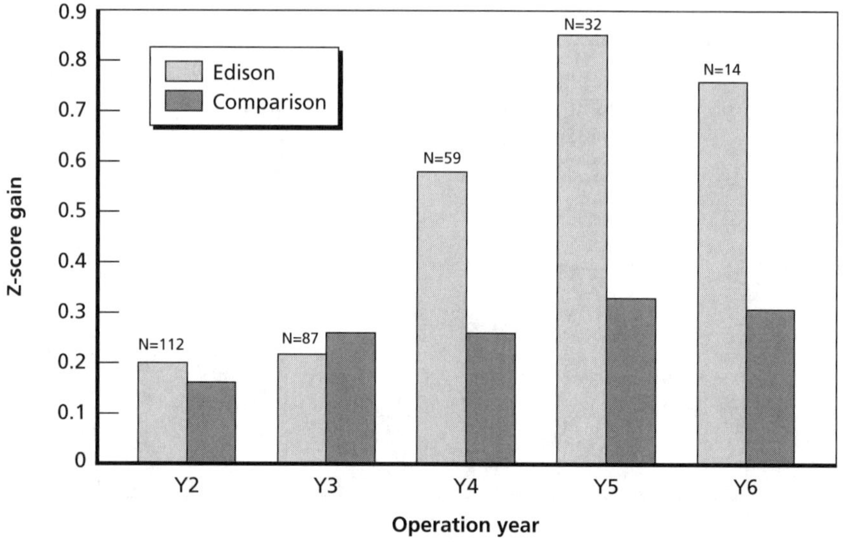

RAND *MG351-S.2*

Edison conversion schools show a decline in average proficiency rates between the pre-Edison year and the first year of Edison operation. Edison results relative to pre-Edison scores are therefore less favorable than they are relative to first-year scores. Edison conversion schools' test-score trends from the pre-Edison baseline fall short of the trends of comparison schools in the first three years of Edison management, in both reading and math, as indicated in Figures S.3 and S.4. As in the first-year baseline analysis, however, Edison results improve as schools gain experience implementing the Edison design. By year five (Y5), conversion schools that remain under Edison's management appear to catch up to comparison schools in reading and exceed the gains of comparison schools in math (although the sample is small

Figure S.3
Z-Score Changes in Reading from Y0 Baseline, Edison Conversion Schools and Matched Comparison Schools

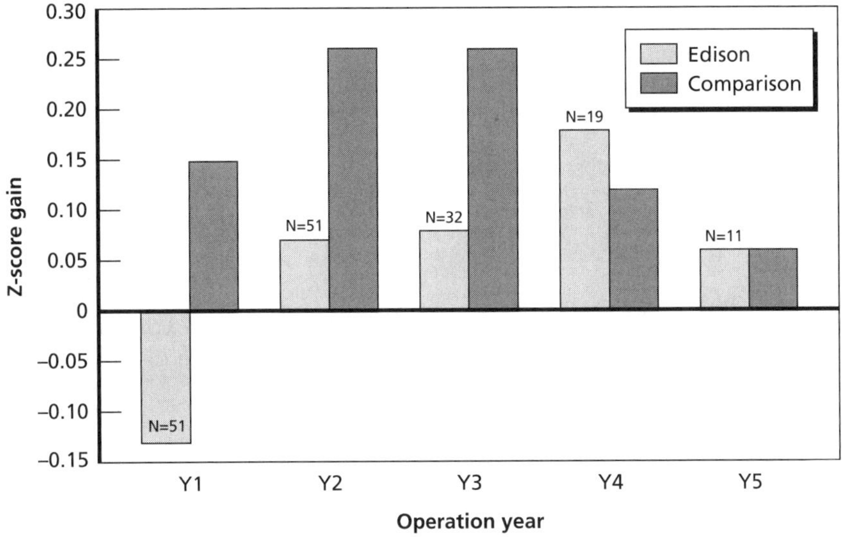

RAND *MG351-S.3*

and the favorable math results in Y5 are not statistically significant).[4] Again, a policy impact analysis that includes post-termination results as well as results for continuing Edison schools shows slightly less favorable estimates in years four and five, with gains that are statistically indistinguishable from those of comparison schools.

The out-year results from the Y0 baseline should be interpreted with considerable caution given the small number of schools involved: We have a fifth year of data from pre-Edison baselines for only 11 Edison schools. Moreover, those 11 schools experienced substantially larger first-year declines than did other Edison conversion schools—which, if current trends continue, may show better results by the time they reach Y5.

[4] Again, as operation year increases, the number of Edison schools with data decreases (as indicated in the Edison sample sizes provided in the charts), so these figures should not be interpreted as depicting trends over time for a common set of schools.

Figure S.4
Z-Score Changes in Mathematics from Pre-Edison Baseline, Edison Conversion Schools and Matched Comparison Schools

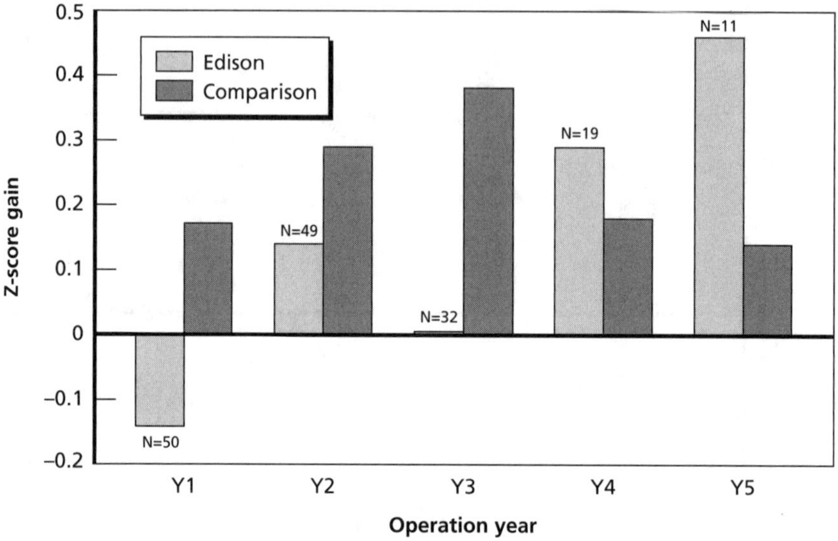

RAND *MG351-S.4*

Still, the first-year decline is apparent across the full range of Edison conversion schools (including 50 schools with data). In reading, Edison conversion schools' first-year deficit relative to comparison schools is approximately equivalent to the Edison schools' relative gain between years one and five. In math, Edison conversion schools' first-year deficit relative to comparison schools is approximately three-fifths as large as the Edison schools' relative gain between years one and five. Including the first year in the analysis substantially reduces our estimates of net long-term Edison effects in conversion schools. Whether the first-year decline occurs in start-up schools is unknowable, unfortunately, with school-level data.

In short, estimates of Edison's effects depend to some extent on the assumptions used in the analysis. Nevertheless, these varied results provide considerable guidance about the range of possible effects. In absolute terms, Edison schools are making gains: Average rates of proficiency in Edison schools improve as schools gain experience with

Edison. In relative terms, Edison schools also improve: On average, gains of Edison schools during the first three years of Edison operation do not exceed the gains of matched comparison schools, but Edison results improve in years four and five. Although the specific trajectories vary in different analyses, all analyses indicate that the performance of Edison schools improves as the schools gain experience with Edison.

Whether those improvements ultimately yield net positive effects is the key question. The positive long-term results from Y1 are comprehensive in their coverage of Edison schools but incomplete in their chronological coverage of Edison management. The results for Edison conversion schools from Y0—which are comprehensive in their chronological coverage of Edison management but incomplete in their coverage of Edison schools—suggest, by contrast, that the improving trends may be only enough to compensate for first-year declines, leaving the Edison conversion schools approximately on par with comparison schools after four or five years. We are therefore left with some uncertainty about whether gains of Edison schools after four or five years are comparable to or superior to those of matched comparison schools. Given this uncertainty, an examination of differences in achievement among Edison schools, and the factors that might explain those differences, is particularly important. We now turn to those differences.

Understanding Variation in Performance Among Edison Schools

The variation in the achievement trajectories of individual Edison schools is extensive, with some schools showing strong performance relative to comparison schools and others falling behind. In most years, achievement gains for Edison schools vary from approximately two standard deviations ahead of matched comparison schools to approximately two standard deviations behind matched comparison schools. These results correspond to differences on the order of plus or minus 30 percent of students achieving proficiency according to state standards. Some understanding of the factors that explain this variation among Edison schools is necessary for predicting how any particular Edison school (or prospective Edison school) might perform in the future.

We examined several factors that might be related to the variation in performance among Edison schools. First, we assessed whether there is any evidence that Edison is producing better results systemwide in recent years than it did in its early years of operating schools. This involved a comparison of test score trends in older and newer Edison schools using a common set of operation years. Schools that opened in 2000 or later showed slightly larger relative gains than those that opened earlier, but sample sizes were small and most of the pre- and post-2000 differences did not achieve statistical significance. Thus, there is some evidence that Edison's effectiveness as an organization might have improved over time, which may justify some optimism about the different overall trends discussed above.

To understand whether any of the variation in the performance of Edison schools could be explained by differences in the types of Edison schools examined, we compared achievement results for Edison's charter schools versus district schools, and elementary schools versus secondary schools. We observed some small differences in a few cases, but trends were generally consistent across categories of Edison schools.

Finally, we used findings from the case study schools to shed light on differences in achievement trajectories among Edison schools. Case study findings are not definitive, because the sample is small and relationships can be measured only in simple, correlational terms, but they are nevertheless suggestive. Among Edison case study schools, curriculum implementation, full implementation of the Edison professional environment, and principal instructional leadership are associated with higher achievement in both subjects. Moreover, implementation of the Edison curriculum in subjects other than reading and math (i.e., science, social studies, foreign language, and the arts) is correlated with stronger achievement results in reading and math, suggesting that schools need not neglect the broader aspects of the curriculum in order to achieve gains in basic skills. Finally, there is limited evidence that Edison schools that operate with fewer local constraints on the model, and where principals have full authority over hiring and firing teachers, may have better achievement trends. In particular, the challenges of the first year of Edison management in some instances appear to be at least partly attributable to local opposition to Edison.

Recommendations

This monograph aims not only to describe Edison's historical record in managing schools, but also to provide guidance to policymakers, clients, prospective clients, parents, and Edison staff about what to expect in the future and how to promote favorable outcomes in the future. The historical record provides considerable evidence that Edison's existing schools, on average, are likely to continue to improve, both in absolute terms (as measured by proficiency levels on state high-stakes tests) and relative to matched comparison schools. Most Edison schools have raised their students' achievement results as they have gained experience with Edison, and there is evidence that Edison's systemwide achievement trends have also improved in recent years.

Unfortunately, the data limitations described above render equivocal the historical evidence for Edison's *net* long-term effects. Predicting future long-term effects is therefore doubly challenging, subject not only to the inherent uncertainty of anticipating Edison's systemic performance over the next four to five years, but also to the ambiguity in Edison's historical long-term effects. In consequence, we cannot make strong predictions for prospective clients about whether they will achieve better long-term results with Edison or with an alternate approach. Nevertheless, Edison's improving trends are encouraging, and some schools have clearly done well under Edison management, making it clear that Edison is capable of producing favorable results.

Together, our achievement results and our case study observations suggest some actions that Edison and its clients can take to improve the likelihood of successful implementation. We present two sets of recommendations: one for Edison, and another for district staff and other policymakers considering hiring Edison.

Recommendations for Edison

1. Provide improved support and oversight during the first year. In conversion schools with pre-Edison achievement data, Edison's achievement results appear to be weakest in the first year of management, and the case study findings confirm that the first year is difficult. The challenges of the first year were apparent in start-up schools (typically charter schools) and conversion schools (typically district contract schools) alike. Edison provides extensive professional development during the first year as well as in subsequent years, but our interview participants told us they would benefit from additional, ongoing support throughout the first year.

2. Apply value-added assessment (VAA) methods to benchmark data. One of the strengths of Edison's design is its high-quality assessment system for helping principals and teachers track student progress. The benchmark assessments are used not only as a tool to help school staff improve their instruction, but also as a monitoring device to help Edison improve its oversight of and services to schools. To improve the utility of the benchmarks for this latter purpose, Edison should consider applying VAA methods to identify which schools and teachers have been most successful at improving the performance of individual students, and which appear to need more assistance in this regard.

3. Continue to promote a comprehensive vision of the curriculum. Although the achievement measures that are typically used to evaluate public schools focus heavily on mathematics and reading, our case study visits provide evidence that schools need not neglect other subjects in order to improve achievement in math and reading. The schools that had the best achievement results typically had strong implementation of the full range of Edison's broad curriculum.

4. Take further steps to ensure the development of principals' instructional leadership skills. Evidence from the case study schools suggests that principals' instructional leadership is directly related not only to effective implementation of Edison curricula but also to student achievement.

5. Avoid compromises to the design that may undermine the professional environment in the schools. The professional environment component of Edison's school design—its use of house teams, planning time, and on-site professional development—appears to be important, and there is suggestive evidence that its full implementation may contribute to better student achievement outcomes.

Recommendations for Clients and Prospective Clients

1. Manage the transition with care. The first year often presents challenges that hinder effective implementation of Edison's design, and Edison's achievement trajectories from pre-Edison baselines suggest that these challenges reduce early levels of student achievement in some schools. Our case studies suggest that some of those challenges (at least in conversion schools) are attributable to local opposition to Edison. District staff (or chartering authority staff, in the Edison schools that are chartered by organizations other than the local district) should work closely with Edison before and during the first year of Edison operation to reduce problems associated with the transition or start-up.

2. Give Edison full authority to implement its design. Implementation of the Edison design is stronger in schools where clients have imposed fewer constraints on Edison's operation. Moreover, Edison schools operating under more local constraints appear to have lower achievement gains. Edison's comprehensive approach to school management is designed on the assumption that all aspects of schooling need to be addressed in order to promote real reform. School districts that hire Edison should accept what the contracting model requires.

3. Ensure that teachers and principals support the model. Committed principals and teachers are critical for the effective implementation of the Edison design, and Edison schools should be staffed only with those educators who believe in the approach and want to work toward the goal of fully implementing the model.

4. Do not expect instant improvement. In today's high-stakes accountability environment, district and school staff typically face pressure to demonstrate immediate gains in student achievement. But reforming schools takes time. It is important that everyone involved in the decision to bring in a school management company understand that the desired results might not materialize for a few years.

5. Develop data systems that facilitate following individual students. Longitudinal, student-level data are essential for rigorous evaluation of Edison's effectiveness in individual schools and districts. Such data are not only useful for evaluations of large-scale programs like Edison, but would also be invaluable for districts that want to evaluate their own local initiatives. In addition to promoting better research and evaluation, this type of data system could be used as a resource for teachers and principals who want to use data to inform decisions about curriculum and instruction.

6. Carefully consider the incentives created by state and local accountability systems. All public schools are currently facing pressure under NCLB to increase proficiency levels on state achievement tests, and districts often impose their own accountability systems to supplement the state rules. Edison's accountability system creates additional incentives to raise test scores, but includes other elements of accountability as well. District staff need to understand the pressures facing schools and the extent to which the goals imposed on schools by the state, the district, and Edison are compatible with one another. If undesirable incentives are identified, districts can work to address them through training or through modification of their own approaches for motivating and rewarding school staff.

As the largest private manager of public schools, Edison's experiences provide a model to help policymakers and members of the public understand the benefits and limitations of nontraditional forms of school management. Interest in alternative management is likely to increase under NCLB as schools and districts that fail to meet their annual targets face some of the more severe sanctions of the law. Our analyses provide evidence regarding what can be expected when schools are turned over to Edison management, both in terms of how the program is implemented in schools and what happens to student achievement over time. Edison has a comprehensive and ambitious set of strategies for school improvement, encompassing both resources and accountability systems. Successful implementation of the Edison model requires a sustained commitment from clients and hard work from Edison's school staff, but there is evidence of an eventual benefit: Given sufficient time, achievement trends in Edison schools generally move upward, particularly when the model is faithfully implemented. Whether Edison's average achievement effects ultimately exceed those of comparison schools is not certain, but the Edison model is capable of producing positive effects: Our case study sample suggests that schools that effectively implement the wide-ranging Edison curriculum, that establish Edison's professional environment, and that operate with strong instructional leaders under limited constraints have positive achievement results. Given that Edison's results have not been uniformly positive, the findings of this monograph suggest some actions that Edison and its current and future clients can take to promote greater consistency of results, in terms of both implementation and student achievement.

Acknowledgments

The research reported here would not have been possible without the assistance of a large number of individuals. We are grateful to the principals, teachers, and other staff at the Edison schools we visited. They welcomed us warmly and gave us candid and extensive information about their practices and their experiences implementing the Edison design. We also wish to thank the large number of Edison central office staff who spoke to us, provided us with documents, and assisted us with data collection. We are especially indebted to John Chubb and Tung Le, who facilitated our access to meetings and staff and who provided timely and helpful feedback on our research throughout the course of the project.

Several RAND staff assisted with this work. Alex Rohozynsky helped gather and format the school-level data. Gina Ikemoto, James Padilla, Karen Ross, and Alice Wood assisted with various aspects of data collection and analysis. Natalie Weaver provided invaluable administrative assistance and helped with document production. We are also grateful to Lisa Price, who skillfully and promptly edited the document, and to Lynn Rubenfeld, who guided the document through the production process.

A number of RAND colleagues provided helpful substantive advice to the project as well as reviews of earlier drafts of the monograph, particularly Sue Bodilly, Sheila Kirby, Dan McCaffrey, and Brian Stecher. And the monograph was markedly improved through the thoughtful comments and suggestions of our external reviewers, Frederick Hess, Paul Hill, Henry Levin, and Patrick McEwan.

Acronyms

AFT	American Federation of Teachers
AIR	American Institutes for Research
AYP	adequate yearly progress
CCD	Common Core Data
CDF	cumulative distribution function
CEO	chief executive officer
DIBELS	Dynamic Indicators of Basic Early Literacy Skills
EMO	education management organization
ESL	English as a second language
FASST	Family and Student Support Team
FRL	free or reduced-price lunch
GAO	Government Accountability Office
GM	General Manager
K–x	kindergarten through x, where x is a school grade (fifth, sixth, eighth, or twelfth)
n	number
MIT	William E. McGee Institute of Technology
NCC	National Curriculum Coordinator
NCE	normal curve equivalent
NCES	National Center for Education Statistics
NCLB	No Child Left Behind

OLS	ordinary least squares
PD	professional development
PFT	Philadelphia Federation of Teachers
PLC	Principals' Leadership Conference
PSSA	Pennsylvania System of School Assessment
Qx	quarter in a year, where x is the quarter (one, two, three, or four)
RAPAH	Renaissance Academy of Pittsburgh, Alternative of Hope
SAP	school achievement plan
SES	supplemental educational services
SFA	Success for All
SRC	School Reform Commission
SRI	Scholastic Reading Inventory
TLI	Texas Learning Index
VAA	value-added assessment
WMU	Western Michigan University
Yx	year of operation, where x is the number of years of operation (zero, one, two, three, four, five, or six)

CHAPTER ONE
Introduction

Laura S. Hamilton and Brian P. Gill

Edison Schools, Inc. is the nation's largest private manager of public schools. During the 2004–2005 school year, approximately 65,000 students were enrolled in over 100 Edison schools in 18 states and the District of Columbia. Most of Edison's schools are operated under contract with local districts that have sought new management of schools, often because the schools have a long history of academic failure. Other Edison schools are brand-new start-ups, typically charter schools that Edison operates under contract with a local organization holding the charter. And Edison manages a few schools under contracts with states that have instituted takeovers as a result of chronic failure. Although a variety of other for-profit and nonprofit education management organizations (EMOs) now operate public schools, none have achieved the scale—or the public attention—that Edison has. In the context of a growing charter-school sector and No Child Left Behind (NCLB), which makes private management one of the remedies that can be applied to schools that repeatedly fail to meet state academic standards, EMOs may become increasingly prominent on the landscape of American kindergarten through grade 12 (K–12) schooling.

Purpose of This Study

Private operation of public schools has generated vigorous, often rancorous debate in the education policy and research communities, and

Edison has often found itself at the center of that debate. To date, however, there has been little empirical evidence to inform public opinion and policymaking with respect to EMOs. In 2000, RAND Education contracted with Edison to conduct a comprehensive evaluation of achievement in Edison schools, and to examine Edison's design and how it is implemented in schools. This monograph represents the final product of that evaluation. It is intended to help Edison evaluate its own progress and to inform policymakers, educators, and other members of the public who are interested in engaging with Edison in efforts to improve student achievement.

This evaluation was designed to be comprehensive, particularly with regard to the analysis of student achievement in Edison schools. Both RAND and Edison were interested not only in examining how student achievement has changed in Edison schools, but also in exploring the ways in which the Edison design is implemented in schools to understand how implementation varies and what barriers and facilitators influence implementation. Therefore, we designed a study to address the following research questions:

- What are Edison's strategies for promoting student achievement in the schools it manages?
- How are Edison's strategies implemented in schools it manages?
- How does Edison's management of schools affect student achievement?
- What factors explain differences in achievement trends among Edison schools?

By addressing questions regarding implementation and achievement, and by examining, where possible, the relationships between implementation and achievement, this study seeks not only to provide summary information about student performance in Edison schools, but also to explain some of the sources of differences in achievement trends among Edison schools. The findings should be of interest not only to those directly involved with Edison, but to anyone who is curious about the promise as well as the challenges of nontraditional forms of public school management.

In addition to conducting this evaluation, RAND has also assisted Edison with its own annual reports in the past three years. Each year, Edison publishes a report that summarizes student achievement in its schools and that also includes school-by-school test-score reports. For the fifth, sixth, and seventh annual reports (published in 2003, 2004, and 2005, respectively), RAND staff examined Edison's data and the report text. RAND staff provided Edison with comments on Edison's analysis and discussion of the data. In addition, where possible, RAND staff confirmed that the achievement data reported for Edison's schools were consistent with data from state sources or from test publishers. Similarly, RAND staff confirmed that the figures Edison reported for the states and districts where it works were consistent with publicly available data. This activity was conducted separately from the evaluation described in this monograph.

Data and Methods

Addressing these research questions required a variety of data-gathering methods and analytic strategies. We conducted several rounds of interviews with Edison staff at all levels of the organization, and examined documents to understand Edison's strategies for school improvement and how these strategies translate into a concrete set of design components. To examine implementation, we visited 23 Edison schools that were selected to provide a range of school contexts and student populations.

Our student achievement analysis relies primarily on school-level test scores in mathematics and reading. We focus on state tests, which are now the primary measures of accountability for Edison schools and for other public schools. We were primarily interested in understanding how well Edison schools are doing relative to other public schools that serve student populations similar to those enrolled in Edison schools. Therefore, our analytic approach relies on the use of comparison schools chosen from the districts and states in which the Edison schools are located. We compare the test-score trends of

Edison schools with those of comparison schools, and examine changes in achievement over time.

Our first set of achievement analyses was designed to examine recent changes in the performance of Edison schools and to estimate the total effect of Edison management on reading and mathematics achievement by calculating trends back to a baseline score and comparing the test-score changes in Edison schools with the changes attained by comparison schools. We then use both the school-level, systemwide achievement data and the case study data to examine differences in achievement trends for different types of Edison schools. Using the systemwide data, we compare trends for several categories of schools: (1) schools that opened recently versus schools that had been opened earlier; (2) charter versus district schools; and (3) elementary versus secondary schools. Our small sample of case studies, which provide rich data on implementation and local context, allows us to examine achievement variations in greater detail, though with a smaller degree of generalizability.

Limitations of This Study

There are several critical questions that this study does not address. In particular, we do not examine the costs of the Edison design or the ways in which financial resources are distributed and used in Edison schools. Such a study would be extremely valuable for evaluating the cost effectiveness of the Edison model, but obtaining the information to do this type of study would be time- and labor-intensive and was beyond the scope of our evaluation. Moreover, even for the questions we do address, the degree of confidence we can place in the results is limited by the quality of data available to us. Perhaps most notably, the fact that most of the achievement analyses rely on school-level data rather than on individual student-level data limits the inferences we can make, in particular with regard to the causal effects of Edison on student achievement. We also lack implementation data for most Edison schools and therefore cannot examine in detail the ways in which variations in implementation are related to student achievement across the entire Edison universe. Finally, although some Edison schools have been open for many years, most are still relatively new, and more time would be needed to understand Edison's long-term effects on student achievement.

How This Monograph Is Organized

The next chapter presents a brief history of Edison schools and summarizes the existing literature that is relevant to our evaluation. In Chapter Three, we describe Edison's strategies for school improvement and how they have been translated into a set of resources and accountability systems. Chapter Four presents the results of our implementation analyses in our case study schools. The achievement methodology and results are presented in the next three chapters. Chapter Five describes the data and statistical methods. Chapter Six presents the results of the analyses that address the first of our achievement-related research questions, and includes a discussion of the extent to which the findings can be interpreted as providing information about the overall causal effect of Edison management. In Chapter Seven we discuss our analyses of variation in achievement among different types of Edison schools. We conclude with a chapter that summarizes the findings and presents recommendations for Edison and for Edison's clients.

CHAPTER TWO

A Brief History of Edison Schools and a Review of Existing Literature

Julie A. Marsh, Ron W. Zimmer, Deanna Hill, and Brian P. Gill

This chapter presents background information that provides context for the analyses and findings discussed in subsequent chapters. First we describe the history and growth of Edison as an organization, and then we review the small body of existing research literature that has examined Edison schools.

Emergence of Private Educational Management Organizations

Private firms, both for-profit and nonprofit, have long maintained contractual relationships with public schools in the United States. Historically, such contractual relationships were often limited to the provision of materials, such as textbooks and testing materials, or support services, such as transportation and food services (Hentschke, Oschman, and Snell, 2003). Although some firms provided educational services, they did so through contractual relationships with multiple school districts, and then only for particular students (e.g., students with special educational or behavioral needs) (Hentschke, Oschman, and Snell, 2003) or for specialized programs. In recent years, however, several firms have expanded their contractual relationships with public schools to include the management and day-to-day operations of entire schools. Commonly referred to as EMOs, these firms—many of which are operated for profit—provide comprehensive educational services to all students in a host of district contract schools, charter schools, and public schools taken over by the state.

In the past two decades, the EMO industry has experienced tremendous growth (Hentschke, Oschman, and Snell, 2003; Miron and Applegate, 2000). Many factors have supported this growth, most notably the proliferation of charter school legislation as well as accountability policies giving school districts the option, and in some cases, the mandate to contract out services for low-performing schools. Indeed, EMO management of public schools may continue to grow in the future, because the federal No Child Left Behind (NCLB) Act of 2001 includes private management as one of the strategies that school districts may use to improve chronically low-performing schools. In 2004–2005, more than 50 for-profit EMOs operated 535 schools across the country (Molnar, Garcia et al., 2005). The largest of these EMOs is Edison Schools, Inc.

History of Edison Schools

As one of the oldest EMOs in the country, Edison has spent more than a decade building its organization and system of schools—a history marked by significant "ups and downs" (Chubb, 2004, p. 489). In 1991, Christopher Whittle, founder of Whittle Communications and Channel One News service for schools, launched the Edison project (renamed Edison Schools, Inc. in 1999). His goal was to "reshape education in America by providing state-of-the-art schools to communities nationwide and a state-of-the-art example for others to follow" (Henriques, 2003, p. C3). Whittle's vision was to apply business concepts and best practices—such as economies of scale, research and development, and efficiency—to public education and to operate 1,000 for-profit schools one decade later (Chubb, 2004, p. 487). Whittle believed Edison could make a profit at the same time that it was dramatically improving academic outcomes for the students it served; it aimed to offer a "world-class" education to all of its students, at no greater cost than current expenditures in conventional public schools. In short, Edison was founded with the goal of realizing a classic American entrepreneurial ambition: to do well while doing good.

In order to actualize his vision, Whittle raised tens of millions of dollars in private capital and hired a team of business, technology, and education experts to develop a school design and an implementation strategy. In 1992, he recruited then-president of Yale University, Benno Schmidt, to lead this research and development effort. Over the next three years, the Edison team developed a comprehensive school design that it regarded as exemplifying the best ideas from both education and business about curriculum, teaching methods, assessment, educational technology, staff development, and management (see Chapter Three for further details on design).

Initially, Edison planned to employ its design in a nationwide network of private schools. When large-scale, publicly funded voucher programs failed to materialize, however, Edison modified its strategy to follow the money: It would contract with school districts, charter-authorizing agencies, and charter holders to manage new and existing schools with this new design. Under these contracts, Edison would operate all aspects of the school, including curriculum, instruction, budgeting, hiring and firing, and staff development. The company would receive the same total average per-pupil funds available to local districts and "invest its capital up front on all new instructional materials, technology, and training to give the school a fresh start" (Chubb, 2004, p. 488). Edison never promised to save its clients money in educating students—its sales pitch claimed that, for the same money,[1] it would achieve better academic results. The company hoped that, over a five-year period, the initial investments would pay off in terms of improved student achievement and that, with efficient management and rapid growth, the company would earn a profit.

In 1995, Edison opened its first four schools, in Boston, Massachusetts; Wichita, Kansas; Mt. Clemens, Michigan; and Sherman,

---

[1] The assumption that Edison's services would not cost districts extra money depended on the notion that districts could save the portion of expenses attributable to district-wide spending, since Edison would be paid the full per-pupil average cost, including the share that would normally support district administration.

Texas. For the next five years, the company experienced rapid growth, opening 58 new schools from 1996 to 1999.

In November 1999, Edison became a publicly traded company. With an initial public offering price of $18 a share, the stock increased in value to more than $38 in early 2001. With the influx of additional capital from the stock offering, Edison's expansion continued apace. Starting in 2000, the company's growth became more concentrated in large contracts to manage multiple schools in individual districts. For instance, in 2000, Edison began operating seven schools in Dallas under a district contract, three schools in Baltimore under a contract with the state, and all four of the public schools in Inkster, Michigan, after the state threatened to take over if significant improvements—both academic and fiscal—were not made (Michigan Education Digest, 2001). A year later, in 2001, Edison took over the management of seven schools in Las Vegas and the majority of schools (six of ten) that the state took over in the Chester-Upland school district in Pennsylvania. The company was soon managing nine of ten schools in Chester after it merged with LearnNow, Inc., a smaller EMO.

During this period of rapid growth, Edison leaders discovered that they "needed systems" to better support school design and implementation across a large number of schools (interview with Edison executive, June 13, 2002). Having spent much of the early history developing and refining the school design, Edison leaders built up new systems to better support and monitor operations and achievement. Many of these systems are described in Chapter Three.

In 2002, Edison's expansion slowed down and the company faced what Edison leaders characterized as "a perfect storm" (Whittle, quoted in Walsh, 2002) and "a near-death experience" (Schmidt, quoted in Henriques, 2003, p. C1). *The New York Times* described the year as "one of compounding horrors for the company, for its shareholders and for H. Christopher Whittle, Edison's controversial founder and chief executive" (Schmidt, quoted in Henriques, 2003, p. C1). In early 2002, a complaint was filed over Edison's accounting practices with the Securities and Exchange Commission. Although later settled, the action prompted a series of class-action lawsuits by

Edison shareholders. These moves sparked declines in the company's share price (closing at $5.13 at the end of April 2002) and damaged investor confidence as well as the company's public image. At the same time, Edison waged a highly publicized political battle to put in place its largest single contract ever in Philadelphia.

Edison's involvement in Philadelphia began in the fall of 2001, when Pennsylvania governor Tom Ridge awarded Edison a $2.7 million no-bid emergency contract to evaluate the district and to make recommendations for improvement. In October 2001, Edison released its report on Philadelphia, finding the district to be facing "grave academic and fiscal crises" (Edison Schools, 2001b, p. 1). Edison recommended, as one of several options, that the district hire a private firm to take over its central management and operations of numerous low-performing schools (Edison Schools, 2001b). The following day, the new governor, Mark Schweiker (who had taken over for Ridge when he accepted the post of U.S. Director of Homeland Security), proposed the state take over the district and turn over its central management to Edison.

In response to Edison's anticipated involvement in Philadelphia, various interest groups, school personnel, taxpayers, concerned citizens, parents, and students waged public protests throughout the city. In the most dramatic show of protest, the city council filed a lawsuit to stop the state takeover and the Philadelphia Federation of Teachers (PFT) and others filed a lawsuit to stop Edison from benefiting from any such state takeover. Both lawsuits, while politically damaging, proved unsuccessful in the courts.

In December 2001, the state took over the district. By February 2002, a seven-member School Reform Commission (SRC) had been appointed and was poised to hire a new district leader. In June 2002, the SRC hired Paul Vallas, the well-respected former Chicago public schools chief executive officer (CEO) (1995–2001). Vallas denied Edison the central management role and, instead, approved contracts for Edison to run just 20 of 45 low-performing schools turned over to private firms. The remaining 25 schools were split between four other EMOs and two local universities.

The political turmoil in Philadelphia further damaged investor confidence. Company stock was downgraded almost immediately after the announcement that Edison would manage only 20 schools, triggering a sell-off. By October 2002, Edison stock was trading as low as 14 cents per share. Edison leaders were equally rattled by these events. In a 2003 interview, Whittle (2003) commented, "A decade of work kind of went up in smoke. For me to sit here and say that the loss of my entire net worth was not bothersome? . . . Yeah. It hurt."

By 2004, however, the political environment had calmed for Edison, in Philadelphia and elsewhere. Student gains on the terra nova had CEO Vallas "singing Edison's praises" (Snyder, 2004, p. B01) and the SRC chairman touting "the promise of the partnership management model." Further, gains on the Pennsylvania state assessments had district and Edison officials celebrating side by side as they publicly announced the results (Gewertz, 2004, p. 6). In an Edison press release (2004a), Vallas praised Edison for its willingness to take on 20 of the most difficult schools and for clearly demonstrating "their ability to take on this challenge and make a critical contribution throughout a period of transformation."

Meanwhile, Edison launched a series of new strategies to bolster public and investor confidence. First, the company decreased its growth targets. In contrast to its historic strategy of building economies of scale based on rapid growth, Edison decided to slow down the number of new schools it opened each year (Molnar, Wilson, and Allen, 2004). In 2003–2004, Edison had its first-ever net decline in the number of schools managed, with only three new schools opening and 25 schools ending relationships with Edison. As of 2004–2005, 103 schools were operating under Edison management (Figure 2.1 charts the number of Edison schools under contract in each academic

Figure 2.1
Number of Schools Managed by Edison, 1995–2005

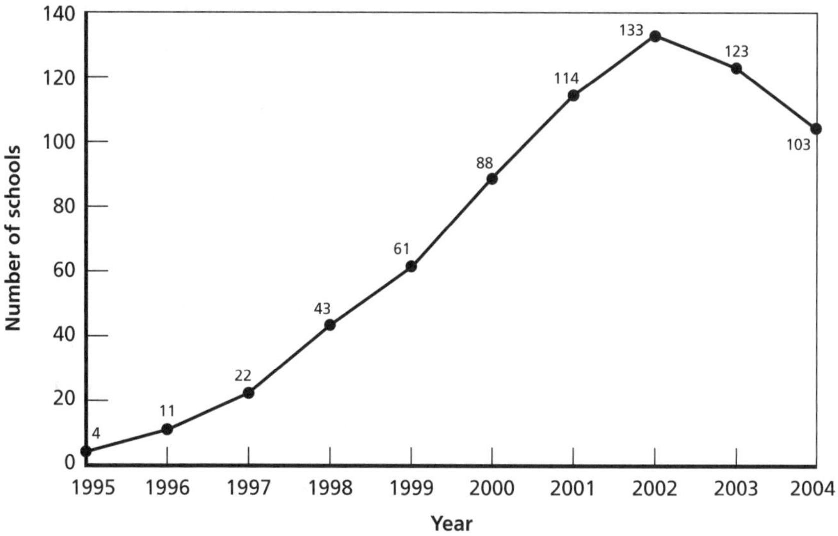

RAND *MG351-2.1*

year since the first schools opened in 1995).[2] Leaders also overhauled management—laying off 15 percent of the staff in its New York headquarters (Gewertz, 2002)—and ended some of its unprofitable contracts. And in July 2003, Edison was removed from publicly traded status and returned to private ownership—permitting a welcome retreat from the public eye.

While Edison continued to refine its system-level support (described in Chapter Three) for the schools it manages, it also diversified the portfolio of services it offers. In addition to its whole-school management partnerships with school districts and charter authorizing agencies, the company currently offers and supports the following business channels:

---

[2] Here we count schools in the conventional way: Regardless of the number of grades served, each school with a single principal and (typically) a single site counts as one school. Later, in the achievement analysis, it becomes necessary to divide some schools with unusually wide grade configurations (e.g., K–8, K–12) into separate units corresponding to elementary, middle, or high schools, to be able to find appropriate matched comparison schools.

- **Tungsten Learning**, offering "achievement management solutions" for schools and school systems, including the interim benchmark assessment system, school-based server technology, and technical assistance with data. Tungsten Learning partnerships were serving 81,000 students in 230 schools and ten states in 2004–2005 (Edison Schools, 2005).
- **Edison Schools UK**, offering comprehensive school improvement programs to schools in the United Kingdom. This partnership currently involves 20 clients across the United Kingdom (Edison Schools, 2005).
- **Newton Learning**, offering summer and after-school programs to school districts. Summer school programs currently operate in more than 80 districts in California, Missouri, and New York; after-school services have been launched in ten districts across California and Missouri (Edison Schools, 2005).
- **Newton Learning supplemental educational services (SES) partnerships**, providing schools that are identified for improvement under the federal No Child Left Behind (NCLB) Act with on-site, SES supported by Title I funds. Newton Learning is an approved SES provider in 37 states, with operating programs serving 45,000 students in 17 states in 2004–2005 (Edison Schools, 2005).
- **Edison Alliance**, offering customized achievement programs designed to assist schools and districts in improving achievement and meeting adequate yearly progress (AYP) targets. Alliance currently (2004–2005) consults with two districts in South Carolina, providing services to 4,700 students in 13 schools (Edison Schools, 2005).

In sum, in a decade of operating schools, Edison has gone from spectacular growth to spectacular controversy and retrenchment, but has thus far survived the turmoil. Widespread predictions in 2002 and 2003 of Edison's impending demise (e.g., the 2003 Frontline documentary on Edison schools described it as "a fragile company with a fading vision") proved inaccurate, although the number of schools under Edison management has declined. Whether Edison's core business in managed schools will grow, or whether it will increasingly rely on its other business streams, is yet to be seen.

Number and Types of Schools

Counting only the schools for which Edison has whole-school management contracts, Edison has operated 144 schools throughout its history (through 2004–2005). Of those 144 schools, 87 (60 percent) have been district contract schools while 57 (40 percent) have been charter schools. The number of Edison schools in operation in each year since 1995 is charted in Figure 2.1. In 2004–2005, Edison operated 103 schools in 18 states and the District of Columbia. Of these schools, 45 (44 percent) were charter schools and 58 (56 percent) were district schools. In 2004–2005, 76 percent (78) of the schools Edison operated were elementary schools.

Review of the Literature on Edison Schools

Although various studies have examined Edison schools over the past decade, research findings appear to have had little influence on Edison's political or economic fortunes. This is perhaps appropriate, because none of the existing studies have produced results that are both comprehensive and methodologically persuasive. Most studies have lacked sufficient data to permit rigorous analysis, and the few that have had access to high-quality student achievement data have encompassed too few Edison schools to be useful for generalizing to Edison as a whole (see GAO, 2002).

Some studies have examined Edison as part of a larger examination of privatization or charter schools. For instance, the Government Accountability Office (2003) conducted an analysis of privately managed public schools, including Edison schools, in which it compared the performance of students in privately managed schools with that of students in a matched set of conventional public schools[3] in six major

[3] Comparison schools were matched based on school size, grade arrangements, and student characteristics, including demographic and socioeconomic characteristics.

urban districts using both cross-sectional and longitudinal analyses and found mixed achievement results in privately managed schools across the districts. Not enough Edison schools were included, however, to form a general conclusion about Edison's performance.

Other studies have focused specifically on the performance of Edison schools. A major contributor to this literature has been Edison's self-evaluations. As part of its operation, Edison has produced annual reports of performance for the schools being managed by Edison that year (Edison Schools, 1997, 1999, 2000, 2001a, 2003, 2004b, 2005).[4] Initially, Edison reported the achievement gains of its schools without comparison groups, but beginning in 2003, Edison began comparing its schools to a demographically matched sample of non-Edison schools within the same districts. In 2003, these matches were created using baseline data from the first year of Edison management (Edison Schools, 2003). Edison found that the annualized gains of its schools from 1995 through 2002 were higher than the annualized gains for demographically similar schools over the same time frame. In the last two annual reports (Edison Schools, 2004b; Edison Schools, 2005), Edison compared recent gains of its schools relative to a demographically matched set of schools within the same school districts.[5] Edison found that its schools outgained the comparison schools by more than three percentage points from 2002 to 2003 and by more than six percentage points from 2001 to 2003. Our own analysis examines Edison achievement in recent years and from the beginning of each school's Edison operation; in Chapters

[4] Edison reports have also addressed four other performance areas: customer satisfaction, implementation, financial management, and system growth (Edison Schools, 1997).

[5] Based on the most recent year of data available, Edison created within-district matches of schools within plus or minus ten percentage points of the Edison school's percentages of free or reduced-price lunch students and African-American or Hispanic students. If no schools matched both restrictions, Edison matched schools based on one of the two restrictions, while limiting the second one to within 30 percent. In total, this process created 390 matched schools to 63 Edison sites. The remaining 56 Edison sites were not included in the analysis because no data were available to create the matches or the site only had baseline data at this point.

Six and Seven, we present results and discuss the interpretations and limitations of each of these methods.

In addition to Edison's own annual reports, there have been a limited number of external evaluations, including studies by Western Michigan University (WMU), the American Federation of Teachers (AFT), and Caroline Hoxby of Harvard University. WMU examined the performance of ten Edison schools that had been operating at least four years, which the researchers argued is sufficient time for Edison schools to overcome any transitional issues (Miron and Applegate, 2000). The researchers first compared the performance of individual Edison students over time compared with national norms on standardized tests, which suggested that Edison students were improving from year to year at a rate that was consistent with grade-level advancement. The analysis also compared school-level criterion-referenced test scores[6] of consecutive cohorts of students in ten Edison schools relative to schools in their surrounding school district as well as within their states. Using these comparisons, Edison schools, in the majority of cases, lagged behind their comparison schools.[7] But only ten Edison schools were included in the study, and the data are now at least five years old.

The AFT has released a series of reports (1998; Nelson, 2000; Nelson and Van Meter, 2003) since the inception of Edison schools and has relied primarily upon school-level data across states in which Edison schools operate. The 1998 and 2000 reports found Edison schools generally perform on par with or worse than comparison schools and only occasionally do better, but these studies included only a limited number of then-operating Edison schools. The most recent AFT report used a 2000–2001 national database of school-level ethnic and socioeconomic composition as well as test scores that

[6] These criterion-referenced tests were different for each state.

[7] WMU researchers Horn and Miron (2000) also examined the performance of Edison charter schools in Michigan as part of a larger statewide evaluation of charter schools and reached similar conclusions. In this evaluation, the researchers compared the percentage of students earning a passing grade on achievement tests in individual charter schools and in noncharter schools within the same district.

included a larger sample of Edison schools. Using these data, the researchers compared the performance of Edison schools to schools with a similar proportion of low-income students within the same states.[8] Overall, each of 80 Edison schools was compared on average to 40 non-Edison schools. In general, the report suggested that Edison schools are performing poorly, especially in the early years, but some Edison schools show improvement over time. Edison schools with a high concentration of African-American students were more likely to improve their ranking among comparison schools in math.

Hoxby and Rockoff (2004), in contrast, found favorable results for Edison in a cross-sectional comparison of the performance of Edison schools to a matched sample of non-Edison schools within the same districts. To create the matched sample, Hoxby used a propensity score approach in which schools were matched based on the statistical probability of being an Edison school given the demographic characteristics of the individual school. Using school-level outcomes and controlling for school-level aggregates of student characteristics in a regression analysis, Hoxby found that Edison schools had average proficiency levels about two percent higher than the matched set of schools. It is not clear from the report which Edison schools were included in this analysis.

Several reports have examined subsets of Edison schools operating in individual districts. Two reports that have used student-level data, examined longitudinally over time, have been conducted by Miami-Dade and Dallas independent school districts.[9]

---

[8] Their analysis varied state to state, and in some states the analysis was longitudinal. For instance, in California, all schools are evaluated from 1998–1999 to 2000–2001, no matter what year the school started. In only one case (Edison Bethune) was the 1998–1999 school year prior to the year Edison started. In other states, the time frame varied from school to school, but generally, did not use pre-Edison test scores to see improvement before and after Edison's "treatment."

[9] Studies have also been conducted of Minneapolis and Wichita Edison schools (Minneapolis Public Schools, 2000; Wichita State University, 1996). Hoxby (2003) analyzed three charter schools, including one Edison school using a randomized design with student-level data in Chicago. However, she did not examine the effect of the Edison schools separately from the rest of the charter schools. Overall, she generally found positive effects for the charter schools.

Capitalizing on the student-level data, Miami-Dade (Gomez and Shay, 2000) used a "value-added" approach to measure the performance of students over a three-year period using test scores for individual students. The study design compared the performance over a three-year period of students in the one Edison school in Miami to a random sample of students drawn from the district in the same grade, socioeconomic status, ethnicity, and achievement levels, as measured by a pre-Edison test score. Using two different analytical approaches, the study found that despite a disappointing performance in year one (Y1), Edison students, by year three (Y3), were progressing at similar rates to conventional public school students. The authors acknowledge that their analysis has limited implications because it is of a single elementary school serving low-income African-American students in Miami.

The Dallas evaluation examined seven elementary schools over a two-year period (Dryden, 2004). Each Edison school was matched to non-Edison schools within the district based on prior reading achievement, proportion of students receiving free or reduced-price lunch, proportion of students in special education, proportion of students in bilingual and English as a second language (ESL) programs, proportion of students in gifted and talented programs, proportion of white and black students, school size, and school climate variables. Once schools were selected, continuously enrolled Edison students[10] were matched to non-Edison students from the pool of matched schools based on grade level, prior achievement, similar school cluster identification, free and reduced-lunch status, bilingual and ESL status, special education status, talented and gifted status, race, and gender.[11] From the matched sample of schools and students, the author compared the performance of Edison students to non-Edison students over time and found that the Edison schools are neither

---

[10] Continuously enrolled Edison students were students who remained at the same school from the end of the first six-week grading period during Y1 to the time of testing at the end of year two (Y2).

[11] Not all Edison students were matched based on the full range of characteristics and some criteria had to be dropped for individual students.

meeting nor exceeding the performance of comparison students from comparison schools. However, the author noted that the evaluation examined only a two-year period, which may not be sufficient time to implement Edison's design, and that Edison schools faced a tenuous political climate in Dallas.

Analysis of Reform Implementation

There is a large and growing literature that has examined implementation of reform efforts which suggests that myriad factors can affect the implementation, including whether there is teacher or school buy-in (Bodilly and Berends, 1999; Ross, et al., 1997; Smith et al., 1997), district support (Spillane, 1996), teacher union support (Timar, 1989), school autonomy (Bodilly, 1996; Haynes, 1998), community support (Newmann and Wehlage, 1995), and sufficient resources (Wehlage, Smith, and Lipman, 1992). Like comprehensive school reform models, Edison incorporates a broad set of services that are intended to be implemented at all of its schools. These services include a comprehensive curriculum package, enrichment programs such as foreign languages and art, instructional techniques, frequent assessments, professional development, extended school day and year, career ladders for teachers, and technology. Unlike many of the comprehensive school reform models discussed above, little research has examined the level of implementation of Edison school design.

The GAO (2002) examined the implementation of three different for-profit management organizations, including Edison, within the District of Columbia, relying primarily on interviews with company officials, officials of the district's oversight authority, and representatives of the schools. The GAO concluded that four of the six Edison schools were completely implementing the Edison design.

Two other studies provided a more thorough evaluation of Edison implementation in a single school: the Miami-Dade school district (Gomez and Shay, 2000) and the University of Maryland's Lauren Morando Rhim (2002) both conducted in-depth studies of an individual Edison school.[12] In the Miami-Dade evaluation, the research team examined school documents, surveyed teachers, interviewed the school principal, and conducted classroom observations across a three-year time period in Henry E.S. Reeves Elementary School. The analysis generally revealed that the Edison design was well implemented. It also provided some evidence that implementation varied by year, growing stronger as the school remained under Edison's management over time.

Rhim (2002) conducted 61 interviews with teachers, administrators, support staff, charter board members, parents, and state officials for in-depth analysis of one (unnamed) Edison school. Rhim found that Edison was able to implement some aspects of its strategies, but not others. Specifically, she found that "Edison struggled to implement its ideals for a rich and challenging curriculum, purposeful instruction, assessments that provides accountability, teachers who are professionals, integrated technology, and a partnership with families. Aspects of its model that Edison was able to implement with greater uniformity include: operating an extended school day and extended school year; providing a structured curriculum; and arranging for teachers to have daily professional development periods" (p. 10). Rhim also noted that the rigorous demands required by the Edison design promote a high level of teacher turnover, and perpetuate the challenge of implementing the model.

Cookson, Embree, and Fahey (2000) examined the academic climate and classroom culture of Edison schools, which is indirectly related to implementation. They visited six schools located in Colorado, California, and Michigan and found that Edison is generally effective in implementing its design. Specifically, the report noted that investment in professional development led to higher teacher morale and that teachers are enthusiastic about the curriculum. How-

---

[12] AFT (1998), while not focusing on implementation, noted that some Edison schools more fully implement the Success for All (SFA) reading program than others. For instance, they highlighted that the Wichita Edison schools had the prescribed number of certified SFA tutors, while Edison's Miami school did not. They hypothesized that this was the reason they found stronger performance in the Wichita schools relative to the Miami school.

ever, they note that there is a high level of teacher burnout due to the stress of longer school days and years, and that Edison's relationships with unions have been problematic.

In the next chapter, we describe the results of our investigation of Edison's strategies for managing schools, and then turn to our analyses of implementation and achievement in subsequent chapters.

CHAPTER THREE

Inspiration: Edison's Strategies for "World-Class" Education

Brian P. Gill, Julie A. Marsh, Deanna Hill, Laura S. Hamilton, and Shana Pribesh

The stated educational aim of Edison's school-management business is the provision of "world-class education" to all of its students. Edison has defined a "world-class" education as one that "cultivates the mind to be ready for opportunities of every kind" in a rapidly changing world (Edison Schools, undated Web page [e]). In Edison's view, this means that its students should have access to the breadth of content—including art, music, and foreign languages beginning in the primary grades of elementary school—that is available to students of elite independent private schools. Edison also defines the critical primary measure of "world-class" education, however, to be proficiency on annual state high-stakes assessments in reading and math (and additional subjects in some states). A focus on measurable progress on high-stakes tests has been a central characteristic of Edison since it opened its first schools a decade ago. As a matter of corporate policy, Edison welcomed and endorsed the aims of the federal No Child Left Behind Act; its passage served to reinforce Edison's prior attention to student outcomes as a key means of accountability.

In the service of "world-class" education, Edison has devised a range of strategies to promote in its teachers and principals not only the capacity to deliver high-quality instruction, but also the motivation and opportunity to do so. The attention to all three of these components—capacity, motivation, and opportunity—makes Edison's strategies for student achievement unusually comprehensive. In Edison's view, "to change schools thoroughly, it is essential to change everything at once. Incremental reforms are too easily undone by those elements of the school that have not yet been changed. When everything changes at once, there are fewer old habits to break" (Edison Schools, 2004b, p. 11). Edison's strategies were inspired by research on effective schools, visits to high-performing schools, and interviews with recognized school leaders, all conducted during several years of development prior to the launch of the first Edison schools, and refined over a decade of operating schools. Edison's Web site credits education scholars such as Robert Slavin, James Coleman, and James Comer for some of the inspiration for its strategies (Edison Schools, undated Web page [e]). Another uncredited but nonetheless prominent intellectual source was *Politics, Markets, and America's Schools*, the 1990 volume by political scientists John Chubb and Terry Moe. Chubb soon thereafter became one of Edison's original partners, and he remains Edison's chief education officer today.

Edison's strategies for school improvement can be broadly classified into two categories:

1. Providing resources in support of a coherent and comprehensive school design.
2. Implementing accountability systems that aim to ensure that the resources for the design are in place and used as intended.

Figure 3.1 characterizes these strategies graphically. The resources Edison seeks to provide include technical capital (including curricula, assessment systems, and computer systems), human capital, social capital, and time, and are directed at teachers, principals, and at students and their families. Edison's accountability model includes direct line and staffing authority, monitoring and rewards, parental involvement and market accountability, and the reduction of political and bureaucratic accountability that is prominent in conventional public schools. Edison's model is ambitious in its use of resources, but it is most clearly distinguished from conventional public schools (and from other providers of comprehensive school designs) in its accountability systems.

As Edison grew from a system of four schools in 1995 to over 100 schools just a few years later, the bulk of its leaders' attention shifted from resources for its school design—which has remained relatively stable for a decade—to accountability and support systems that would help to cope with the challenge of bringing the school design resources to scale across a large number of schools (Edison central office staff interviews, June 13, 2002). These systems are particularly important, given that implementation at scale has been a difficult problem for many school reform models (see, e.g., Kirby, Berends, and Naftel, 2001; Berends et al., 2001; Bodilly, 1998). Meanwhile, the resource components of the school design have been continually fine-tuned over the years. Moreover, even at the beginning, Edison's strategies included a set of accountability systems embedded in the school design and intended to promote the motivation and opportunity of its school-level staff to improve instructional performance.

Figure 3.1
Edison's Strategies for Promoting School Performance

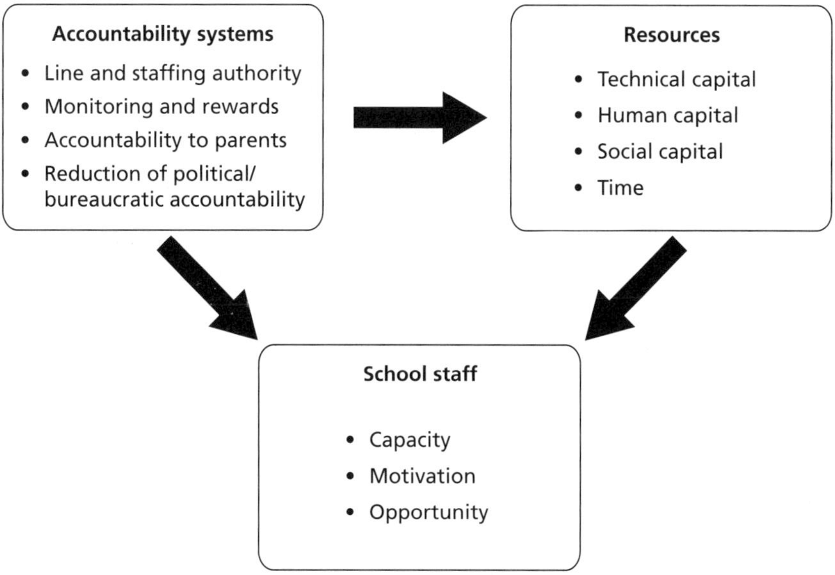

RAND *MG351-3.1*

This chapter describes the resources and accountability systems that Edison has devised over the years to support "world-class education" for its students, as revealed in public and internal Edison documents, and through an extensive set of interviews of Edison central office staff. We began our data collection efforts with a series of semistructured interviews of Edison headquarters staff in New York in the fall of 2000, discussing Edison's school improvement strategies with the chief operating officer, the chief education officer, the director of curriculum and instruction, the chief technology officer, the director of assessment, and various others with responsibilities in operations, finances, and education. Because Edison is an evolving organization, it was important to update our understanding of Edison's central strategies and operations through the course of the study. We therefore returned to New York for a second round of interviews in June 2002, and again for a final round of central office interviews in the fall of 2004, with some follow-up telephone interviews in winter 2004–2005.

Throughout this chapter, the reader should keep in mind that we are describing Edison's ideal model rather than the actual conditions in the schools. The following chapter describes what RAND learned about the implementation of Edison's strategies in visits to schools around the country. As we will explain in Chapter Four, we found considerable variation in the extent to which Edison schools resemble the Edison ideal. While some aspects of the Edison model were present in virtually all of the case study schools we visited, other elements were less consistently implemented, for a variety of reasons. We postpone that discussion until the next chapter; the current chapter seeks to describe Edison's general strategies and its ideal model.

Resources

The resources that Edison seeks to put in place to support the capacity of teachers and principals are substantial and wide-ranging, encompassing technical capital, time, human capital, and social capital. A school is expected to progress through four stages of the implementation of these resources—beginning, developing, proficient, and exemplary, as defined in detailed rubrics provided to school staff—and to move up one level per year.

Technical Capital

Curriculum. One of the key elements of the technical capital that Edison provides to its schools is "A Rich and Challenging Curriculum" (Edison Schools, undated Web page [e]). The curricular programs that Edison offers, across subjects and grades, represent those that Edison's design teams have viewed as best supported by rigorous research, supplemented in some instances by Edison-designed programs. They do not clearly place Edison in a progressive or traditional camp in the ongoing pedagogy wars. In elementary-grade mathematics, for example, Edison has stayed for a decade with its original decision to adopt Everyday Mathematics, an inquiry-based program that was developed by the University of Chicago School Mathematics Project with the support of the National Science Foundation—and that is often under attack as too progressive by pedagogical traditionalists affiliated with organizations such as Mathematically Correct. In elementary-grade reading, by contrast, Edison has long offered Success for All (SFA), a highly scripted reading program developed at Johns Hopkins University by Robert Slavin and colleagues. Recently, Edison began offering its schools Open Court, another highly scripted reading program, as an alternative to SFA. In short, in curriculum issues, Edison's decisions appear to be driven by a simple desire to choose the most effective (or most cost-effective) programs rather than by adherence to any particular pedagogical ideology. Crusaders in the math wars and the whole language versus phonics debate are notably absent from the halls of Edison's New York headquarters.

Similarly, the teaching methods that Edison endorses are eclectic, encompassing "project-based learning" and "cooperative learning" as well as "direct instruction—explicit teaching combined with skilled questioning and observing to assess student understanding" (Edison Schools, undated Web page [e]).

In keeping with its aim of "world-class" education, Edison's curriculum goes well beyond basic skills in reading and math to include explicit components in writing, social studies, science, art, music, world language, and fitness/health (Edison Schools, undated Web page [e]). In its ideal, Edison's curriculum aims to offer its students—who are predominantly low-income and nonwhite—the kind of breadth that is available to students in independent private schools (Edison central office staff interviews, September 2000 and June 2002). For example, Spanish is introduced to Edison students in kindergarten (continuing twice weekly through elementary school and increasing to daily instruction in middle school); science, history, and social studies are part of the daily curriculum from elementary school onward; and fine arts instruction is provided to elementary students every other day. Edison also specifies a set of "core values"—wisdom, justice, courage, compassion, hope, respect, responsibility, and integrity—that it expects schools to integrate into the regular curricula. And Edison provides materials and support for other specialized areas, including English as a second language and special education.

Instructional materials for all elements of the Edison curriculum are provided new to each Edison school at the beginning of its first year of Edison operation, via a purchasing and delivery system that seeks to ensure that the full complement of materials is available before school opens. Edison estimates that it spends more than $600 per student on instructional materials when launching a school (Edison Schools, 2004b).

Edison has sought to balance the need for standardization—considered essential for scaling up the model nationwide—and the need for flexibility—considered essential for promoting buy-in and adaptation to local norms (Chubb, 2004, p. 491). Standardization of curriculum is essential to enabling the system to support schools across the country effectively. Nevertheless, Edison recognizes that the many states in which it operates schools have their own academic standards and their own tests to measure student performance. Edison leaders admit that in the early years, they may have "erred in leaving too many of the details of the design to be filled in at the school level" (Chubb, 2004, p. 491) and soon developed greater specificity and guidance, such as implementation guidelines and operating manuals. Over time, leaders believed they found the right balance between site autonomy and accountability, realizing just how much "management [could] tell a school to do and still expect the school site to feel responsible for getting the results, instead of just following orders" (Chubb, 2004, p. 491). As part of negotiating a balance between standardization and local needs, Edison's strategies include extensive work to align its curricula with state and local standards, including the development of specific "embedding" strategies that incorporate preparation for high-stakes state tests into the standard Edison curricula.

Diagnostic technology. One of the key supports for the alignment of Edison's instructional programs with local standards and assessments is the Edison benchmark system, an online system of monthly assessments developed by Edison. The benchmarks are monthly assessments in mathematics and reading, delivered online to Edison students in grades 2 through 11. Because the benchmarks are administered by computer, they can be scored automatically and instantly, providing immediate results and information to help teachers identify student needs and adjust instruction to meet those needs. As such, the benchmarks constitute a potentially powerful diagnostic system for data-driven decisionmaking at the classroom level.

Although the content of the benchmarks (within a grade and subject) was originally the same Edison-wide, the monthly tests are now customized for each state in which Edison works, with the aim of helping Edison teachers track progress toward meeting state standards, and preparing Edison students for the local high-stakes state assessments. Edison designs benchmark test items to resemble the content and format of state assessment items, and it has shown the predictive value of benchmark results using statistical correlations of those results with student results on state tests in various states where Edison schools are operating. The benchmark results therefore are available to teachers and principals not only to diagnose the particular academic strengths and weaknesses of a student or a class, but also to predict the likelihood that a student will achieve the state's standard of proficiency on the end-of-year, high-stakes test. Edison uses the confidence intervals calculated from the previous year's results to provide each of its schools with a target to aim for on the benchmarks to ensure a 95-percent probability of achieving proficiency on the state test. Its schools in turn have the opportunity to use the benchmark results to identify students in need of additional educational assistance prior to the state test.

Edison's benchmark system allows school staff to generate a series of reports that are designed to present appropriate information formatted in a user-friendly way. These reports include schoolwide proficiency snapshots, grade-level and teacher-specific results, longitudinal tracking over the course of the school year, and results confined to specific skills within reading or math. In recent years, Edison has encouraged schools to use additional assessment data to guide instruction and instructional decisions, including the Dynamic Indicators of Basic Early Literacy Skills (DIBELS) to gauge early elementary school student reading skills, the Scholastic Reading Inventory (SRI) to determine student reading levels, and, for some schools, its own "principal's" test providing snapshots of student learning of skills taught that week. At annual training sessions, Edison regularly provides school staff hands-on training on how to interpret and use these data. It also provides schools with various tools to help staff record and track a variety of student, classroom, and school-level data over time, such as color-coded Excel spreadsheets and charts to identify the number of students "at risk" or those performing below, at, or above grade level.

Computers in instruction. The benchmark system represents what is today perhaps the most important component of Edison's investments in computer and communications technology. Although the electronic benchmark system has been put into place only over the last three years, telecommunications technology has represented a well-publicized part of Edison's academic model since the launch of its first schools a decade ago. Edison created a publicity splash in the mid-1990s by announcing that it would supply home computers to the families of all students in the third grade and above. Home computers are no longer a standard part of Edison's program, because Edison determined that they were not producing a sufficient educational return on the investment. Nevertheless, Edison continues to make substantial investments in technology in its schools.

According to Edison's Web site, "Edison believes that information technology can make students, teachers, and schools more effective—but only when used as a tool and not as a teaching machine. In Edison schools, technology should be fully integrated with the education program and used to facilitate communication, research, writing, and analysis just as it is used in the real world" (Edison Schools, undated Web page [e]). In support of this vision, teachers and administrators are given laptop computers, each classroom typically has a few desktop computers, and each school has a dedicated computer lab for communal use (in which benchmark assessments are administered, as well as instruction in computer skills). Edison has also created an intranet called The Common, a Web-based "message, conferencing, and information system" that provides links to current research, curriculum materials, lesson plans, and discussion groups.

Communication technology. To support communication among teachers and between teachers and parents, Edison's technology investments include not only laptops and the common but also more mundane but no less important forms of technology such as telephones in every classroom and voicemail for every teacher. Telephones and voicemail have constituted an explicit part of Edison's academic program since the beginning, regarded by Edison as essential to promoting better, more frequent, and more efficient communication between teachers and parents. They are expected to improve home-to-school links by providing parents with easy access to homework assignments and by providing teachers with easy opportunities to speak with parents about academic and behavioral challenges.

Human and Social Capital

As in any school, the most important resources that Edison employs to promote student achievement are professional staff. Edison's strategies aim to promote both human capital and social capital in its schools, addressing not only the capacity of its teachers and principals, but also their motivation. Edison seeks to develop the human capital of its school staff through a variety of centrally provided professional development programs aimed at new and continuing Edison teachers and principals. More important, in Edison's view, are the schools' site-based resources that are designed both to develop teachers' knowledge and skills and to promote elements of social capital such as morale, trust, and school spirit. Social capital in Edison schools is also promoted through a "culture of achievement" that aims to motivate students and parents as well as professional staff. We describe each of these elements below.

Centrally provided professional development and support. Edison believes that professional development is critical to preparing school staff to implement the Edison design effectively. Edison offers a wide range of professional development opportunities to its teachers and principals, beginning in the summer prior to the initial hiring of new staff (or the launch of the Edison school). All teachers new to Edison are expected to attend highly intensive, weeklong "teaching academies" in the summer prior to their first year in an Edison school. Some sessions are geared toward novice teachers (new to the profession and to Edison), while others are geared toward experienced teachers (new to Edison). A major emphasis of the summer teaching academies is understanding and knowing how to implement the curricula. They also aim to promote pedagogical skills in "Teaching Methods That Motivate" (Edison Schools, undated Web page [e]), the analysis of student achievement data for diagnostic purposes, and effective methods of classroom management. And, not least important, the summer teaching academies are used to begin building social capital, providing opportunities to establish relationships with teachers from other Edison schools and using motivational programs that introduce teachers to Edison's "culture of achievement" (which we discuss below). In 2004–2005, Edison reports training approximately 1,800 teachers in these academies (Edison Schools, 2005).

In large part, experienced trainers whom Edison has certified as trainers deliver training in Edison's teaching academies. Training is delivered by grade level and content area, with the intention of modeling classroom instruction in the delivery of training. Sessions focus on reviewing curriculum—including the goals, materials (e.g., lesson guides, scope and sequence, parent resources), example lessons, and activities—and on providing suggestions on pacing, classroom management strategies, and ongoing assessments.

Meanwhile, Edison principals—both new and continuing—receive approximately two weeks of leadership training during the summer. Like teachers, principals receive training in the analysis of data, and specifically the use of the Edison benchmark system. In addition, their summer training includes seminars on building management, improving curriculum and instruction, promoting staff capacity, supervision and evaluation, and the creation of a strong school culture. Edison's leadership training is aimed not only at principals, but also at other school administrators and teacher leaders, and is intended to build cohesion and morale among leadership teams—and also to connect staff from around the country, to build an identity as belonging to the larger Edison community. In this sense, the leadership training aims to promote social capital as well as human capital.

Edison's centrally organized professional development (PD) program also includes "achievement academies" conducted regionally during the fall, and aimed primarily at principals and school-level curriculum coordinators—teachers who have accepted responsibility for coordination of site-level implementation and PD for a particular subject. The major emphasis of the achievement academies is to provide strategies that will enable schools to increase achievement for all students, with a focus in recent years on aligning Edison curricula and state standards. Edison recognizes that schools may be at different levels of development. Thus, the first two days of the achievement academies are devoted to providing information and concrete examples that are applicable to all schools (e.g., data analysis, instructional tools), yet also tailored to state contexts (e.g., state standards and assessments). The final day is then reserved for work sessions, in which school teams utilize the strategies to update and revise their own individual school achievement plan (SAP).

In fall 2004, Edison organized three of these achievement academies for approximately 700 educators (Edison Schools, 2005). The achievement academy that RAND researchers observed focused on literacy, including topics such as creating a culture of literacy, reading and writing in mathematics, and reading strategies in social studies and science. Session participants reviewed various curricular packages and strategies aimed at building literacy skills across disciplines and throughout the school. The final day focused on designing and operationalizing a SAP to address schoolwide proficiency goals, reflecting on lessons learned and sharing best practices. One final session gave educators examples of how schools at various stages of implementing the Edison design (i.e., beginning, developing, proficient, exemplary) achieve these goals and effectively utilize the SAP. These included strategies to align instruction and assessment, monitor instruction, monitor data for mastery of standards, efficiently use time and resources to monitor the SAP, and prepare for state assessments.

Each fall, Edison gathers its principals in a Principals' Leadership Conference (PLC), at which it provides additional leadership training and offers recognition to the principals of high-performing schools. At the 2004 PLC, sessions led by corporate, regional, and, at times, school staff covered a range of topics: how to build a community of committed professionals, standards and guidelines for the principalship, professional portfolios, upholding the tenets of the Edison design, what do you need to know and be able to do about NCLB, the five points of accountability, using reading data, using Edison tech tools, community relations, and charter board relations. Generally held at a different resort each year, the conferences also feature motivational speeches from Edison leaders and panels of principals sharing their experiences.

In addition to the various conferences that Edison sponsors every year, in recent years Edison has begun offering an ongoing series of small-dose professional development opportunities in the form of "Edison evenings," voluntary training sessions on particular topics, delivered via conference call and computer linkup to interested Edison teachers across the country.

Typically, members of Edison's national curriculum staff conduct Edison evenings and the training in curriculum and pedagogy offered at the conferences. In each subject area, Edison maintains a small staff of full-time curriculum experts (often individuals who previously taught in Edison schools), known as National Curriculum Coordinators (NCCs), who provide systemwide professional development and also support individual schools as needed, via email, telephone, and occasional site visits.

The schools' primary contact for instructional support purposes is an Edison regional achievement vice president. Edison maintains a cadre of achievement vice presidents, each assigned to about seven schools, to provide support and assistance to principals and school staff on all matters related to instruction and student achievement, as well as design implementation and student discipline. The achievement vice presidents—who like the NCCs are usually former school-level staff, either principals or teachers—assist schools in making plans for student achievement, in analyzing test results, and in complying with the demands of NCLB and state accountability systems. The achievement vice presidents also monitor and help principals stay on track with executing basic program components, such as ensuring that teacher self-assessments and evaluations occur, that curriculum coordinators develop observation schedules, that newly hired teachers attend central Edison office professional development, and that tutoring programs are in place.

Site capacity and school-based professional development and support. Edison's understanding of professional development is substantially broader than the traditional definition. It includes not only conferences and evening training sessions, but also a variety of day-to-day activities conducted at the school site, and usually led by school staff. Edison leaders believe that "on-the-job training is by far the most important kind of training," because it encourages school personnel to take responsibility for results and allows teachers more regular opportunities to try out new ideas and receive immediate feedback (Chubb, 2004, p. 501). This kind of routine, daily support and coaching cannot be delivered from afar; it depends on capacity at each school site, within the regular school staff. Internal capacity at the site is also critical to ensure the endurance of the implementation of the design over time, in the face of external political pressure and inevitable staff turnover (Chubb, 2004). Edison therefore seeks to develop site capacity for instructional leadership and support in the hands of administrators and teachers in the schools.

Edison takes seriously the now-commonplace notion that principals should be instructional leaders, as well as good managers of building and budget, and facilitators of a strong school culture. Edison leaders believe that all three types of leadership are essential for ensuring school results in five key areas—student performance, school design, customer satisfaction, financial management, and operational excellence. In support of this view, Edison has developed detailed standards and rubrics specifying principal expectations around instructional leadership, site-based management, and building school culture. To hold principals accountable, Edison staff formally assess principals' performance in all three areas in an annual appraisal process. Principals are rated on a four-point scale in each area, ranging from not meeting expectations to exceeding performance expectations. Principals are also asked to reflect on these areas in their self-appraisals, in the development of professional growth plans, and in the collection of evidence for a professional portfolio demonstrating their accomplishments.

In Edison's view, instructional leadership is particularly important: It "is essential to improving student achievement" and includes such responsibilities as improving curriculum and instruction, data-driven decisionmaking, building staff capacity, and setting and holding high expectations (Edison Schools, 2004b, p.7). Edison expects principals to be intimately engaged with instruction in the school. The principal should know the curriculum content, be aware of pacing, and visit classrooms daily. Edison's instructional leadership standards cover four "essential elements":

1. Implementing core programs: principals are expected to monitor program implementation and student achievement.
2. Supervising and evaluating staff: principals are expected to monitor teacher development, use supervision and evaluation to ensure that quality instruction and student achievement are priorities, and create systems to support peer coaching.
3. Building the learning environment: principals are expected to monitor the learning environment to ensure that "the look and sound of all classrooms" meet Edison's performance standards and guidelines, and to ensure that teacher appraisals are in place and aligned with learning environment goals.

4. Creating a professional culture: principals are expected to ensure the development of individual teacher, house, and schoolwide professional growth plans, to create effective house and leadership teams, and to focus staff meetings on instruction and student performance.

Detailed rubrics define what it looks like to be beginning, developing, proficient, and exemplary in each of these areas.

As noted above, Edison's central training for principals and for academy directors (similar to assistant principals, with responsibility for an "academy" consisting of three or four grades) includes substantial emphasis on instructional leadership, with a particular focus on the analysis of student achievement data. One PLC session researchers observed in 2004 entitled "Developing Instructional Leaders: Using Leadership Rubrics to Improve Leadership Capacity" articulated Edison's leadership expectations and engaged principals in developing rubrics to generate growth plans identifying skills that needed improvement. Other sessions focused on specific leadership skills, such as how to build a culture of continuous improvement and committed professionals, and how to organize, analyze, and utilize reading data.

In addition, the Edison school design tries to distribute instructional leadership responsibilities and capacity among teacher leaders in the school. Each school has a leadership team that is responsible for helping the principal develop, adjust, and monitor school policies, procedures, and programs. The leadership team includes not only the principal and the academy directors, but also the lead teachers for each of several small "houses" into which the school is organized.

Each house consists of about six teachers, usually representing two or three grade levels (within an "academy"). Students are expected to stay in the same houses as they progress through several grades, so that the team of teachers in the house can be responsible for instructing and managing a common group of students over a period of time. The lead teacher for each house is expected to serve as a mentor for the other teachers with respect to both pedagogy and classroom management (Chubb, 2004), and (where permitted by contract) to take some responsibility for the evaluation of junior colleagues within the house. Within each house, each teacher is expected to "become a resource for teammates by developing a specialty in a subject area, in ESL, in technology, or in special education" (Edison Schools, 2002b, p. 4). Each house team is expected to meet daily, and each daily meeting is intended to be an opportunity for teachers to work together and develop their skills, whether with respect to curriculum, instruction, student behavior, data-driven decisionmaking, or the use of technology (Chubb, 2004, p. 501).

The distribution of instructional leadership and the expectation of collaboration among teachers require a school culture in which classroom doors are routinely open to colleagues and administrators. In support of such a culture, the house structure is intended not only to develop the particular skills of teachers (i.e., their human capital), but also to promote morale and trust—elements of social capital that have been shown to have a substantial impact on school performance (Bryk and Schneider, 2002). Edison intends that both teachers and students will identify with their house teams and that the teachers in a house will provide mutual social support as well as training and mentoring. Student behavioral challenges are addressed at the house level prior to becoming matters of schoolwide concern; both the collaborative structure of the house and the fact that the same students remain in a house for several years are intended in part to help with behavioral challenges. Meanwhile, teachers can expect that their house leads will represent their interests and concerns in meetings of the schoolwide leadership team. In short, Edison aims to create in each school a collegial, professional environment for teachers that gives them significant leadership responsibility and simultaneously ensures substantial support.

Each subject area has a curriculum coordinator in the school, who is generally a teacher given additional responsibilities including managing curriculum materials, providing ongoing professional development in the curricular area, conducting classroom observations, modeling instruction, and offering general support to teachers around the curriculum. In some instances, house meetings focus on a particular subject matter, in which case the school's curriculum coordinator for that subject may attend.

Beyond the administrators, lead teachers, and curriculum coordinators, site capacity under the Edison design also includes full-time staff who are responsible for the school's special education program and for student and family support related to behavioral challenges and special needs.

Culture of achievement. Edison seeks to promote social capital in its schools not only through the school structure, but also by "envelop[ing] teachers and students in a new culture of high achievement" (Chubb, 2004, p. 507). For students, this involves a variety of methods to increase their motivation to achieve, from pizza parties to posting examples of exemplary work on classroom and school walls (in Edison schools, the walls are expected to be almost entirely covered with student work and instructional materials). Edison also seeks to enlist parents in the culture of achievement. It expects every school to have a parent advisory council; its Family and Student Support Team (FASST) process seeks to actively engage parents in addressing students' academic, social, and behavioral challenges; and it expects a parent to come to the school and meet with the teacher to receive every report card.

Meanwhile, Edison promotes a culture of achievement among school staff by recognizing and rewarding high-achieving schools. The most prominent example of this comes at Edison's annual PLC, which concludes with a black-tie dinner at which schools that achieved "four-star" status under Edison's customized star-rating system (described in the discussion of accountability systems) are publicly honored. Strong performance on Edison's star rating system comes with material benefits as well (also discussed in the section on accountability systems). Edison intends that these opportunities for recognition and reward will serve not only as a direct incentive for performance, but also as an opportunity to develop team spirit and camaraderie among staff members and students in each school.

Time

Edison describes "A Better Use of Time" as one of the key strategies it employs to promote student learning (Edison Schools, undated Web page [e]). This involves, first of all, a substantial increase in total instructional time for students. Ideally, the standard Edison school year is expected to be 198 days, about 10 percent longer than the 180 days required in most states. And Edison expects its standard school day to be longer as well, stretched by an hour or more beyond the time expected of most public-school students. Students who attend Edison schools throughout kindergarten through grade 12 (K–12) would ultimately have the equivalent of up to four years of additional instructional time, according to Edison's estimates (Edison Schools, undated Web page [a]).

The additional time is used, first of all, to fit in the wide-ranging components of the Edison curriculum. Ideally, the additional time permits Edison students to have their cake and eat it too: They can devote a substantial amount of attention to core academic subjects without sacrificing the "specials" that identify the Edison program as "world-class," including art, music, physical education, and foreign language. Edison expects its schools to block out substantial chunks of time for reading (at least 90 minutes daily in elementary school) and math (at least 60 minutes daily). In reading, and sometimes in other subjects, students who need extra help (often identified by their benchmark results or results of other assessments) are given supplemental tutoring one-on-one or in small groups, during the school day, before or after school, or on Saturdays. After-school and Saturday sessions typically ramp up in intensity in the weeks prior to the local high-stakes assessment.

The lengthy Edison school day is organized not only to pack in an extensive curriculum, but also to provide teachers with more daily opportunities for planning and professional development. Edison's scheduling model gives its teachers two periods a day free of instructional responsibilities, so that they can plan, collaborate, and learn. One of these two periods is intended for a meeting of the teacher's house team.

Finally, "a better use of time" involves the creation of a "safe and orderly learning environment" (Edison Schools, 2002c, p. 5) that permits teachers to focus on teaching—as opposed to discipline problems and other related issues that detract teachers' time and attention away from instruction. To support such an environment, a "character and ethics" curriculum promotes the teaching and modeling of core values—wisdom, justice, courage, compassion, hope, respect, responsibility, and integrity—throughout the school. These core values are reflected in a school code of conduct and expected to be integrated into all areas of instruction and daily practice. Some schools, for example, highlight one core value a month and celebrate its meaning through special projects, displays of student work, and awards to students exemplifying the value. In addition, consistent classroom management techniques are taught to all Edison teachers as part of their initial training at the time of hiring. And each Edison school backs up the classroom learning environment with a family and student support team that serves to address the needs of students with ongoing behavioral (or academic or emotional) challenges.

Accountability Systems

Although the resources that Edison aims to provide in support of its schools are wide-ranging and substantial, what makes Edison (like other EMOs) novel on the American K–12 education scene are the accountability systems it puts in place both within its schools and across its system. Unlike other providers of educational services, EMOs have operational authority over the schools in which they work. Edison seeks to use this operational authority to impose accountability systems that supplement or replace many of the conventional accountability systems of American public schools. Edison's accountability model begins with straightforward line and staffing authority, adding an ambitious system of monitoring and rewards, and including the reduction of conventional political and bureaucratic authority.

Line authority. The most important distinction between Edison and other "comprehensive" school reform designs (such as Roots and Wings, Accelerated Schools, America's Choice, Modern Red Schoolhouse, Atlas, and other designs including those promoted by New American Schools) is that Edison has operational authority over its schools. Edison regards this distinction as crucial. In the words of John Chubb: "Getting great education results requires great schools, and getting great schools requires running them—not just supplying them, training them, or advising them" (2004, p. 490). Principals in Edison schools report to regional "General Managers" (GMs), who in turn report to Edison executives in the New York headquarters. Edison's chief education officer (Chubb) serves a role analogous to that of a school district's chief academic officer. Meanwhile, Edison's chief executive officer is much like a district superintendent.

Staffing authority. In Edison's view, one of the key aspects of operational authority over schools is the ability to select staff. "The ability to hire and fire principals and teachers" is a critical component of Edison's reform model (Chubb, 2004, p. 495). Staffing authority, according to the Edison model, is important not only for ensuring the effective operation of line authority but also for promoting the buy-in of staff: "Reform has the best chance to succeed . . . when reformers have the authority to carry it out and when educators have the right to choose whether they want to participate in it" (Chubb, 2004, p. 495). Because Edison's school design is demanding and highly specified, it is especially important that its principals and teachers are supportive; voluntary transfer in and out makes that support more likely. The transfer option may give Edison more ability to ensure a good fit between staff and programs than conventional school districts have, given that conventional school districts generally cannot transfer staff to other districts.

Edison tries to maximize the value of its staffing authority with a national recruitment system that aims to identify teachers and principals who are well suited to its program. Recruitment strategies include attending conferences, advertising, communicating with headhunters, and screening internal references (e.g., academy directors are often seen as natural candidates for principal openings). The search process for principals at Edison charter schools, for example, generally involves a committee of parents, teachers, board members, and other school staff. For candidates it considers highly qualified, Edison tries to offer salaries that somewhat exceed what might be available in conventional public schools.

Edison views the qualifications of applicants—whether teachers or principals—primarily in terms of expertise rather than years of experience. In principal candidates, Edison seeks a demonstrated track record of academic growth for students; the ability to talk to parents and achieve customer satisfaction; a commitment to the Edison program and the ability to get staff to buy in; familiarity with, ability to use, and understanding of the value of data; and strong financial management skills, including the ability to "think outside the box" in managing a budget (e.g., a willingness to look for outside grants and an entrepreneurial spirit). Principal candidates are asked to take an Edison-developed assessment to identify personal attributes, interests, attitudes, and behaviors, as well as strengths and weaknesses. Applicants may be asked to produce a writing sample on site, based on a topic selected by the school's recruiting committee (often with guidance from the national recruitment manager). The instructions might explain that a goal of Edison is to create, develop, and sustain learning communities that meet the needs of all students. Applicants might be given 30 minutes to describe the components of a learning community and how they would ensure that the Edison school becomes a successful learning community.

Authority over staffing involves more than just hiring and dismissal. Edison has developed a career ladder for teachers that specifies opportunities for advancement internally. The career ladder aims to give teachers opportunities to advance to greater responsibility and salary—in positions such as school-level curriculum coordinators and house lead teachers—without leaving the classroom for administration. Edison expects advancement in the career ladder to be based on demonstrated competence in instruction and instructional leadership, and it does not require that a teacher have greatest seniority to advance. Teachers also have opportunities to earn additional salary and develop professionally by taking on training responsibilities at Edison's summer teaching academies in addition to their school responsibilities. And a few teachers move out of the classroom and into Edison corporate positions, working on Edison's national curriculum teams. All of these opportunities are intended to ensure that Edison has the most qualified staff in teacher and teacher leadership positions, and to provide additional motivation to classroom teachers to develop their skills and perform their best.

Less formally, Edison has also developed a career ladder for principals. Those who demonstrate success at the school level are given opportunities to advance into supervisory and training positions at the regional and corporate level. Edison often publicizes these opportunities for career growth as an incentive when recruiting new principals.

Monitoring and rewards. Edison attends to the motivation of its teachers and principals not only with opportunities for advancement, but also with systems to monitor performance and reward it directly.

School visits and review calls. Edison's monitoring systems include in-person visits to schools by general managers, achievement vice presidents, and members of the national curriculum staff. As noted in the preceding pages, visits are conducted for purposes of support and professional development—but they also provide Edison's central office with critical information about the implementation of the school design. Edison's two achievement executive directors—who report directly to Edison's chief education officer, John Chubb—preside over monthly conference calls during which each of the regional achievement vice presidents, with support from national curriculum staff as well as general managers, summarizes conditions in the schools, one by one. The conference calls are preceded by the submission by the achievement vice presidents of summary information in spreadsheet form to these two executive directors. The spreadsheets and conference calls address a wide range of issues related to conditions in the schools, from curriculum implementation to student behavior to benchmark results to the staffing of leadership positions. In keeping with a relentless focus on achievement, benchmark results and preparation for high-stakes state tests are always prominent on the agenda.

Benchmark review. Indeed, Edison views the monthly benchmark results as perhaps the most important indicator of a school's instructional performance that is available during the course of the school year. As noted earlier in this chapter, Edison's computerized benchmark assessments are designed to monitor students' progress toward state standards and their preparation for state tests. Using data available retrospectively, Edison has been able to verify the predictive validity of the benchmarks, determining empirically that benchmark results are good predictors of state test results. Moreover, the fact that the benchmarks are administered and scored by computer means that they are immediately available for analysis, not only by teachers and principals but also by regional achievement vice presidents and other Edison corporate staff.

Customer satisfaction. Each year, Edison also commissions the Harris Interactive polling organization to conduct systematic surveys of the satisfaction of teachers, parents, and students in each of its schools. Edison regards these surveys as important measures of client satisfaction, and they are included in Edison's evaluations of its schools and principals.

Star rating system. More generally, Edison's "star rating" system is its key instrument for determining a school's eligibility for performance-based rewards. The system is designed to be "an objective measure from which we can celebrate success or set targets for improvement" (Edison Schools, 2002a, p. 3). Each year, Edison rates each of its schools in terms of five characteristics or "points of accountability," which it defined for its principals at their 2004 leadership conference as follows:

- **Operational excellence** measures "the factors that we know are keys to healthy and successful schools," including student attendance, staff attendance, student mobility, teacher turnover, and graduation rate.
- **Customer satisfaction** measures "a school's ability to please its students, parents, and staff" and averages student, parent, and staff ratings from Harris surveys to determine overall customer satisfaction.
- **School design** measures implementation of the "Edison ten fundamentals" (enumerated on Edison's Web site), including school organization (i.e., performance of house teams, lead teams, curriculum coordinators), use of time (i.e., amount of time spent in each subject area and in required design elements such as meetings and professional development), curricular program, instruction and pedagogy, assessment and accountability

(i.e., benchmark participation), professional development, technology, partnership with families, communications and community outreach, and system growth (e.g., number of development trips or tours, number of conference presentations). Edison expects schools to achieve proficiency in all school design areas, including curriculum, by the third year of operation (Edison Schools, 2004b).

- **Financial management** measures the fiscal health of the school and is determined in multiple ways, depending on the nature of Edison's contract with its client. Usually, successful financial management in an Edison school requires the school to meet an enrollment target.
- **Student achievement** measures "the school's ability to meet its most important and primary function—to advance, improve, and enhance the learning done by students (as reflected in state and district mandated assessment results)." Ratings in this area are determined by a complex formula that emphasizes relative growth in schoolwide proficiency rates as measured by state-mandated tests—and, more recently, by the ability to meet adequate yearly progress (AYP). To align further with NCLB, the formula more heavily weights results in the mandated tested areas of reading and math and includes rewards and penalties for meeting or not meeting AYP.

Edison staff have developed detailed criteria and rubrics for awarding each school one to four star ratings in each of the five areas. Over the years, Edison has revised and refined this rating system, most recently to align with and emphasize the importance of the federal No Child Left Behind legislation.

Edison uses the star rating system to recognize and reward school and individual performance. Schools earning four stars in the areas of student achievement and financial management are publicly recognized at an annual black-tie event for principals known as the "Edi Awards" ceremony (held at the conclusion of the principals' leadership conference). Edison's central office staff view the event as a key component of a more general strategy to affirm and celebrate successful schools (and thereby to contribute to the culture of achievement). Where allowed by contract, principals and teachers are also eligible for monetary bonuses based on weighted star ratings, which primarily emphasize student achievement (ratings in this area count for 40 percent of principal and 60 percent of teacher bonus eligibility) and factors tied to academic success (ratings for school design, operational excellence, and customer satisfaction each count for 10 percent of bonus eligibility for principals and teachers). And on occasion, Edison has rewarded the principals of high-performing schools by giving them brand-new sports cars.

Accountability to parents. Consistent with Edison's general faith in market-based accountability, it expects its schools to be responsive to parents. All of Edison's schools are at least nominally schools of choice—at minimum, parents have the opportunity to opt out in favor of another public school, and in many cases (especially the charter schools), parents must actively choose to enroll their children. Edison believes this imposes a healthy measure of customer accountability on its schools. Edison seeks to reinforce that accountability and to make it flow in both directions by creating a parent advisory council at each school, by commissioning parent satisfaction polls at every school every year, and by asking all parents to attend a meeting with the teacher in order to receive every report card. Meanwhile, the communication tools that Edison provides to teachers (telephones, voicemail, laptops, and email) are intended to facilitate communication with parents. Edison believes that actively engaged parents will contribute to the culture of achievement.

Reduction of political and bureaucratic accountability. Edison's strategy for promoting school performance involves not only installing new accountability systems for principals and teachers, but also removing aspects of existing accountability systems that it views as constraining and unproductive. Several aspects of political and bureaucratic accountability that are typical elements of the operation of conventional public schools are notably absent from Edison's accountability strategies.

First of all, Edison seeks to give principals more authority over budgeting than they would have in conventional public schools—

and, as a corollary, more freedom from the bureaucratic constraints that are typically imposed by districts. This freedom is easy to grant in Edison's charter schools, but involves challenging traditional governance structures in district schools. Edison believes that its own accountability systems, coupled with state-level systems that operate in accordance with NCLB, are sufficient to promote high performance in its schools. In Edison's view, bureaucratic accountability systems that go beyond its own structures may only muddy the waters, sending schools confusing signals and perhaps constraining schools' ability to act in ways to promote high performance. Consistent with the demands of outcomes-based accountability, Edison seeks to ensure that its principals have maximum freedom to lead their schools.

Edison's corporate structure, of course, includes a bureaucracy of its own, but Edison aims to make that bureaucracy as limited and efficient as possible. In pursuit of this end, Edison's regional organization—organized in a matrix structure—gives each school a single point of accountability for operations (the general manager) and a single point of coordination of support for achievement (the achievement vice president). Edison intends that this system—accompanied by the reduction of district-based bureaucratic demands—will not only provide principals with adequate freedom of action but will also produce better communication and support. According to Edison leaders, "Great organizations put in place the systems to provide quality services, however mundane"—including the efficient delivery of materials, technology, and supplies, as well as "running conferences, getting bills paid, providing reports, and even answering phone calls and e-mails" (Chubb, 2004, p. 500). Aware of teacher and principal frustration with the bureaucratic nature of public schooling (e.g., district offices that do not return calls or deliver supplies), Edison hopes to provide a more effective and efficient support system to schools, allowing staff the opportunity to focus on the work of teaching and learning, and to receive the services and help they need, unencumbered by hierarchy, rules, and red tape.

Edison also aims to insulate its schools from local politics, in the hope that this will give them the opportunity to focus on instruction. This aspect of Edison's accountability strategy is derived directly from the insights expressed in *Politics, Markets, and America's Schools* (Chubb and Moe, 1990). Fifteen years ago, Chubb and Moe argued that the direct operation of public schools by elected officials frequently prevents them from focusing intensely on their academic missions. School-board politics too often distracts the schools from focusing on improving instructional performance, in this view. Frequent turnover on school boards yields frequent turnover of superintendents, which in turn yields frequent shuffling of instructional programs—leaving teachers jaded and suffering from "programmitis." In the words of John Chubb (2004, p. 492), "Electoral pressures place a premium on quick fixes." Lacking stability, schools spin their wheels (see also Hess, 1999; Hill, Pierce, and Guthrie, 1997).

Edison, to be sure, does not seek to eliminate all democratic control of public schools. Nevertheless, Edison seeks to insulate its schools from some of the most immediate intrusions of local politics. In theory, Edison's contract with its client will create that insulation, clearly spelling out the terms under which Edison operates the schools, and creating a freedom of action within those terms—so that elected school boards need not be involved in day-to-day operations of the Edison school. In general, Edison's contracts for schools last approximately five years "to ensure time to bring about the tough but requisite changes" (Chubb, 2004, p. 507).

The fact that Edison itself is not a political organization similarly creates opportunities for stability and a focus on academics, in this view. Edison's central office leadership has been quite stable for most of its existence. Chris Whittle, Edison's founder, remains the company's CEO. Chris Cerf, the outgoing president, was in a corporatewide leadership position for seven years before stepping down in spring 2005. And John Chubb, the chief education officer, has been with Edison since its launch. As Whittle says, "If you were to think of Edison as a school district, then I would be the longest serving head of a major U.S. system" (interview, October 4, 2004).

The continuity of leadership is reflected in a similar continuity of the educational program. Although Edison has constantly sought to improve its school design and its support and accountability systems, the changes (such as the implementation of electronic benchmarks) generally reflect the extension of its core ideas rather than fundamental departures. Indeed, Edison continues to rely on many of the same curricular programs that it selected a decade ago (even if it is now using updated editions)—*Everyday Math*, for example, has been consistently used in Edison elementary schools for a decade. With stable leadership and a continuing commitment to a coherent school design, Edison has been able to maintain programmatic stability.

Edison's insulation from political turmoil has the additional benefit, in view of its leaders, that it can take the long view and invest in research and development much more extensively and strategically than most school districts have the capacity to do. The company's ability to invest in research and development, in turn, is intended to support the continuous improvement of the school and system designs and the overall performance of the schools and company as a whole. The most notable product of Edison's research and development investments is the online benchmark system, which was developed in house over several years (initially on paper) and is continuously adjusted year after year (and, indeed, is now sold by Edison as a stand-alone product).

Maintaining and renewing contracts to run schools, of course, requires some attention to the demands of local politics. Edison officials acknowledge that some past contracts have been lost as a result of insufficient attention to client demands. In recent years, Edison has changed the expectations of its general managers, so that a critical part of the job involves maintaining good client relations.

Edison Strategy Summary

In sum, the resources and accountability systems that constitute Edison's strategies for promoting student achievement are, on paper, impressively comprehensive in addressing all elements relevant to high-quality delivery of instruction, including capacities, motivation, and opportunities for school staff. Edison (like other EMOs) is distinct from other "comprehensive" reform models in having operational authority over schools. At the same time, Edison is distinct from conventional school districts in its favored modes of accountability, relying more extensively on outcomes-based and market-based systems, and less on political and bureaucratic accountability. Indeed, Edison's well-developed information systems and focus on achievement-based accountability should make it especially well suited to the high-stakes testing environment of NCLB. In the next chapter, we explore the extent to which Edison's strategies are realized in practice in a number of its schools.

CHAPTER FOUR

Perspiration: The Edison Model in the Schools

Brian P. Gill, Julie A. Marsh, Deanna Hill, Shana Pribesh, Ron W. Zimmer, and Laura S. Hamilton

The ground-level implementation of Edison's strategies—including both resources and accountability systems—is the issue of interest in this chapter. Even if Edison's strategies appear comprehensive and coherent in theory, their success in improving school performance and student achievement is ultimately determined by their implementation in schools. This chapter examines how Edison's accountability systems and resources are implemented in a sample of Edison elementary schools. The discussion reverses the order from the preceding chapter—here discussing accountability systems first, followed by resources—because this structure provides the opportunity to explore the extent to which differences in the implementation of the accountability systems may predict differences in the implementation of resources in the schools. We begin with a discussion of methods.

Methods

To understand the implementation of Edison's accountability systems and resources, we visited a sample of Edison schools across the United States in 2001, 2003, and 2004, and observed and conducted extensive interviews of Edison school administrators, teachers, and staff. Additionally, we conducted interviews of Edison corporate and regional staff as well as the clients or officials responsible for overseeing Edison case study schools; listened to monthly Edison account review calls regarding our case study schools; and observed Edison staff training. Below, we describe our rationale for selecting the case study schools, our various data sources, and our method for analyzing the data.

Selection of Case Study Schools

Throughout this chapter, it is important to recognize that findings are based on examination of a relatively small number of Edison elementary schools that were not randomly selected. The aim of the case study examination was not to assess how Edison schools compare with conventional public schools (thus the absence of a non-Edison comparison group), but (1) to assess the extent to which Edison schools in practice match Edison's ideal in terms of design implementation, and (2) to examine factors that might explain differences in implementation and in student achievement among Edison schools. Given the limitations inherent in a small sample size, we sought a sample that would capture a wide range of Edison elementary schools to ensure sufficient variance in accountability systems, resource implementation, and achievement outcomes to permit us to understand how these various factors might be related. As we describe below, our sample provided variation on a variety of key dimensions. Nevertheless, these analyses should be considered exploratory, and not necessarily generalizable to the full population of Edison schools.

In 2001, RAND selected 15 Edison elementary schools that were intended to capture the range of variation in Edison schools across the country. The dimensions we examined to select the schools included local context (as represented by state and urban versus suburban status), the year Edison began operating the schools (ranging from 1995, when Edison's first schools opened, to 2000), and the form of governance (i.e., charter schools and district contract schools). In addition, the schools RAND selected were typical of Edison-wide averages in terms of Edison's own measures of design implementation, test score gains, and "client satisfaction."[1] We chose

[1] On Edison's four-point scale of school-level achievement gain ratings, the original case study schools achieved an average score of 2.6, virtually identical to the Edison-wide average at the time (five of the case study schools had no achievement ratings as yet, because they had

to focus on elementary schools because they constitute the great majority of Edison's schools, and because we wanted to keep the range of variation manageable, given the small sample size.

By 2003, three of the original 15 case study schools were no longer under Edison operation, and a fourth elected to drop out of the study (and soon thereafter terminated its relationship with Edison). We replaced these four schools with four schools that were new to Edison. This not only maintained our sample size but also permitted us the opportunity to maintain a sample that better represented Edison's current portfolio of schools. Three of the additional schools were located in Philadelphia, where Edison had begun managing 20 schools in the fall of 2002. Given that Philadelphia was Edison's largest, highest-profile contract and involved a number of departures from the standard model, including these schools was an important addition to the sample. Two of the three case study schools in Philadelphia were selected randomly among Edison's elementary schools there. The third school was selected purposively, because it was identified as having especially serious first-year implementation challenges, and we wanted to examine how Edison responded to such challenges. The fourth case study school added in 2003 was a newly opened charter school.

In the fall of 2004, the RAND study team concluded, in consultation with Edison staff, that it would be useful to conduct a few additional school site visits as our study neared completion. Rather than returning to schools we had previously visited, we elected to add four more Edison elementary schools to our sample. These four schools were selected to balance out the sample in terms of governance and number of years under Edison's management. Attrition of our original sample had primarily affected district contract schools, so that the case study schools that remained under Edison operation were disproportionately charter schools (compared to the full universe of cur-

not been open long enough to establish trends). In terms of client satisfaction, the case study schools earned an average score of 2.8 on a four-point scale, versus 2.5 Edison-wide. And in terms of design implementation and "system growth," the case study schools averaged a score of 2.7, versus 2.5 Edison-wide.

rently operating Edison schools). In consultation with Edison staff, we therefore selected four additional district contract schools, two of which had recently opened and two of which had been operating under Edison management for some time and had recently had their contracts renewed. In contrast to the other case study schools, which were selected without regard to the quality of the relationship between Edison and the client, these additional four schools were described by Edison as examples of good client relationships.

Summary statistics on the sample of Edison schools, as compared with the full universe of Edison schools, are captured in Table 4.1. As the table indicates, the sample fairly represents the Edison universe on most key dimensions.

The one respect in which the case study schools differ notably from the larger Edison universe is that, looking retrospectively at their full Edison histories to this point, their achievement results are

Table 4.1
Descriptive Characteristics of Case Study Schools and All Edison Schools

	Case Study Sample (N=23)	All Edison Schools Operating 1995–2005 (N=144)
Charter school	43%	40%
District/state contract school	57%	60%
Start-up school	39%	31%
Conversion school	61%	69%
Opened 1995–1997	26%	15%
Opened 1998–2000	48%	47%
Opened 2001–2003	26%	35%
Located in Michigan	9%	14%
Located in Pennsylvania	17%	24%
Average total enrollment	581	662
Average % Asian	2	2
Average % Hispanic	16	21
Average % black	60	62
Average % white	22	15
Average % students eligible for free or reduced-price lunch (FRL)	70	74

somewhat better on average than those of other Edison schools in both reading and math. We describe these differences more specifically in Chapter Seven. Despite these mean differences, however, the case study schools represent the full range of Edison's academic performance, with case study schools appearing in every quartile of the Edison-wide distribution of achievement trends. We are cautious about generalizing descriptive results for the case study schools, but the fact that they capture a wide range of the distribution suggests that they may provide useful opportunities to understand differences in implementation and how those differences may be related to achievement outcomes (an issue we address in Chapter Seven).

Data Sources

We drew on several sources of data to understand the implementation of the school design in our case study schools over time, as well as the overall implementation of Edison's system-level supports and structures.

Edison corporate interviews. These are described in the preceding chapter. In addition to informing our understanding of Edison's strategies, they provided information about how Edison corporate officials understand implementation in the schools, and about how they monitor school performance.

Case study site visits. Prior to undertaking the first case study site visits, we developed a series of interview and observation protocols derived from the elements of Edison's school improvement strategies that were emerging from our headquarters interviews and document reviews. We further customized these instruments to the various respondent groups (e.g., principals, teachers, teacher leaders) and types of schools (e.g., charter versus contract or partnership, start-up school). In spring 2001, we visited 15 case study schools across the nation. Within each school, teams of two RAND researchers spent two days on site, interviewing the principal, academy directors, teacher leaders (including the math coordinator, reading coordinator, and at least one lead teacher), and three teachers randomly selected from a teacher roster. We also collected relevant documents, such as school improvement plans, and observed three randomly selected teachers: one instructing reading, one instructing math, and one instructing science, social studies, arts, or foreign language.

In winter and spring 2003, researchers conducted a second round of site visits, following a similar agenda in 11 of the original 15 case study schools and in four replacement sites. Finally, in the fall of 2004, we visited four additional Edison elementary schools, returned to one of the replacement schools originally visited in 2003, and conducted follow-up telephone interviews with principals and teachers in the other three replacement schools originally visited. All interviews were recorded either by a researcher (usually on computer during the interview) or by audiocassette for later transcription.

Following each round of site visits, we conducted telephone interviews of Edison regional staff responsible for overseeing our case study schools. To enhance our understanding of school operations and achievement at each of our case study schools, as well as Edison's management and support systems, we interviewed the relevant regional staff members (e.g., general managers and achievement vice presidents). In a small number of instances, we were unable to successfully connect with Edison regional staff.

Edison client interviews. Following our school visits, we conducted interviews of relevant Edison clients to understand further the case study schools, their implementation of the school design, and overall context for school operations. In the case of charter schools, we interviewed chartering authority officials or members of the school's local charter board; in the case of state contracts, we interviewed relevant state officials; and in the case of district contracts, we interviewed relevant school district officials responsible for oversight and monitoring.

Edison achievement reviews. To keep up with the changes that occurred in our case study schools during our study and between our visits, and to understand how Edison's own monitoring of schools worked, we observed Edison's annual achievement review meetings that were conducted in 2000, 2001, and 2002. These meetings were held over the course of two or three days each fall, under the supervision of the chief education officer, during which the latest test results and the current year's achievement plan was discussed for each Edison school. The meetings included input from regional achievement vice presidents, general managers, and various members of Edison's national curriculum and instruction staff.

Following the 2002 meeting, Edison switched to monthly "account review" conference calls addressing achievement and operational challenges at each Edison school. From fall 2002 through fall 2004, RAND staff listened to the monthly calls that addressed case study schools, again in order to aid our understanding not only of the case study schools, but also of Edison's monitoring of and support for those schools. The chief education officer or one of his two deputies typically oversaw account review calls. Each call focused on the handful of schools under the purview of one regional achievement vice president, and involved additional input from general managers and national curriculum staff. Our observations allowed us to access more than just a snapshot of our case study schools and greatly enhanced our understanding of the dynamic nature of our case study schools. These calls also informed our broader understanding of the organization, its priorities, and its monitoring and support strategies.

Training observations. RAND staff observed a variety of Edison conferences and professional development meetings in 2003 and 2004. These included, in summer 2003, the week-long Edison leadership development academy (for veteran principals) and Edison leadership team training (for principals and leadership teams) in Snowbird, Utah, and the teaching academy in Valley Forge, Pennsylvania. In summer 2004, we returned to the leadership conferences. In fall 2003 and fall 2004, RAND researchers attended Edison achievement academies for teacher leaders, and in fall 2004, RAND observed the annual principals' leadership conference in Phoenix. These observations provided insights into Edison's professional development activities and priorities.

Data Analysis

Following each case study site visit, researchers analyzed all interview and observation notes and transcripts, as well as all documents collected on site, and developed analytic memoranda summarizing overall findings about the school context and its implementation of the

Edison school design. These memoranda were organized based on the concepts comprising Edison's school-improvement strategies. First-round (2001) reports identified preliminary findings and observations, and second-round (2003) reports built upon the earlier memoranda and noted changes that had occurred or not occurred over time in schools previously visited. For replacement schools visited for the first time in 2003 or 2004, the visiting researchers constructed new memoranda along the same lines. In the final year of the study, researchers used these case study memoranda to identify overarching themes about design implementation across the sample of schools.

In addition, the RAND research team created a series of codes intended to measure the extent to which a wide range of design elements and contextual factors, from the implementation of each curriculum component, to the principal's skill as an instructional leader, to the existence of an extended school day and year, were present in each case study school. To ensure consistency, codes were assigned to each case study school during group meetings that included site visitors and other members of the research team. For most variables, codes were given in one of three categories: weak, moderate, or strong implementation. For some analytical purposes, we collapsed these into just two categories: strong implementation versus anything less.

After coding all measures for each of the 23 case study schools, we combined several related measures into indices representing average results across several variables. Two of these indices figured prominently in our analyses. The first encompasses the implementation of curricula in subjects other than reading and math—i.e., social studies, science, "specials" (art, music, physical education, and world languages), and core values. These subjects constitute important elements of Edison's "world-class" educational model, but NCLB does not attach high stakes to test results in the subjects, so it is worth examining how they are implemented. The second index encompasses major features of what we characterize as the school's "professional environment," including the use of houses, the availability of planning time, and the prevalence of site-based professional development. Both of these indices had high levels of internal consistency, as indicated by coefficient alpha estimates of 0.91 and 0.84 respectively.

We then divided the coded variables into two groups, largely corresponding to accountability systems and resources. We ran cross-tabulations and conducted exploratory statistical analyses that viewed the accountability measures as independent variables and the resource measures as dependent variables, permitting us to assess some of the underlying logic of Edison's strategies by examining relationships between accountability and resources. The aim was to examine in an exploratory way whether schools in which Edison's accountability systems are operating according to plan see better ground-level use of the resources in the Edison design. In addition, by incorporating school-level achievement estimates (derived as described in Chapters Five and Six) for the case study schools, we were able to examine relationships between accountability systems and resources, on the one hand, and student achievement outcomes, on the other. This chapter presents the results of the analyses relating accountability variables to resource variables as well as broader descriptive themes emerging in the case study observations; in Chapter Seven, we discuss the results of the achievement analyses for the case study schools.

Accountability Systems

Edison leaders have acknowledged that they do not always have the opportunity to implement fully all of the accountability systems that their design involves. Each of Edison's contracts to operate schools is unique, and clients sometimes impose constraints that require compromises to Edison's ideal model. In this section, we discuss the extent to which each of the accountability elements of Edison's design was apparent in our observations of the schools and the system.

Line Authority

As intended in the design, Edison had operational authority over all of the case study schools we visited, with principals reporting to Edison's regional general managers. Indeed, Edison's model invests substantial responsibility in the hands of general managers and regional achievement vice presidents (a few of whom are also serving as current principals). But Edison's authority over school operations is not always complete, and in some district partnership schools it coincides uncomfortably with a parallel line of authority through the district itself (see also Bulkley, Mundell, and Riffer, 2004, on the challenges of the EMO-district relationship in Philadelphia). Some of the principals in Edison's district partnership schools complained of the challenges associated with reporting to two masters: Edison and the district. Edison's charter schools usually have fewer problems with competing authority, but local charter boards sometimes seek to assert their influence, occasionally creating challenges similar to those experienced in many district schools.

The challenges of competing authority are not necessarily resolved by contracts that clearly spell out Edison's operational control of the schools. Even when a contract nominally grants full control, a district's power to cancel a contract creates the opportunity for implicit influence in operations. The ability to navigate the political and contractual waters associated with having two masters is therefore a critical skill both for Edison principals and for general managers responsible for maintaining good client relations.

In extreme cases, district clients view Edison as a mere vendor—providing curriculum, professional development, and assessment tools—rather than a manager with both the responsibility and the authority to run the school. Our case studies included a small number of schools where district clients had this attitude, and such schools typically only weakly represented the Edison culture.

If Edison administrators succeed in managing the relationship with their clients, the absence of full operational authority does not necessarily create problems. In Philadelphia, for example, the district and the superintendent remain intimately involved in operational decisions in the Edison schools, viewing Edison as a collaborative partner. Despite the intense political battle that accompanied Edison's arrival in Philadelphia, and despite the design compromises required by limited resources (which we discuss later), over the course of three years Edison staff have developed what they believe is as an effective working relationship with the district. Similarly, the premise of Edison's newly established "Edison alliance" model is that such relationships can be replicated in districts where Edison is explicitly a vendor of educational services, lacking direct operational authority. In Philadelphia, the working success of the relationship has undoubtedly been enhanced by the intensity of support and staff Edison has provided locally, where a critical mass of 20 Edison schools permits local economies of scale that Edison lacks in most of its sites.

Staffing Authority

Along with operational authority, Edison had authority to hire and fire the principal in nearly all of the schools we visited. Indeed, Edison sets high expectations for principals, and it has dismissed more than a few who have fallen short. Edison is not reluctant to apply corporate models to the process; on at least one occasion it has set a target of improving or dismissing the bottom quartile of principals—and followed through on the plan, firing 80 percent of the bottom-quartile group. In 2004–2005, Edison made a point of evaluating principals early in the year—and dismissed at least two in mid-year. Even in Philadelphia, where decisions about changes in school leadership must be made jointly with the district, Edison reports that it has been able to remove and replace principals as needed, in cooperation with the district (a report that appears to be confirmed by principal turnover in Edison's Philadelphia schools).

By contrast, we observed one school in which Edison's nominal authority over the staffing of the principal position was seriously undermined in practice by the principal's personal relationship with the district superintendent. Constrained by the need to maintain a good relationship with an unsupportive superintendent, Edison kept on staff a principal about whom it had serious doubts. The school had a variety of problems—with design implementation, with student achievement, and with teacher morale—all traceable to leadership. Ultimately, the principal was publicly accused of testing improprieties, and Edison lost the contract for the school as a result. This was, to be sure, an extreme and spectacular case, but it represents one end of a continuum; we came across at least one other instance in which an ineffective principal survived longer than might have been justified as a result of a personal connection with the client (in this case, a charter board president). In an Edison school in Rochester, New York (not part of our case study sample), which was recently given an unfavorable review in request for the renewal of its charter, the renewal report for the chartering authority noted that one of a series of unsuccessful principals in the school had been hired by the school's board against the wishes of Edison (Charter Schools Institute, 2005). In short, Edison's de facto authority to dismiss a principal is sometimes less than the letter of the contract might imply.

And the authority to dismiss an ineffective principal matters. It will come as no surprise that Edison case study schools in which RAND researchers gave principals strong ratings for instructional leadership (i.e., principals who appeared to spend a substantial amount of time visiting classrooms, who analyzed achievement data, and who took an active role in site-based professional development for teachers) also showed stronger implementation of both tested (reading and math) and non-tested (science, social studies, specials, and core values) aspects of the Edison curriculum.[2] Moreover, schools with strong instructional principals had better achievement results (as we discuss further in Chapter Seven).

Edison's authority over teacher staffing is more often compromised than its authority over principals, largely because it usually is required to honor existing teacher contracts in its district partnership schools. In most of Edison's charter schools, teachers are employed under one-year contracts that are renewed at the discretion of the principal. But in district schools, Edison teachers usually have the same contractual and tenure protections as teachers in other public schools in the local district. (And we often heard principals in district contract schools long for the staffing authority available to charter principals.) Indeed, Edison teachers in district schools often receive their paychecks from the district rather than from Edison.

---

[2] On a reading and math implementation scale ranging from one to two, Edison schools with strong instructional leaders had a mean score of 1.89, while schools without strong instructional leaders had a mean score of 1.61 (N=18). On a nontested-subjects implementation scale ranging from one to two, Edison schools with strong instructional leaders had a mean score of 1.68, while schools without strong instructional leaders had a mean score of 1.29 (N=18). In both cases, differences were statistically significant at 0.05.

In general, Edison is willing to accept compromises to its ability to dismiss teachers as long as the district makes it relatively easy for teachers to transfer voluntarily out of the Edison school (see Chubb, 2004). Rhim (2005) describes the problems that Edison faces in Chester, Pennsylvania, where it not only lacks authority to hire and fire teachers, but also effectively lacks a voluntary transfer mechanism because it operates nine of the ten schools in the district. Edison believes that, in most instances, the voluntary transfer mechanism ensures that the teachers who do not "buy in" to the Edison model will not stay. Consistent with this view, we saw only one Edison school that had substantial numbers of teachers who were actively opposed to Edison. That school was a Philadelphia school in its first year of operation by Edison, where teacher morale collapsed as a result of poor leadership by the Edison principal (who was ultimately dismissed before the end of the school year). Large numbers of teachers transferred after the first year, removing some of the resistance.

One other case we observed is worth noting. At one of the most successful Edison schools we visited (a conversion school that achieved spectacular achievement gains under Edison's management), the Edison principal had nearly complete discretion to hire and fire teachers, except that the contract included a series of mandatory targets for state teacher certification: Each year, a higher proportion of the school's teachers had to be certified. At the end of each year, the principal was forced to dismiss a number of uncertified teachers, regardless of the achievement results in the school or the principal's desire to keep the teachers. This constraint apparently did not pose a major problem for the school, however, which remained one of Edison's star performers when we visited again two years later.

Within each Edison school we visited, the assignment of teachers to leadership positions—i.e., the use of Edison's teacher career ladder—at least nominally followed the Edison design. Principals have the authority to appoint lead teachers and subject-matter curriculum coordinators in the case study schools, and they are not required to abide by seniority rules in making such appointments. In many district partnership schools, however, existing teacher labor contracts constrain Edison's ability to set salaries commensurate with the teacher ladder (rather than with seniority).

Many of the young teachers we spoke with (and Edison's teachers are often young) looked favorably on the opportunities created by the Edison career ladder, even if those opportunities did not include substantial pay benefits. They appreciated the chance to assume positions of instructional leadership in the school, earlier than would be possible under a seniority system. For instance, a lead teacher told us the career ladder provided teachers with the "incentive to strive, to be there." Some teachers also appreciated the opportunities available to them to take on responsibilities in the Edison system outside their own schools, whether as summer trainers or as full-time members of Edison's national curriculum teams. For young and ambitious teachers, Edison's opportunities for rapid upward mobility, in the school or in the system, were seen as a genuine advantage.

The Edison system uses these opportunities to advantage as well, giving Edison the ability to recruit ambitious, highly effective teachers to regional and national support and training positions. As one young achievement vice president told us, Edison values "what you have to bring to the table first rather than [your] years of experience." Teachers who took advantage of opportunities to take on summer responsibilities as Edison trainers could benefit their schools as well, increasing site capacity. On the flip side, the system opportunities occasionally create a challenge for schools, which sometimes lose some of their best teachers to national Edison positions. In a few of the schools we visited, we heard concerns about this kind of attrition.

As noted in Chapter Three, Edison aims to offer somewhat better salaries to both teachers and principals, in an effort to increase the quality of its applicant pool. In practice, the salary advantage over other local public schools appears to be larger and more consistent for principals than for teachers. In Edison schools that operate with a longer school day and year, teachers usually receive pay in excess of standard local salaries, but many teachers told us that the additional pay was not sufficient to compensate for the additional hours worked. In particular, some teachers told us they were compensated for the extra days in the year but not the extra hours in the day. In some instances, district teacher contracts made it difficult for Edison to offer all of the benefits it sought; we visited one school in which Edison was precluded from offering its standard stock options (at the time it was a publicly traded company) to teachers because the offer was deemed unfair to other teachers in the district.

Monitoring and Rewards

Information collection systems. During RAND's study, Edison was continually seeking to improve its capacity to gather timely and accurate information on design implementation, instructional performance, and student achievement in its schools. Establishing the monthly benchmark system online represented the most important advance in the information available to Edison, giving immediate feedback to the central office every month about the extent to which students in each school are prepared for high-stakes state assessments (for which Edison has undertaken internal statistical studies that confirm the predictive value of benchmark results).

A recent reduction in the number of schools for which each regional achievement vice president is accountable also helped to improve the quality and consistency of information gathered for Edison about each school. In the past, some achievement vice presidents were responsible for as many as 13 schools, but the new organization reduces their load to seven or eight schools each. This is intended to allow each achievement vice president enough time to visit each school at least twice monthly. The two achievement executive directors who now oversee the monthly achievement calls have instituted a systematic spreadsheet for each achievement vice president to fill out for each of the schools every month. These spreadsheets include a wide variety of information related to discipline, curriculum and instruction, organization, teachers, leadership, benchmark implementation, and student support. Regional achievement vice presidents are asked not only to rate the school on each dimension, but also to answer a set of questions, particularly about the school's principal (e.g., has the principal conveyed his or her year-long vision and Edison/AYP goals to faculty and staff? Are lead teachers and curriculum coordinator observation schedules in place for the quarter?). The various pieces of information are aggregated into a global rating for each school: green for schools that appear to be doing well, yellow for schools with some issues of concern, and red for schools that Edison views as having significant problems.

RAND researchers observed the effects of Edison's ongoing monitoring efforts by regularly listening to Edison's monthly account review calls—in which the red schools get most of the attention. In general, we found an impressive level of detail in the conversations, which suggests an understanding by Edison staff of principals' instructional leadership capabilities, of the general quality of instruction in the school (particularly as related to subjects that are included in state assessments), and even of the strengths and weaknesses of teachers. This information permits Edison staff on the calls to develop targeted strategies to address problems that come up.

Implementation of those strategies has been aided by a reorganization of the school assignments of achievement vice presidents so that they better correspond with the assignments of general managers, permitting improved coordination between achievement vice presidents and general managers (who often participate in the monthly calls along with achievement vice presidents).

Although we cannot compare Edison's monitoring systems to those that exist in conventional school districts, the extent of detailed central-office knowledge about instruction in each of more than a hundred Edison schools appears impressive. The integration of monthly test results and qualitative assessments by direct observers appears to represent the kind of data-driven decisionmaking machinery that many school districts are seeking in the age of NCLB. Edison's systems may provide a useful model for providing information necessary to develop rapid interventions for troubled schools.

Edison's systems for monitoring achievement and instruction have some weaknesses. Some of these are driven by economics and geography: Even though each achievement vice president is typically responsible for only seven schools, those schools are in some instances widely dispersed geographically, making it difficult for the achievement vice presidents to visit regularly. Moreover, Edison's corporate retrenchment a couple of years ago forced substantial reductions in the number of visits that national curriculum staff can conduct. And Edison's information about staffing in schools is often unreliable, because data systems for staffing very often run through the local school district rather than through Edison.

Occasionally, even the quality of information provided by the benchmarks is in doubt. A few teachers have viewed the benchmarks as high-stakes tests in themselves rather than diagnostic tools (although interviews in our case study schools suggested that this is not common). Although Edison's explicit accountability system attaches no consequences to benchmark results (unlike state test results, which constitute a major part of each school's Edison star rating), it is not surprising that some teachers would wonder whether benchmark tests might have implicit consequences for their own evaluation. Teachers who view the benchmarks as high-stakes tests may prepare their students in ways that are effective in promoting performance on the benchmarks but ineffective in promoting general academic skills. If this happens, the diagnostic value of the benchmarks is degraded. Recognizing the potential problem, Edison assessment staff are well aware that misuse of the benchmarks will undermine their utility for diagnosis (for teachers, for schools, and for the central office), and they consistently send the message that the benchmarks should not be viewed as high-stakes tests.

Edison is probably unusual in attempting to gather information on "customer satisfaction" from teachers, students, and parents. In the past, this information has been of relatively limited value, because response rates have varied widely in different schools (among all three groups of respondents). Edison now provides schools with a direct incentive to promote response rates, however, incorporated in the star rating system; this may help to improve the rates in future years.

Star ratings and associated rewards. In the schools we visited, Edison's star rating system has mixed success in getting the attention of teachers, and substantial success in getting the attention of principals. This difference is almost certainly related to the fact that substantial bonuses tied to star ratings are available to most (but not quite all) Edison principals, while contracts often preclude bonuses being given to teachers. Moreover, even where teacher bonuses are available, the bonus pool depends on the performance of the entire school rather than individual teachers. Within a school, distribution of bonuses among teachers is typically at the principal's discretion.

Some principals expressed frustration at the complexity of the star rating system, perceiving it as mysterious, arbitrary, and at least partly beyond their control (particularly with respect to the financial management component). But among the principals who spoke with us, this was a minority view. More often, principals reported that their own motivations were primarily intrinsic, but that the availability of bonuses was a nice benefit. As one principal put it to us, "I don't really think that, if a principal gets up everyday, a bonus is what they're truly after. It's a nice ending to a year of hard work, but I don't think that's what really pushes them to reach that. I think it's the children."

In addition to and apart from the bonuses, Edison hopes the star rating system will motivate performance via the recognition of "four-star schools," which are given public acknowledgment at the conclusion of the Annual Principals' Leadership Conference (PLC). The black-tie award ceremony is modeled after the Academy Awards, and principals clearly appreciate being honored and "treated as professionals."

To the extent that the star rating system motivates behavior in the schools, it is reinforcing the same signals that are created by NCLB and attendant state high-stakes testing systems. Edison's calculation of a school's achievement star rating does not exactly follow NCLB—Edison focuses more on achievement gains, while NCLB focuses primarily on achievement levels—but it relies on the same school-level data, and Edison recently revised the formula to explicitly include the school's success in meeting adequate yearly progress (AYP) under NCLB as one component.

Since it opened its first schools a decade ago, Edison has always used student achievement outcomes as a key measure of accountability, and its focus on achievement outcomes has actually increased during the period of RAND's study. This undoubtedly reflects in part the changes in the external policy environment: NCLB went into effect in 2002, and in its wake, public schools across the country are increasingly focused on student test results.

In fact, we observed an intense focus on achievement in many of the Edison case study schools. This clearly had a payoff, as the case study schools had generally positive achievement trajectories in both reading and math. In some instances, however, a focus on test scores created a tension with Edison's broader goal of promoting "world-class" education. In a few of the schools we visited, some teachers admitted that the broader Edison curriculum is sometimes pushed aside by narrowly focused test preparation activities. Non-tested subjects such as art, music, foreign language, and (in many states) science and social studies are in some instances downplayed in favor of additional practice in basic skills in reading and math. And the ambitious, problem- and concept-focused mathematics curriculum used by Edison is sometimes displaced by worksheets used for test preparation in basic math skills. The most egregious instance we encountered (and the only such instance of which we are aware in the case study schools) involved one Edison principal who was dismissed after the district discovered evidence of cheating on a high-stakes assessment.[3]

We have no evidence that the narrowing of the curriculum in favor of test preparation is any more prevalent in Edison schools than in other public schools responding to NCLB. Various studies indicate that principals and teachers who are subject to high-stakes testing programs report a number of changes to their instructional practice. These changes include shifts in emphasis among tested and nontested subjects, shifts in emphasis among tested and nontested topics or skills within a subject, and the adoption of curriculum materials that are designed to mirror the styles and formats of items on the high-stakes test (Hamilton, 2003; Koretz et al., 1996; Pedulla et al., 2003; Shepard and Dougherty, 1991; Stecher, 2002). Indeed, Edison's explicit advocacy of a broad curriculum—and the additional time provided in its school day and year—may help to blunt the pressure to

[3] We are aware of one other instance of alleged cheating by staff of an Edison school. As this report was being completed, an Edison principal in Chester, Pennsylvania, came under investigation for alleged irregularities in the administration of the Pennsylvania state test.

focus excessively on test preparation. Again, Edison is aware of the tension. Edison's curriculum staff invest a large part of their energy into reducing the tension by providing maps of alignment between the Edison curriculum and state standards and by consistently preaching the embedding of test skills in the curriculum rather than the replacement of the curriculum with test preparation. Nevertheless, it must be acknowledged that to the extent that Edison's accountability systems reward test results, they will reinforce both the productive and unproductive incentives associated with NCLB.

Another consequence of NCLB that we increasingly observed in Edison central office discussions and in schools during the course of our study is a focus on "bubble kids"—i.e., students whose current achievement levels place them near the state's cutoff for determining proficiency in reading and math. The standards movement in K–12 schooling has encouraged schools to move away from achievement measures defined by reference to a larger population (e.g., percentile rankings) and toward achievement measures defined by external standards of proficiency in a particular content or skill area. NCLB cemented this trend by requiring all states to establish school accountability systems based on the proportion of students achieving proficiency. Many public schools around the country have rationally responded to the policy by seeking to identify and direct interventions toward those students who are closest to the cut-point for proficiency—the bubble kids (Pedulla et al., 2003). Edison has responded similarly: Its monthly benchmark assessments give its schools unusually good information for identifying bubble kids, and Edison actively encourages schools to identify such students and develop interventions to prepare them for state exams.

The Edison schools we visited had some variation in attention to bubble kids. Some Edison principals and teachers embrace the concept as a logical and appropriate way to have data drive instructional decisionmaking. Others, however, are disturbed by the possible implication that students on both ends of the achievement spectrum—high achievers and low achievers—might be neglected in favor of those in the middle. These educators try to maintain an instructional focus on improving the achievement of all the children in their schools, regardless of their current proficiency levels. Like the narrowing of curriculum, the bubble kids issue is not unique to Edison, and is an inevitable consequence—not only a rational response, but perhaps even intended by policymakers—of tying accountability for schools to proficiency cut points on state assessments. (See, e.g., Rubin, 2004, on the new attention to bubble kids across public schools.)

Many Edison schools seek to engage the students themselves in test-based accountability. Much of the extensive amount of information on the walls in Edison schools and classrooms is devoted to ensuring that students have clear targets for performance and to recognizing good academic work. And many schools reward classes that achieve strong participation in tests with pizza parties and other minor benefits.

Finally, we observed some Edison schools responding to test-based accountability by moving their best teachers into the tested grades. Again, this is rational given the law, and Edison recognizes it as a short-term, incomplete solution.

Accountability to Parents

Our site visitors had little opportunity to observe the case study schools' interactions with parents. Nevertheless, our conversations with Edison teachers provided one indication of effective school-parent communication: In nearly every Edison school we visited, teachers reported high levels of parent participation (typically better than 90 percent) in quarterly report card meetings. Edison's requirement that its report cards be given to parents in person appears to be effective in bringing them to the school several times a year to meet with teachers.

The fact that Edison schools are schools of choice is intended to create an implicit accountability system, inducing Edison schools to be responsive to parent concerns in order to keep their customers. In practice, the extent to which parents and students actively choose Edison schools varies considerably across our sample. Enrollment in an Edison charter school usually requires an active choice by the family. This is sometimes true in Edison's district contract schools as well, but others retain neighborhood assignment schemes in which parents must actively opt out if they wish their children to go to school elsewhere. We did not observe substantial differences between charter schools and district contract schools in terms of the implementation of Edison's curricula or of elements of the school's professional environment (i.e., houses, planning time, and site-based professional development).

Reduction of Political and Bureaucratic Accountability

Edison's effort to clear away some of the bureaucratic constraints on its principals, providing them with greater freedom of action than is available in conventional public schools, has had only mixed success in the case study schools we visited. Many of the case study principals have greater authority over school budgets than they would have in conventional public schools, but this authority varies widely across the Edison universe, depending on the particular contract that Edison has with its client. Edison principals who are constrained by district requirements sometimes express frustration that they lack the authority available to their colleagues in charter schools. Principals in district contract schools more often have to deal with external bureaucratic challenges, related to issues such as building maintenance, budgets, paperwork, materials, or district-sponsored professional development. Here our conclusions are consistent with those of Rhim (2005), who found an extreme case of bureaucratic confusion and blurred accountability in the Chester, Pennsylvania, school district, where Edison operated nine schools as a result of a state takeover, but where the district's central office continuesD to operate despite losing some—but not all—of its operational authority over the schools.

The additional local bureaucratic and contextual obstacles that some Edison schools face may have an effect on the implementation of the design. In our case study sample, schools where staff reported more local constraints had weaker results on the professional environment index, suggesting more difficulty in implementing the Edison house structure, the planning periods, and site-based professional development.[4] In some schools, for example, Edison is unable to implement its longer school day, which in turn prevents the implementation of its standard of two daily planning periods for teachers. But we did not observe a relationship between local constraints and the implementation of the curriculum.

Edison's own bureaucracy received mixed reviews from the school-level staff we interviewed. Their complaints about Edison, however, were more often related to a perceived insufficiency of support and communication than to excessive red tape. Maintaining consistent support and communication is an ongoing challenge for a widely dispersed "virtual school district" such as Edison. The corporate reorganization that reduced the number of primary Edison contact points for each school (focusing on the general manager and the achievement vice president) was intended to improve Edison's communication and responsiveness.

In terms of support and communication, Edison's schools in Philadelphia have a unique advantage over their counterparts elsewhere. With 20 schools operating in the district, Edison has enough economies of scale to support a 16-person local team that forms its own district office. Staff we interviewed in the case study schools in Philadelphia generally viewed Edison as very responsive to their needs. This was less true in Edison schools that were single and geographically isolated rather than being part of larger contracts.

Edison aims to achieve long-term stability in its schools by insulating them from political turmoil. As noted in Chapter Three, Edison has maintained an impressive stability of corporate leadership and model design, even in the face of a rapidly changing economic and political climate. The school design has remained coherent and focused, permitting modifications at the margins (initiated both centrally and locally) without accreting an incoherent array of competing programs.

---

[4] Schools without substantial local constraints had a mean score of 1.77 on the professional environment index (for which scores ranged from one to two), while schools with substantial local constraints had a mean score of 1.57. The difference is statistically significant at $p < 0.05$.

From the perspective of any particular Edison school, however, the stability of Edison's leadership and design is useful only for the duration of Edison's contract. Sustainability has been a challenge for comprehensive school reform models (which might be viewed as Edison's competitors). Datnow (2005) studied 13 schools operating six comprehensive reform models in one urban district, and found that six of the 13 schools had dropped their models within three years after the initiation of the study. The largest longitudinal study of the sustainability of comprehensive school reform models—including 395 schools in 21 districts—is reported in Taylor (2005), who finds that one-third of schools had dropped their models within two years of the initiation of the study. A study of 78 Pennsylvania schools that adopted comprehensive reform models found that 36 percent were no longer implementing those models after five years (Evans et al., 2004, as cited in Taylor, 2005).

It is difficult to compare directly Edison's record of maintaining relationships with these results, because the other studies typically do not follow a cohort of schools from the first year of implementation; attrition rates during the course of a three- or five-year study may not be equivalent to attrition rates during the first three or five years of implementation. Nevertheless, Edison's record of sustaining relationships with schools appears reasonably strong relative to observed results for comprehensive reform models. The great majority of Edison's contracts—a total of 89 percent of contracts initiated by 2001, which include 87 percent of schools that began working with Edison by 2001[5]—have lasted at least four years. Figure 4.1 shows the four-year survival rate of Edison contracts by the starting year.

[5] The number of contracts is not identical to the number of schools, because some contracts involve multiple schools.

Figure 4.1
Proportion of Edison Contracts Remaining in Place for at Least Four Years by Year of Opening

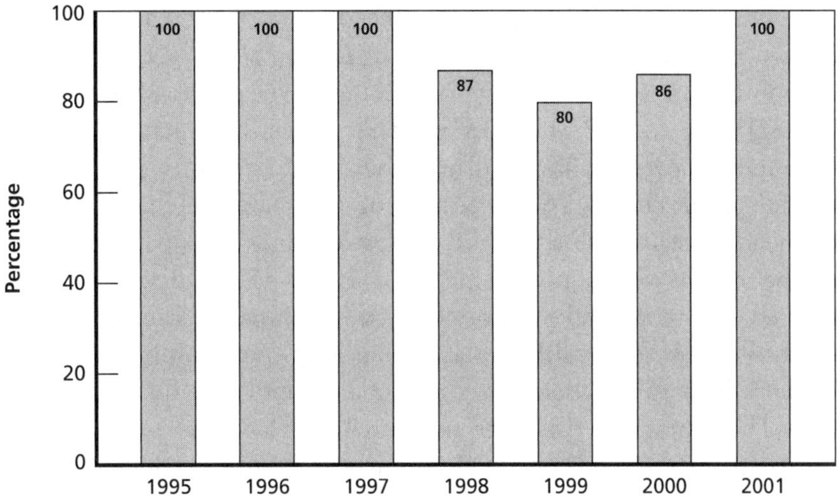

RAND *MG351-4.1*

A majority of the schools that opened in Edison's first three years no longer operate under an Edison contract today. Nevertheless, all of those early contracts lasted at least five years, a record that was not matched in the next three cohorts of Edison schools. Contracts have ended for a variety of political and practical reasons, including insufficient enrollment, low academic performance or failure to meet expected achievement gains, and high costs of maintaining the contract. Turnover of local superintendents has led to difficulties in keeping contracts in a number of districts where Edison has worked; turnover on school boards can have a similar effect. The increase in cancellation rates for schools opened in the late 1990s may be related to the fact that this was Edison's period of most rapid growth. In recent years, Edison has recognized that its success in holding contracts has been less than perfect (see Chubb, 2004), and it has responded by placing greater expectations on its regional general managers to maintain and cultivate its relationships with clients. Such efforts are particularly important during a period when Edison is not seeing rapid growth in the number of new clients for its managed schools business. Whether these efforts will pay dividends in improved contract longevity will be seen over the next few years.

Edison's charter contracts have been more stable than its district contracts. Eighty percent (20 of 25) of Edison's contracts for district schools opening between 1995 and 2001 survived at least four years, while 95 percent (38 of 40) of Edison's charter contracts initiated in the same time period lasted at least that long. Examining the survival of individual schools, 76 percent (31 of 41) of Edison charter schools opened between 1995 and 2000 remained under Edison operation in spring 2005, while only 36 percent (17 of 47) of district schools opened during the same period were still operated by Edison. Edison has been more successful in establishing long-term stability, and, perhaps, in insulating schools from political turmoil, in the charter context. This is not surprising, given that charter laws are specifically designed to remove schools from the direct control of local, elected school boards.[6] It suggests, however, that Edison has a greater challenge in ensuring long-term stability in its district contract schools.

Resources

We now turn to the implementation in the case study schools of the resource components of the Edison design, including technical capital, time, human capital, and social capital.

Technical Capital

Curriculum. Nearly all of the Edison schools we visited, in all parts of the country, were immediately recognizable as Edison schools, by virtue of the curriculum materials and examples of student work covering nearly every wall, in classrooms and hallways

---

[6] Even in charter schools, political insulation can sometimes be a challenge. One of our case study schools was a charter school whose charter had been granted by the state on appeal, after being denied by the local district. The district was therefore given responsibility to act as the authorizing and supervising agency over a school it had not wanted to open. Not surprisingly, the school's relationship with its authorizing agency is tense.

alike. Only two of the case study schools demonstrably deviated from the standard Edison appearance, and in those two schools the absence of Edison wall displays was a clear sign of much deeper problems with the commitment of the staff to the implementation of the Edison model.[7] The various materials associated with the Edison curricula (including textbooks and manipulables) were consistently present in the schools we visited, although many schools reported delays in receiving the materials during their first year of operation. Edison teachers with prior experience in non-Edison settings were often pleasantly surprised at the availability and quality of the materials provided by Edison.

Our teacher interviews and classroom observations could provide only a very limited view of the implementation of the curriculum in the classroom. Not surprisingly, there appeared to be more implementation challenges during the first year of Edison operation, when many teachers encountered the curricula for the first time. In most schools we visited, implementation appeared strongest in reading (Success for All or Open Court) and math (Everyday Mathematics)—consistent with the emphasis of Edison's central office, and with the incentives created by most states' test-based accountability systems. Nearly every school followed a schoolwide daily schedule involving 90 minutes of simultaneous, mandated reading instruction for all students and at least 60 minutes of daily mathematics.

Given the high-stakes accountability environment and the importance of state assessments, many of the case study schools supplemented the reading and math curricula with additional materials designed to prepare students for state examinations. Edison does not discourage the use of supplemental materials as long as the curriculum is not displaced. Although Edison works aggressively on alignment and embedding issues, teachers are not always convinced that curriculum is well aligned with their state's tests. We were told of occasional displacements, but saw no evidence that they occurred fre-

---

[7] One of these schools was a very troubled first-year Edison school in Philadelphia, while the other was a long-time Edison school that not long after our visit ended its contract. Both schools had serious problems with leadership and morale.

quently. Edison's flexibility in allowing schools to supplement the curriculum to meet the needs of local standards and assessments and its efforts to provide teachers with tools to embed test skills within and alongside the existing curriculum—as well as the time available in the long school day—may contribute to maintaining the fidelity of implementation of its core programs in reading and math.

We heard more reports, by contrast, that nontested elements of the Edison curriculum were sometimes displaced by test preparation or other priorities. Implementation of Edison's curricula in social studies, science, and specials, including art, music, and foreign language, was less consistent than the implementation of the reading and math curricula across the case study schools. A few teachers suggested that this displacement resulted in part from Edison's own focus on reading and math; external pressure from states' test-based accountability systems (which usually focus on reading and math) undoubtedly contributes as well (as it does in other public schools).

Compromises in the implementation of nontested subjects were in some case study schools related to resource limitations. In Philadelphia, for example, Edison's contract with the district did not provide sufficient resources to implement the model fully, forcing the abandonment of the longer day, the longer year, and some of the fine arts curricula.[8] According to Edison central office interviews, the budget crises that hit states and local governments across the country in the early part of this decade led to similar compromises in many of its schools.

Regardless of the year of operation, schools with principals who were stronger instructional leaders saw better implementation of nontested and tested subjects alike, as noted above.

---

[8] At the time Edison's contract was awarded in Philadelphia, there was considerable local controversy about the fact that the Edison schools were receiving additional funds beyond those available to other schools in the district, on the order of $750 per pupil. But the assumption that the Edison schools are receiving more funds does not account for variations in teacher experience and salary, which are often substantial within districts. It is not clear that, when teacher salaries are accounted for, the Edison schools in Philadelphia actually receive more funding per pupil than do other schools in the district.

Computers in instruction. Our case study schools provided a few examples in which Edison's investments in computers and audiovisual technology were being well-used by students as well as teachers, for example, in conducting a daily student-run live video announcement delivered to all classrooms at the beginning of the day. And by 2003, virtually all of the case study schools were participating in the monthly online benchmark assessments. But with the important exception of the benchmarks (which we discuss separately below), we saw little evidence of a systematic, Edison-wide plan for the use of computer technology in the curriculum, despite some splashy investments (such as state-of-the-art experimental computer labs installed at a couple of schools). Moreover, school staff frequently complained to us about technical problems—especially in the first year of the school's operation—and insufficient technical support from Edison. The schools that were making extensive use of computers in instruction appeared to be doing so largely at local initiative. We have no reason to believe that Edison schools are trailing other public schools in the use of computers in instruction, but the reality in the Edison schools is well short of the high expectations that Edison created for its clients.

Some Edison leaders privately acknowledged that the use of computer technology in the schools was a weak point of implementation. Indeed, Edison's recent move away from providing home computers to the families of its students was driven largely by the recognition that the computers were not providing an educational return on their investment. Edison recognized some of the fundamental economic challenges associated with the use of computers in the public-school funding context, and its technology staff have been working creatively to design novel solutions to the problem—for example, entering at one point into a partnership (since abandoned) with a major manufacturer to create a new computing device designed specifically for the K–12 environment. But although such efforts may bear fruit in the future, we did not yet see evidence of a substantial impact in the case study schools.

Communication technology. By contrast with instruction, communication in Edison schools was clearly advanced by Edison's technology investments. Teachers generally appreciated Edison's provision of laptops and email (except in the few cases where budget constraints precluded the provision of laptops), and many teachers used them to correspond both with colleagues in the school and with Edison's regional and national staff. Edison's intranet, known as The Common, was used less consistently, but was regarded as an asset by the teachers and principals who took advantage of its resources.

As noted above, the home computers purchased by Edison for the families of its students did not appear to improve home-school communication dramatically in any of our case study schools. But Edison's investments in the less flashy technologies of classroom telephones and voicemail for teachers had clear benefits for parent communication, in the opinion of many teachers with whom we spoke. The phones and voicemail made it easier for parents and teachers to communicate about homework assignments and behavioral challenges. In addition, teachers valued them as an indication of professional respect, so the investment actually aided teacher morale in some schools.

Diagnostic technology: benchmarks. Edison's investment in technology has a clear impact with the benchmark system. As previously noted, electronic benchmark development was the most notable improvement during the course of our study in Edison's ability to monitor and diagnose academic challenges in the schools. But the purpose of the benchmark system is only secondarily to provide information to the Edison central office. Its primary purpose is to provide monthly diagnostic information to teachers and principals so that instruction can be modified and improved at the school site in a timely way, with the specific needs of students and teachers in mind.

Early in the development of the benchmark system, we observed a variety of implementation challenges in the schools. Benchmarks were originally issued on paper, which meant they required time to assess. The launch of the electronic benchmark system was plagued by a variety of technical problems, leading to frequent frustration in many schools when the system was overwhelmed. By the time of our second round of visits, however, these problems had been largely ironed out, and the system appeared to be used faithfully and reliably at nearly all of the case study schools (with the exception of some new start-up schools).

More importantly, reports indicated that many teachers and principals found the benchmarks valuable, and were using the results effectively and as intended to diagnose instructional challenges and develop interventions. Reports of benchmark misuse (for example, interpreting them as high-stakes assessments and providing preparation specifically for benchmark tests) were rare in case study schools, and were vigorously countered by clear messages from Edison's central office about appropriate use. Given the success of the benchmark system, it is not surprising that Edison is finding customers for it outside of its own managed schools. Alongside the benchmarks, Edison now provides its schools with various additional diagnostic instruments (such as Dynamic Indicators of Basic Early Literacy Skills [DIBELS]), which, based on conversations at the principals' leadership conference, are also valued and much used.

A note on charter-school facilities. Physical facilities are an important aspect of resources provided to Edison schools as well. Although a unique building is not an explicit part of Edison's model, the building is necessarily a major focus of attention in Edison's start-up charter schools. Two-thirds (37 of 55) of Edison charter schools were new start-ups at the time Edison began operating them. Edison's conversion schools inherit their buildings, while start-up charter schools must procure a facility. Start-up charter schools all over the country have experienced major challenges in finding and improving buildings to house their students (see, e.g., Zimmer et al., 2003). Although Edison's start-up charter schools have sometimes had access to considerable amounts of private financing, they have faced many of the same challenges, particularly in the first year of operation, as they have struggled to get their buildings ready for students. Despite Edison's considerable experience in opening new schools, case study evidence suggests that these challenges may be just as serious for recently opened Edison charters as for those that opened nearly a decade ago.

Time

Most of the case study schools we visited in fact used an extended school day (19 of 23 schools) and an extended school year (15 of 23 schools), as intended in the Edison design. Edison's Philadelphia schools do not operate with a longer day and year, as a result of contractual and resource limitations there. Outside of Philadelphia, some Edison schools have shortened their academic year, in part because of resource limitations and in part due to concerns about teacher burnout. Edison leaders believe they have been more successful with the longer school day than with the longer year, for several reasons. Attendance is usually lower during the additional weeks of school, because families may have other children in schools using conventional calendars and therefore may be unprepared to have their children in school. Students themselves sometimes resist the extra weeks while their friends are on vacation. And state attendance requirements can create unintended problems for schools with a longer year, if attendance is measured during those weeks.

Despite these challenges, many Edison schools not only maintain longer standard schedules, but also operate after-school and Saturday programs to provide additional skill training, especially for bubble kids and especially in the weeks prior to state exams.

The availability of two periods of time daily for planning and professional development varies across the case study schools. Most were able to put the periods in place as intended, but some had difficulties related to local contractual issues. Reducing this time was one of the compromises that Edison made in Philadelphia, for example, where the shorter school day and the reduced availability of fine arts instruction reduces flexibility.

With respect to the quality of classroom instructional time, our observers were impressed to see the effective use of Edison's classroom management techniques in most case study schools. Various simple classroom management techniques that Edison teaches all teachers in the teaching academy were in evidence in the classrooms of case study schools across the country, and appeared to be effective in keeping students focused and alert, and maintaining a "safe and orderly learning environment." In addition, teachers in many schools made effective use of the house support structure to handle behavior problems before they required the school administration's attention. Many lead teachers took responsibility for helping to handle discipline challenges for all of the teachers in their houses. In a few schools with serious and chronic discipline problems, the problems appeared to be associated with weak building management on the principals' parts.

Human and Social Capital

We now turn to Edison's investments in the skills, morale, and trust of its school staff, addressing first the professional development resources provided by Edison's central office, and then the school-site mechanisms for professional development.

Centrally provided professional development. Edison's up-front investment in the skills of teachers and principals who are new to its schools is impressive. Edison teachers often describe the summer teaching academy as overwhelming in its intensity and breadth of its content, and they report that the value of the seminars varies with the skills of the presenter, but they are typically pleased with the simple fact that Edison pays for their participation in a week-long conference at an out-of-town hotel. Like the classroom phones and voicemail, the professional development conferences—including both the summer sessions for new teachers and the fall achievement academies for curriculum coordinators and other teacher leaders—are viewed by many Edison teachers as a sign that they are respected as professionals. This has benefits in terms of morale and trust even apart from the direct benefits the training may have for the skills of teachers.

Perhaps the primary concern about Edison's professional development conferences for teachers is that the investment is often lost as a result of attrition. Edison-wide, rates of teacher attrition are unclear,[9] but it was a serious challenge at many case study schools—as it is at high-poverty urban public schools generally, which, like Edison,

[9] Edison schools typically report some sort of teacher turnover rate, but reported rates are based on local definitions of turnover and are therefore not necessarily comparable across Edison schools. We were unable to calculate an Edison-wide teacher turnover rate with confidence.

rely extensively on early-career teachers who have the highest rates of departure from the profession. Edison recognizes that its efforts to build site capacity in schools are often hampered by attrition, and it has incorporated retention of teachers into its star-rating formula in an effort to encourage principals to promote stability.

Like teachers, many principals value the summer leadership academy and the fall PLC as indicators of professional respect. We spoke to a number of Edison principals who appreciate the responsibility and support that Edison provides them, particularly in the area of instructional leadership. Relatively new Edison principals were pleased not only to be attending the conferences as learners, but also to be given the opportunity to present to their colleagues. Nevertheless, like new Edison teachers, many new Edison principals find the experience overwhelming, particularly if they do not have experience acting as instructional leaders or managing budgets; a number of new principals told us they would like more support from Edison. Given the high expectations that Edison has for principals, and the extensive demands it places on them, the PLC and its annual awards ceremony are particularly important for promoting morale and a sense of Edison-wide community among principals (although we heard some disgruntlement from a small number of principals who felt that unfair financial targets made it impossible for them to win awards).

Ongoing support from Edison achievement and curriculum staff. Edison's reorganization reduced its reliance on in-person school visits from its national curriculum staff, in favor of greater reliance on the regional achievement vice presidents. In total, the number of support visits to Edison schools probably declined with the reorganization, as Edison tried to reduce travel costs incurred by its central staff. The curriculum staff has tried to replace some reduced school visits with remote support, via email, phone, and regularly scheduled "Edison evenings," professional development programs conducted by conference call. School staff generally appreciated their email and telephone access to Edison's national curriculum staff, but many of them would have liked more in-person support. Philadelphia, again, offers an exception to the general model, because the concentration of 20 schools there allows Edison to keep a local team of staff who can give direct support to schools; this model appears to work well. We heard more complaints about insufficient support in schools that were relatively isolated geographically than in those schools in Philadelphia.[10]

School staff who deal with Edison's national support staff were usually quite pleased with the quality of the support, although many of them would have liked it in greater quantity. We heard some complaints, however, about areas like science (where Edison has invested fewer resources than in math or reading, and where many states do not yet have accountability tests). In addition, at the small number of our case study schools that had opted to use the Open Court reading program rather than Success for All, we heard some complaints that Edison's support for the program was disappointing in quality. Edison only recently began to offer its schools the option of using Open Court, after many years of working exclusively with Success for All.

School-based professional development (site capacity). As noted in Chapter Three, Edison relies extensively on professional development conducted in formal and informal ways at the school site. Indeed, Edison believes site-based learning opportunities for teachers are more important than its centrally organized annual conferences and the support it offers via the achievement vice presidents and national curriculum staff.

Ideally, Edison wants its principals to play a prominent role in leading instruction and in developing the skills of teachers. In practice, we saw wide variation in the case study schools in the extent to which the principal was viewed by teaching staff as an effective instructional leader. Some Edison principals focused on the more traditional responsibilities associated with building management. Others, however, appeared to be highly successful at leading training sessions, modeling instruction, and motivating teachers.

In our case study sample, there was some evidence that charter schools were more likely to have strong instructional principals than

---

[10] For example, one staffer at a relatively new, and struggling, Edison school complained, "I feel like we've been left in the lurch."

were district schools.[11] We can only speculate on the reason for this, but it may be related to the fact that charter schools were less likely to be bound by teacher contracts that narrowly define the scope of a principal's instructional supervision responsibilities.

As previously noted, strong instructional leadership by principals was associated, in the case study schools, with stronger implementation of both tested curricula (reading and math) and nontested curricula (science, social studies, specials, and core values). Moreover, Edison schools with weaker instructional leaders were found to be more likely to end their contractual relationship with Edison subsequently than were schools with strong instructional leaders.[12] In addition, as we discuss in Chapter Eight, schools with stronger instructional principals achieved greater achievement gains in both reading and math.

The extent to which Edison's ideal of shared leadership was implemented in the case study schools varied widely. In the best-functioning schools, the teaching staff viewed the opportunity to participate in schoolwide decisions via the school leadership team as one of the best features of the Edison design. In such schools, lead teachers appreciated the empowerment represented by participation in the leadership team. As one lead teacher noted, "to have ownership in something, you need to feel [you are a] part of it." The extent to which the leadership team involved genuine collaboration in decisionmaking depended almost entirely on the personal style of the principal; some welcomed shared leadership while others preferred a more autocratic model (but we did not observe that this difference predicted a school's achievement results).

---

[11] Five of eight charter schools in the sample were coded as having strong instructional principals, while only two of ten district schools were rated with strong instructional principals. (In five schools, we lacked sufficient information to make a judgment about instructional leadership.)

[12] In the small sample of case study schools for which we were able to rate instructional leadership, only one of seven (14 percent) schools that later ended relationships with Edison had strong instructional leaders, while six of eleven (55 percent) schools that remain with Edison had strong instructional leaders.

Similarly, the house structure was formally present in virtually every Edison school we visited, but its effectiveness and use depended very much on the skills and ambition of the lead teachers. We saw great variation among the case study schools, and even within individual schools, in the extent to which lead teachers take on the leadership role that Edison seeks to give them. We encountered examples of houses in which lead teachers provided active mentorship to their junior colleagues, in which they took responsibility for assisting with behavior problems in the classrooms of other teachers in the house, and in which they played an active role on the school leadership team. In such instances, the lead teachers were often respected and admired by their colleagues, and houses functioned as the closely knit teams that Edison envisioned them to be.

By contrast, some lead teachers lacked the capacity, the motivation, or the respect from their house members that would be needed to take on the leadership responsibilities. In some schools, particularly in the start-up year, principals had difficulty finding experienced and motivated teachers to take on the role. Apart from the limited training that Edison provided them, few lead teachers had any prior training or experience in the evaluative role of the lead teacher—a role that represented a substantial cultural shift for nearly all teachers (although in many instances, this problem was rendered moot, because lead teachers were prohibited by the teacher contract from serving as evaluators). Edison challenges longstanding norms in public schools with its notions that classroom doors should be open to colleagues and that some teachers should have the responsibility of evaluating other teachers; those norms have retained force in many Edison schools.

Some of the challenges facing both lead teachers and school-level curriculum coordinators, however, are inherent in Edison's model. In particular, although Edison seeks to give substantial instructional leadership responsibilities to lead teachers and coordinators, the model does not give them additional time during the school day to pursue those responsibilities. In schools using Success for All, the reading coordinator is freed of teaching responsibilities for half of the day; but in other subjects, coordinators are full-time teachers who are expected to fulfill their responsibilities during their standard professional development periods and when principals can find occasional substitutes so they can observe the instruction of their colleagues and provide coaching support. Curriculum coordinators in Edison schools across the country told us that they rarely had opportunities to get out of their own classrooms and act as coaches—a key task of a curriculum coordinator, according to the Edison design. As a result, many curriculum coordinators defined their jobs largely in terms of keeping track of the inventory of materials for their subject matter.

Culture of achievement. One of Edison's key strategies for developing social capital in schools is the creation of a culture of achievement. Much of Edison's efforts at its annual conferences for teachers and principals are motivational, aimed at creating a companywide culture of achievement that will be fully represented in each school building. In this respect, as in other elements of Edison's strategies, we observed mixed success in the case study schools. A few schools had serious morale problems, driven in part by teacher burnout; burnout in turn contributed to high rates of staff turnover, making it difficult to sustain a unifying culture. But we also saw principals, teachers, and entire schools where Edison's culture of achievement was everywhere in evidence, from the explicit achievement goals posted throughout the building, to the intensive focus on the use of data to improve instruction, to the attention and engagement of students, to the devotion of staff who willingly worked many hours beyond the last bell.

Conclusion

The best-functioning Edison schools demonstrate the promise inherent in Edison's model. They are schools with strong instructional leadership, motivated teachers, effective use of achievement data, high-fidelity implementation of the Edison curricula, and high levels of social capital. Although realization of this ideal is not universal across Edison schools, nearly all of the Edison schools we visited across the country showed enough consistency of implementation to be clearly recognizable as Edison schools.

Among the schools we visited, several factors appear to be important in explaining some of the variation in implementation of the Edison model:

- Full implementation of Edison design takes time. Schools in the first year of operation had frequent challenges in implementing various elements of the design. Edison has been largely, but not entirely, successful in keeping its contracts long enough to ensure the opportunity for full implementation; its charter schools tend to be more stable contractually than its district schools.
- Strong instructional leadership by the principal is associated with stronger implementation of the curriculum, in both tested and nontested subjects.
- Among the case study schools, strong instructional leadership by principals appeared to be more prevalent in charter schools than in district schools. But charter status did not appear to be directly related to curriculum implementation.
- Local constraints, sometimes resulting from compromises required by local contracts, sometimes undermine the implementation of Edison's preferred professional environment.

The discussion so far has focused on Edison's design and its implementation. We now turn to our analyses of student achievement in Edison schools, beginning with a discussion of the methodology. Later, in Chapter Seven, we present some analyses of achievement results in the case study schools to explore whether variation in implementation is related to differences in achievement trends across Edison schools.

CHAPTER FIVE

Methodology for Examining Academic Achievement in Edison Schools

J. R. Lockwood, Laura S. Hamilton, Brian P. Gill, and Ron W. Zimmer

Chapters Five through Seven describe our analyses of students' academic achievement in Edison schools. In this chapter, we describe the statistical methodology we use to examine students' academic achievement in Edison schools. We begin with a discussion of the research questions that this study addresses. We then describe our methodological approach, which was designed to address the research questions within the constraints of the available data. The subsequent two chapters present the results and discuss their interpretation.

Defining the Research Questions

Before turning to the specific features of our analysis, it is important to understand the questions that the study was designed to address and to acknowledge the ways in which limitations in our data prevent us from fully understanding Edison's effects on achievement. Our study addresses the following questions related to achievement:

1. How does Edison's management of schools affect student achievement?
2. What factors explain differences in achievement trends among Edison schools?

The first question is the one that is of greatest interest to most parents, educators, and policymakers—namely, whether the achievement of Edison students is higher, lower, or unchanged compared to what it would have been if the students had attended conventional public schools. Ideally, this would involve examining the achievement trajectories of individual students longitudinally over time for students in Edison schools as well as students in non-Edison schools. Unfortunately (as we discuss later), such information is unavailable except in a small subset of Edison schools. In consequence, we must rely on publicly available schoolwide achievement results for the bulk of our analysis.

Using school-level data to estimate an overall Edison achievement effect requires that we make some assumptions about how the Edison schools would have done if Edison had not been managing them. In technical terms, it requires estimating a counterfactual outcome. We conduct several different analyses involving different assumptions about the appropriate counterfactual, described below. All of these analyses rely on longitudinal data that examine the achievement progress of Edison schools over time. We present these results in Chapter Six, along with a discussion of how the various results might be interpreted.

The second major question is intended to go beyond systemwide averages and explore variation in the performance of different Edison schools. In Chapter Seven, we report the results of several analyses designed to peer "inside the black box," examining a few factors that might explain why some Edison schools have positive achievement trends while others do not. First, we explore whether Edison's performance has changed as the company has gained experience managing schools. In addition, we examine whether there are differences in achievement results between Edison's charter schools and district schools, between its start-up schools and conversion schools, and between its elementary and secondary schools. Chapter Seven concludes by revisiting the case study schools, for which we were able to measure several aspects of design implementation. We report some exploratory analyses that involve examining relationships between implementation and achievement in these schools.

Estimating the Counterfactual

The first research question, examining Edison's effect on student achievement, is the study's critical causal question. In this section, we briefly discuss how our approach is designed to examine this causal question. Readers who are interested in a more technical explication of the reasoning applied to these analyses should refer to Appendix A, where we provide additional details about our statistical methods and the extent to which they support causal inference.

As noted above, estimating Edison's causal effect on student achievement requires estimating a counterfactual—the hypothetical achievement outcome that the Edison students would have attained if they were not attending Edison schools. The difference between the actual achievement results of Edison students and the estimated counterfactual results can then be interpreted as an approximation to the effect of Edison management on student achievement.

Random assignment of study participants to treatment and control groups, which is often considered the gold standard of research designs, is not possible: Students are not randomly assigned to Edison schools, and schools are not randomly assigned to Edison's management. An alternative is to obtain longitudinally linked, student-level data, which would allow us to follow students as they enter and exit the Edison program, comparing the achievement gains of students in Edison schools and non-Edison schools. We hoped to be able to obtain student-level data Edison-wide, but were able to do this for only a small number of schools, as we discuss in Appendix K.

In the absence of student-level data in most Edison sites, we must rely on school-level data for most of our analysis, using student-level data from a small sample of schools as a source of supporting evidence.[1] Implicitly, the use of school-level data involves shifting the

---

[1] Ideally, we would have used student-level data from all Edison schools and comparison schools for our main analysis. Edison collects student-level data for its students and offered to provide these data to us. However, our analytic approach required data from comparison students in schools not under Edison's management. We made efforts to obtain such data from as many schools and districts as possible, but ultimately were able to secure only a small number of agreements to obtain these data.

counterfactual from individual students to groups of students who attend particular schools: School-level data permit us to examine Edison's impact on schoolwide achievement and to consider the question of what might have happened to average student achievement within a school in the absence of Edison management. Schoolwide results are of some interest in themselves, particularly given that NCLB focuses on improvements at the school level, and educators are now held responsible for demonstrating progress on a school-level metric. But their importance depends primarily on the extent to which they are reliable indicators of effects on individual students. In Chapter Six, we discuss the extent to which the evidence suggests the school-level results are reasonable approximations of student-level effects.

Chapter Six begins by presenting the results of a straightforward longitudinal examination, examining achievement trends in currently operating Edison schools between 2002 and 2004 (which we henceforth describe as the recent trends analysis). We begin with this analysis in order to show how Edison schools have been performing in the most recent years for which we have data; this analysis is similar to the one reported by Edison in its recent annual reports. This is a descriptive analysis that sheds light on the causal question *if we implicitly assume that the counterfactual would have involved no change in achievement*. That is, gains achievement in Edison schools over the last year and over the last two years can be viewed as reasonable estimates of average Edison effects on achievement if the schools otherwise would have seen no gains in achievement over the same period.

We then present a variation on this approach, by offering a counterfactual that involves the achievement trends of a set of matched comparison schools that are not managed by Edison. If we can accurately identify schools that are similar to Edison schools in relevant respects, then their achievement results may provide a useful counterfactual estimate.

Edison schools and students are atypical in a variety of ways, so selecting an appropriate comparison group is a challenging but critical step in this type of analysis. The selection of a set of comparison schools is made difficult by the fact that all Edison schools offer some degree of parental choice, and a number of Edison schools are charter schools that are fully enrolled on the basis of choice rather than neighborhood assignment. Moreover, many of Edison's district contract schools are turned over to Edison's management because they are chronically low performing. In both of these instances, it is likely that some features of the students attending these schools will differ from those of other public schools that serve similar student populations but that are not operated by Edison. In particular, there are likely to be motivational or other factors that make certain students or parents more likely to choose an Edison school than a typical family would be, making it difficult to identify an appropriate comparison group of non-Edison schools.

Given the difficulty of finding appropriate matches for Edison schools, our analyses rely on longitudinal analyses that examine changes in aggregate performance over time rather than on cross-sectional analyses that examine levels of aggregate performance at a single point in time. Both longitudinal and cross-sectional analyses would be appropriate for addressing the causal question if we were successful in finding comparison schools that were well matched to the Edison schools of interest. If, however, there is reason to believe the matches are imperfect, then a longitudinal analysis of changes over time is superior to a cross-sectional analysis, because it helps to account for differences in initial levels of achievement. In fact, Edison is often asked to manage schools that have performed extraordinarily poorly, even in comparison to schools that appear on the surface to serve similar student populations. It is possible that Edison management leads to gains in scores that are larger than the gains achieved by non-Edison schools, but that the absolute performance in Edison schools remains below that of other schools. Our interest in understanding how Edison management affects student learning leads us to focus primarily on score changes rather than levels. We estimate a counterfactual—how might students in Edison schools have done if they had attended non-Edison schools—by comparing Edison's achievement trends to the achievement trends of other schools serving similar populations of students.

No set of comparison schools provides a perfect counterfactual, and even an analysis of gains can provide misleading information if schools are not well matched. In particular, the factors that influence which students opt to attend an Edison school might increase or depress achievement in ways that are difficult to measure. For example, when Edison takes over a school with longstanding achievement problems, the families who choose to remain or enroll might be families who are unconcerned about education or who have exhausted other options. An analysis of test-score gains rather than levels partially addresses this concern but does not eliminate it. There is no way to know definitively that the matched schools provide an accurate estimate of what would have happened in the Edison schools if Edison had not been managing them.[2]

We estimate several different matched schools' counterfactuals in Chapter Six. As noted, the first of these compares achievement gains in Edison schools over the last two years with achievement gains in matched non-Edison schools. This analysis is useful for understanding how Edison schools have been performing relative to conventional schools in recent years. The primary concern about such an analysis is that it is incomplete: It includes only Edison schools that are currently operating, and only part of the treatment period for Edison schools that have been open for longer than two years.

Our next analysis seeks to provide a more complete estimate of Edison's effects by tracing achievement trajectories in each Edison school back to the first year of Edison's operation of the school, including all schools that Edison has operated in its ten-year history for which the necessary data were available (we henceforth describe this as the analysis from Y1). The question is this: How do achievement trends from the first year of Edison management in each school compare to achievement trends in non-Edison schools serving similar populations? We examine trends covering the first five or six years of operation for each Edison school (the numbers of Edison schools op-

[2] There is also a theoretical possibility that the introduction of an Edison school to a district creates competition that induces improvement in the performance of nearby schools. Using such schools for counterfactual estimates would therefore underestimate Edison's true effect on student achievement. Although this is theoretically possible, our matched schools are taken from statewide samples, and a statewide competitive effect seems unlikely. We discuss matching further later in this chapter.

erating more than six years are small, so we do not provide estimates for these later years). In addition, we separately examine five-year trends for all schools ever operated by Edison, including those that terminated contracts prior to the end of five years. This latter analysis helps to assess the importance of attrition of Edison contracts, and also provides a global estimate of the long-term impact of turning a school over to Edison.

Although an examination of all years of Edison management for each school provides a more complete measure of the Edison treatment than does looking only at the last two years, it nevertheless does not include all of the period of treatment. Achievement tests typically are administered in late winter or spring, so a baseline using scores from the first year of Edison's operation omits the first several months of Edison's impact. Our final set of analyses in Chapter Six therefore examines achievement trajectories beginning from the year prior to Edison's management (year zero or Y0). These analyses are necessarily incomplete, because many Edison schools (typically start-up charter schools) did not exist prior to Edison's operation of the schools. Moreover, there are reasons to be concerned that pre-Edison scores in takeover schools may not be directly comparable to scores achieved during Edison management, as we discuss in depth in Chapter Six. Nevertheless, we believe it is important to consider pre-Edison scores, as they provide the only way to encompass the entire Edison treatment period. The question examined is this: For schools existing prior to Edison management, how do achievement trends from pre-Edison baselines compare to achievement trends in non-Edison schools serving similar populations?

Methodology

In the remainder of this chapter, we describe our data collection efforts, the set of schools included in the analyses, the measures used for assessing achievement, and the statistical methodology used to address each of the research questions described above. Most of this discussion focuses on our school-level analyses, which provide the core results of the study. We also conducted a supplemental set of analyses using limited student-level data to help inform our interpretation of the school-level results. These results are discussed in Appendix K.

Data Collection

Our analyses were designed to include information on as many of Edison's schools as possible in order to estimate an overall Edison effect and to explore factors that might be correlated with the size of this effect, such as whether schools are operated as district contract schools or as charter schools. To obtain a complete set of school-level test scores and demographic information for the relevant years, we combined data from several sources. We began with a database that had been assembled by the American Institutes for Research (AIR). The database contains average scores by school, grade, and subject on a variety of assessments that have figured prominently in state accountability systems both historically and currently. The data are organized by state and provide longitudinal outcomes back to as early as the early 1990s for some states, and later 1990s for others. Each year, researchers at AIR obtain the relevant outcomes for each state directly from the states themselves (most recently, directly from state Web sites) and append the data to the database containing prior-year scores. The scores are reported in a variety of metrics, but have transitioned steadily to reporting percentages of students falling into various proficiency classes as more states have moved to this type of standards-based reporting with the onset of NCLB.[3] We used the AIR data as the primary source of information on Edison schools and on comparison schools, which we selected on the basis of criteria discussed in a later section.

Although the AIR database included much of the information we needed, it was missing at least some data for a substantial number of schools. In addition, when we collected the data, scores from the 2003–2004 school year were not available in the AIR database. We

[3] The latest datasets, which as of January 2004 contained merged data up to and including the 2002–2003 school year, are available at http://208.253.216.16/Assessment/ as of June 17, 2005.

obtained this missing information from states. In some cases, the data were available for download on state Web sites, but in other cases, we had to request the data from state departments of education or enter the data by hand into a database, because the state data were not in an analyzable form (e.g., a few states provided scores in the form of interactive report cards on a Web site but did not provide a usable data file). In a small number of cases, where Edison is responsible for only a subset of the student population (i.e., the "schools within schools"), we obtained the data directly from Edison, because state and district reports did not allow us to separate Edison students' performance from that of non-Edison students. In addition, for a small number of states, we obtained 2002–2003 data directly from the state Web sites because of missing information in the AIR database.

We obtained school-level demographic information from the Common Core Data (CCD) collected by the National Center for Education Statistics (NCES). These data include information on race and ethnicity and participation in the free and reduced-price lunch program, as well as total enrollment for each year.

Achievement Test Scores

Using the AIR data and other sources, we gathered state test scores for all Edison schools and potential comparison schools for all years included in the analyses. For states with more than one test, we chose the test that was the state's primary measure of accountability in the particular year in question, which in general is the same measure Edison uses to evaluate its own performance in its annual reports. We identified these tests based on publicly available information about state accountability systems. Although some schools administer additional tests, the state accountability assessments are the tests for which Edison schools are held accountable by states and districts as well as by Edison itself, and therefore might be considered the most appropriate measure of the extent to which Edison schools are meeting their achievement goals. Moreover, these tests provide the best opportunity to identify comparison schools where the same assessments are administered.[4] In some cases, states changed their accountability tests from one year to the next, and our data reflect these changes.

The analysis includes only mathematics and reading (or language arts) tests. Although Edison's design addresses a much broader set of subjects, the availability of state test scores in subjects other than reading and mathematics varies widely across states, so we could not do a comprehensive analysis of performance in other subjects.

In most cases, the primary metric for reporting scores on state tests is the percentage of students at a school, grade, and subject scoring at or above the proficient level. This type of standards-based reporting is now required under NCLB, but many states were using this method before the implementation of NCLB. For states in which a percent proficient metric was not available in certain years, we used the metric that the state was using at that time. For example, California did not administer its standards-based California standards tests until spring 2002. Before 2002, its primary measure of accountability was the Stanford 9, which was reported in terms of percentile ranks. Our analysis uses these percentile ranks for pre-2002 years. Later in this section, we discuss our approach for combining different reporting mechanisms across states and over time.

For each Edison and comparison school in each year, we created a single measure of mathematics achievement and single measure of reading or language arts achievement by calculating an average score across all grades of the Edison school that were tested in a particular year. Because numbers of students tested in each school, grade, and subject were not available for all cases, for consistency we used a simple unweighted average of the aggregate (school by grade by subject by year) scores to produce an overall (school by subject by year) average.[5] The average created for each year and subject for each compari-

[4] Although there are documented validity problems with high-stakes tests in some contexts (Linn, 2000; Hamilton, 2003; Koretz, 2003), we believe that these concerns are outweighed by the need to use measures aligned with the goals Edison schools are expected to attain, as well as the need for comparable data across Edison and comparable schools. However, readers should keep potential validity issues in mind when interpreting these results.

[5] We also examined an alternative approach for aggregating results across grades. We standardized the outcomes within each grade level for each subject, school, and year to address

son school was taken over the precise set of grades for which scores were available for that year and subject for the matched Edison school. This was important because the set of tested grades has changed over time in some states, and because many Edison schools, particularly new start-up charter schools, have expanded their grade configurations over time. Calculating the averages as we did ensured that for every Edison school, subject, and year, the Edison school was being compared to an analogous quantity for its comparison schools.

In addition, Edison schools that had grade configurations that extended beyond traditional elementary, middle, and high school boundaries were split and treated as separate schools in the analysis (with appropriate corrections made to standard errors calculated for estimated effects). This was necessary to find sufficient numbers of comparison schools when otherwise not enough potential comparison schools would have the appropriate grade configurations. Our school splitting rules were analogous to those used by Edison in its own annual reports. Schools that served only kindergarten through grade six, grades six through eight, or nine and above, or any subset of grades within these ranges, were generally kept intact. Schools that served kindergarten through grade eight or beyond were split into subschools of kindergarten through grade five, grades six through eight, and, if necessary, nine and higher. For any other nonstandard grade configuration that straddled grade six (e.g., a school serving grades four through eight), the school was split into a subschool containing all grades up to and including grade five, another containing the middle school grades (six through eight), and, if necessary, a third containing the high school grades.[6] Although we tried to keep kindergarten through grade six schools intact, in some cases this resulted in an inability to identify comparison schools because the district or state lacked a sufficient number of kindergarten through grade six

---

the possibility that differences in the meaning of "proficient" across grade levels might affect results. A sensitivity test that used this metric showed that it did not affect our results.

[6] An exception to this rule occurred in Philadelphia, where a large number of Edison and non-Edison schools contained grades five through eight. Because this configuration was common throughout the district, we kept these grade five through eight schools intact and matched them with other grade five through eight schools.

schools. In these cases, we kept kindergarten through grade five together and treated grade six as a middle school grade.

Choosing Comparison Schools

An important feature of our analytic approach is the inclusion of a sample of comparison schools that are not under Edison's management but that serve populations of students similar to those in the Edison schools, as measured by the proportion of students participating in free and reduced-price lunch programs and the proportion of students who are African-American or Hispanic. For each Edison school and each major analysis (one-year gains, two-year gains, Y1, and Y0), we obtained two sets of comparison schools. One set was restricted to schools within the same districts as the Edison schools, whereas the other set included schools throughout the entire state in which the Edison school was located, both within the same district and in other districts. Below, we discuss our approach to selecting comparison schools and then provide the rationale for exploring both district and state matches.

We used a window-matching or caliper-matching (Cochran and Rubin, 1973) procedure for selecting comparison schools.[7] Within each state or district, we identified all schools serving similar grade spans (i.e., elementary, middle, or high schools, based on the splitting rules discussed earlier) in which both the percentage of students receiving free or reduced-price lunch and the percentage of students from traditionally underserved minority groups (African-American, Hispanic, and Native American) were within ten percentage points of the corresponding percentages for the Edison schools, and in which baseline achievement scores fell within five percentile points of the Edison school's scores, where percentiles are calculated with respect to

---

[7] We considered using a propensity score matching procedure, which involves creating a set of matched schools based on the estimated probability of school being a "treatment" school, in this case an Edison school. This approach was not feasible due to the small number of Edison schools in most districts and states. Using a national matching approach rather than relying on in-state matches would fail to capture differences in student populations among states and could result in poor matches for some Edison schools.

the statewide distribution of scores in the matching year.[8] The year that was considered the baseline varied across analyses: For example, for the one-year gain analysis, the baseline was spring 2003, whereas for the Y1 analysis, the baseline was the spring of the first year during which Edison managed the school.[9] Using this matching procedure, we selected two different sets of comparison schools (state and district) for each set of analyses.

As we discuss below, in its reports on achievement, Edison uses a comparison sample of schools matched on demographics but not on baseline achievement. We decided to match on both demographics and achievement to ensure a comparison sample of schools facing similar achievement challenges and to enhance the comparability of test-score gains between the two groups. As we noted, Edison schools are often initially low achieving, even when compared to other schools serving demographically similar student populations. By including achievement as a criterion when choosing comparison schools, we could ensure that our comparison sample was similarly low achieving. This is especially important because low-achieving schools often make larger test-score gains than do schools whose achievement is closer to average, in part because of regression to the mean but also because of other factors including greater accountability pressures in schools where achievement has been unusually low (Greene and Winters, 2004; Kirby et al., 2002; Hanushek, 1979).

Another important decision regarding comparison schools was whether to limit the sample to schools within the Edison school's district or to include schools throughout the entire state where the Edi-

[8] For a small number of schools that had no matching schools within five percentile points, we used a ten-percent window to select comparison schools. We also conducted sensitivity tests to examine the effects of using wider windows, and found that the five-percent window produced the best set of comparison schools in terms of placing the Edison schools near the middle of the comparison school distribution.

[9] We also explored matching on each school's average demographic characteristics over the years for which the school was included in the analysis (as opposed to matching only on baseline-year demographics), but this did not affect our findings, so we report only the results that used the baseline-year matching.

son school was operating.[10] Each of these approaches has advantages as well as limitations. Schools within the same district as the Edison school might be more similar to the Edison school than those outside the district in some respects. In particular, they are likely to be facing some of the same challenges, in terms of district governance as well as student and community factors such as crime rates and poverty. At the same time, there are at least two problems with within-district comparison schools. First, it is possible that the Edison schools exert competitive effects on other schools in the district. That is, staff at the other schools might engage in efforts to improve student performance as a result of pressure from the presence of the Edison school (e.g., they may feel compelled to keep up with the new school in some way). This hypothesis is supported by research that has shown competitive effects associated with charter schools; these findings are directly relevant for Edison's charter schools and indirectly relevant for Edison contract schools of choice (Hoxby, 2001; Holmes, DeSimone, and Rupp, 2003; Bifulco and Ladd, 2003; and Booker et al., 2004). A second problem inherent in the use of within-district comparison schools is a problem of selection bias. To the extent that district leaders select their lowest-scoring (or, alternatively, their highest-scoring) schools to be converted to Edison schools, the schools not selected will be inherently different from those selected. This selection could bias the results against Edison if districts tend to convert schools facing the most intractable problems, or it could bias results in Edison's favor if districts selected the schools perceived as most likely to benefit from Edison's management.

An additional consideration is the need to find comparison schools for each Edison school. When the pool of prospective comparison schools is limited to schools within the Edison school's district, we encounter a number of cases in which no comparison schools can be identified. This problem is especially likely to occur in small districts and in cases where Edison manages all or almost all schools in the district. As a result, an analysis using within-district

[10] It was not feasible to explore the use of comparison schools outside the state because of the need to have common achievement measures for each Edison school and its comparables.

comparison schools not only includes a smaller number of Edison schools than an analysis using statewide comparison schools, but the schools included come disproportionately from large districts, producing results that fail to reflect the range of contexts in which Edison operates. To address these problems, we report all of the results using state comparison schools, but we include two appendices that compare the results obtained using both sets of comparison schools for a common set of Edison schools. These comparisons revealed that the choice of whether to use district or state comparison schools does not materially affect our results.

It should be noted that any matching procedure is limited by the characteristics that can be adequately measured. There are a number of reasons schools become Edison schools, and these cannot be fully captured by matching schools based on observable, quantifiable characteristics. Student mobility in both Edison and comparison schools adds another source of error to the estimates of school-level score changes. Therefore, any set of comparison schools provides an imperfect indicator of what the Edison schools' performance trajectories would have been in the absence of Edison's management.

Exclusions

Although this study was designed to be comprehensive, certain factors resulted in the need to exclude some Edison schools from the analysis. Some schools did not have data available in either AIR or in a state database for one or more years, and we were unable to obtain the data from other sources. A few schools were excluded because we were unable to identify comparison schools for them.

We also excluded some schools from the analysis that started with a pre-Edison baseline (i.e., the Y0 analysis) if the schools experienced unusually large enrollment changes between the pre-Edison year and the first year under Edison's management. We present the details of these exclusions in Chapter Six. Similarly, we excluded a small number of schools from the Y0 analysis because they experienced a change of 20 percent or more between Y0 and Y1 in the percentage of minority students or students receiving free or reduced-price lunches.[11] Finally, in a small number of cases there were concerns about possible testing irregularities (e.g., the use of nonstandard test administration procedures) that would have affected the validity of scores, particularly between the pre-Edison year and the first year of Edison's management. These exclusions are also discussed in Chapter Six. Appendix B lists all Edison schools that were open at any time during Edison's history, and indicates those analyses in which each school was included.

Analytic Approach

One of the challenges in conducting an analysis of achievement across multiple states is that each state has its own assessment system and its own methods for reporting scores. Although NCLB has imposed some constraints, such as the requirement that schools test in specific grades and that they report scores using a percent-proficient metric, states continue to have considerable latitude in what and how they report. A consequence of this latitude is great variability in test content and format and in the level of difficulty represented by the "proficient" label (Linn, 2000; Olson, 2005). Moreover, there have been numerous changes in testing programs within states during the period in which we are evaluating Edison's performance, with some schools adopting entirely new instruments during this period and others making smaller but still important modifications such as changing the level of difficulty of the cut score representing proficient performance. More than 40 percent of the Edison schools included in our various achievement analyses have experienced such changes. Conducting a straightforward analysis of test-score gains over time and across states was not feasible under these conditions, except in the recent trends analysis that examines only the period from 2002 to 2004.

As we discuss below, we analyzed the achievement data using several different approaches, with a focus on comparing each Edison school's trajectory to the trajectories of comparison, non-Edison

---

[11] Demographic changes could well be directly correlated with changes in students' prior achievement levels, so we chose a cutoff of 20 percent rather than 50 percent.

schools within the same states. We created an index of each Edison school's performance relative to its set of matched comparison schools, and then combined the results across all Edison schools to obtain a global estimate of Edison's progress relative to comparison schools. Creating this index required devising a method that could be carried out even when tests changed over time within a state, and that could be reconciled across all Edison schools to facilitate inferences about aggregate performance changes.

Our method relies primarily on z-scores, which measure the distance of a score from the mean of the distribution in standard deviation units. The use of z-scores facilitates comparisons across states by putting all of the test scores on a common scale regardless of the original metric or the nature of the score distribution in each state. Z-scores also produce results that are expressed in terms of an effect size, which is a commonly used metric in research for indicating the magnitude of a difference between two groups (Cohen, 1969).

As an initial step, we calculated the school-level level outcome y (average score across all tested grades, as described above) for each subject, school, and year. Separate outcomes were calculated for reading and mathematics. If a comparison school lacked an outcome for one of the tested grades of the Edison school in a given year, its outcome data were excluded for that year. From this set of scores, we calculated z-scores as follows:

$$z = (y - mean) / sd$$

where *mean* and *sd* refer to the mean and standard deviation of the distribution of all non-Edison schools in the state with observed scores that year.[12]

---

[12] We also explored an alternative measure, a rank-based z-score. Appendix D describes this measure and presents a comparison of results obtained using both the traditional and the rank-based z-scores. These sensitivity tests showed that the two approaches produced similar results. For reporting purposes, we rely on the traditional z-score metric because it is more commonly used, and because it allows us to calibrate the results to a more familiar metric, as we discuss in the next section.

We then calculated the gain on the z-score scale for each Edison school, and compared that gain score to the average gain score of the comparison schools assigned to that Edison school. All gain scores are calculated relative to the baseline of the specific analysis. For the recent trends analyses presented first in Chapter Six, the baseline is either spring 2002 or spring 2003. The subsequent analyses use baselines in the first year of Edison management (Y1) and the pre-Edison year (Y0). The resulting number represents, in standard deviation units, the direction and magnitude of the Edison school's score change relative to the change in average scores of that school's comparison schools. A positive value indicates that the Edison school outperformed its comparison schools in terms of change in performance, though it does not necessarily indicate that the Edison school's scores increased (i.e., a positive value indicates either that the Edison school improved more than its comparison schools or that it declined less than its comparison schools).[13]

After calculating the z-score for each Edison school, subject, and year (which is the difference in gain between the Edison school and the average of its comparison schools), we average these outcomes across Edison schools to obtain estimated average effects for a particular year and subject. For our operation-year baseline results, we estimate effects by averaging across each operation year (i.e., number of years during which a school has been managed by Edison) regardless of calendar years. For example, we calculate the average effect of Edison in operation year two (Y2) from an operation Y1 baseline for both reading and math. These estimates are based on averaging the operation Y2 results across all Edison schools regardless of calendar year. Alternatively, for our recent trends analyses, we average the estimated effects in calendar year 2004, regardless of operation year.

Standard errors of these effects were estimated using specialized methods that account for the different numbers of comparison schools available for different Edison schools, potential correlation in

[13] As an additional sensitivity test, we compared the z-score method with a regression-based approach that involved predicting a school's scores in a given year based on its baseline scores. The results of this test are described in Appendix D.

outcomes of split Edison and comparison schools, and potential overlap in the sets of comparison schools for different Edison schools. These methods are described in Appendix C.

Interpreting Z-Score Changes

One disadvantage of the use of z-scores is that they are unitless, and without a specific context in which to interpret them it is difficult to calibrate how z-scores relate to more familiar metrics of student achievement. The z-scores reported in the tables in Appendix M are further complicated by the fact that they are differences of differences; that is, they are differences of gain scores made by Edison schools and their comparison schools relative to a baseline. If a particular Edison school and its comparison schools had identical baseline scores, the z-scores reported in the tables would be directly interpretable as the differences of the out-year level scores, expressed in terms of the distribution of scores across all schools in the state. The purpose of comparing the gain scores is to examine this out-year difference after adjusting for the degree of difference between Edison and its comparison schools in the baseline year. In the event that the baseline year test is different than the out-year in question, the adjustment is made by assuming that had the newer test been administered at the same time as the baseline test, the difference between Edison and its comparison schools in terms of standard deviations of the newer test would be the same as it was on the baseline test. The z-score metric that we report can be interpreted as an adjusted difference of Edison and its comparison schools in the out-years.

In the recent trends analysis, we report raw gain scores in terms of percentages of students proficient as well as the corresponding z-score differences. We are able to report both quantities for the recent trends analysis because most states did not experience a change in testing programs between 2002 and 2004. Because we cannot directly compute changes in percent proficient for the analyses that examine achievement trends over a longer period of time, we sought an alternative method for helping readers understand the magnitude of a particular difference in z-score change. To do this, we examined the means and variances of the metrics for all tests, years, subjects, and states used in the analysis. The metrics consist primarily of percentages of students proficient, but in some cases are percentile ranks with respect to national norming groups (e.g., California prior to 2002 when the Stanford 9 test was used, and the District of Columbia, which also used the Stanford 9). The means and variances we calculated were of the school-level averages (across grades) that we used as the outcomes in our analysis of each Edison school. Across states using proficiency metrics, the standard deviations had a median of about 19 points of percentage proficient, a mean of about 18 points, and first and third quartiles of about 16 and 21. Taking the value of 18 as representative, this implies that z-score differences of 0.1, 0.25, and 0.5 correspond approximately to 1.8, 4.5, and 9.0 points of percentage proficient.

Sensitivity Tests

In addition to the primary analyses reported in subsequent chapters, we conducted several sensitivity tests to determine whether our results were influenced by particular features of the methodology or of the samples of schools included. First, we examined the effects of using the traditional z-score metric as compared with the rank-based z-score approach and with the regression method described above. These comparisons, shown in Appendices D and E, suggest that choice of method did not materially affect our results in most cases.

Second, we examined the effects of excluding certain categories of schools from our analyses, particularly from the Y0 baseline analysis. These include schools with relatively large changes in enrollment (i.e., greater than 15 percent) between the pre-Edison year and the first year of Edison management. Enrollment changes over this period are a concern because student populations sometimes change substantially when Edison takes over a school, and a change in total enrollment can be a sign of a change in the characteristics of the student population. The results of this analysis are presented in Appendix F and are discussed in Chapter Six because they are relevant to the discussion of differences in interpretation for the Y0 and Y1 baselines.

As an additional check on possible population changes over time, we examined changes in demographic characteristics of students in the Edison schools and comparison schools that were included in our Y4 and year-five (Y5) estimates to determine whether the populations of students being served by the more mature Edison schools differed from those enrolled in the early years of Edison's management of a school. Measured from both a pre-Edison baseline and from the first year of Edison management, differences in demographic changes in years four and five were negligible, as shown in Appendix G. Relative to comparison schools, Edison schools enrolled slightly more minority students and slightly fewer students receiving free or reduced-price lunches in later years than they did in their early years, but the differences were all less than four percent. Of course, change in demographic characteristics provides only limited information about possible population change, and these findings do not guarantee that the results are not affected by differences in the unmeasured characteristics of students attending Edison schools over time.

We also examined the effect of excluding data from schools for which Edison reported insufficient access and control during later years of the contract (i.e., schools technically under contract to Edison but that would not allow Edison to implement the design). Seven schools fell into this category, and we exclude the final operation year for these schools in all of our analyses. The sensitivity test suggested that the decision to exclude these cases did not affect the results.[14]

Finally, we conducted the analyses with and without Philadelphia schools. As was discussed in Chapter Four, implementation of the Edison design in Philadelphia was marked by several compromises, which suggests that it might be worth examining achievement effects in Philadelphia schools separately from other schools. Moreover, Philadelphia represents by far Edison's single biggest contract, with 20 schools. Appendix H presents the comparisons and indicates that the Philadelphia results do not look notably different from re-

---

[14] These cases did not affect the Y0 or recent gains analyses at all because none of the excluded cases had the necessary data or were operating during the relevant years. The effect on the Y1 analysis was negligible in most cases (details available from the authors upon request).

sults in other schools, so we include Philadelphia in the analyses presented in the body of the report.

Testing Statistical Significance

We conducted tests of statistical significance for the primary analyses. For the analyses shown in Chapter Six, we test whether the estimated difference in z-score gains is significantly different from zero using a type I error rate of 0.05. In Chapter Eight, where we compare the achievement trends for different types of Edison schools, we conduct statistical tests of whether the difference between two estimates (e.g., for charter and contract schools) is significantly different from zero.

It is important to recognize that statistical significance depends in part on the number of schools included in the analysis. When the true effect sizes are small to moderate (e.g., 0.20–0.30), power calculations showed that approximately 50–100 Edison schools would be needed to detect statistical significance (the number varies depending on other features of the data). Many of our estimates are based on much smaller numbers of Edison schools, and in these cases a lack of statistical significance might be the results of insufficient statistical power rather than an absence of effects. Lack of statistical power is especially a concern for estimates of Edison effects in Y4 or later, for which the number of schools is quite small. The reported indicators of statistical significance should therefore be interpreted with caution.

Limitations of Our Analyses

It is important to acknowledge some additional limitations of these analyses. The primary drawback is that school-level results do not necessarily tell us what is happening to individual students. A year-to-year test-score comparison for a school will include a nontrivial number of students whose scores are present in one year but not the other, and in some cases (e.g., when only a single grade is tested), virtually no students will have scores for both years. These problems affect both Edison and comparison schools. Although there is a high degree of correspondence between the student-level and school-level results for those Edison schools for which student-level data are available (see Appendix K), we do not know how well these results generalize to the larger population of Edison schools.

In addition, although we attempted to assess the degree to which our positive later-year results are affected by differential selection of schools out of Edison management, we cannot definitively dismiss concerns about selection. A more systematic analysis of the reasons for terminations is needed to understand the differences between schools that remain with Edison and those that do not.

These analyses are limited by the fact that they focus on mathematics and reading achievement, which are only two among a broad set of outcomes that Edison's design is likely to address. In particular, the fact that the design requires schools to devote time and resources to social studies, science, the arts, and foreign language suggests that Edison might be expected to exert a positive influence on performance in these subjects, but unfortunately we have no way to measure that performance consistently across the districts and states in which Edison operates.

We also lack good measures of design implementation across all of the Edison schools, which would be informative for understanding the source of differences in schools' achievement trajectories. Furthermore, because we were unable to examine the financial resources that districts and others (e.g., private donors who provided supplemental funding to some Edison schools) devoted to implementing the Edison design, we do not know whether some of the differences in results are attributable to different levels of resources. Clearly, some Edison schools are more effective than others, and a focus on average performance across all Edison schools masks these differences. In Chapter Seven, we present some analyses that go beyond systemwide averages and examine the black box of Edison implementation, but these analyses are limited to a small number of school characteristics for which we have data, and they cannot tell us whether the results we have obtained will generalize to future Edison schools that might differ from the current set of schools in resources or other factors that influence the effectiveness of implementation.

The need to combine results across different tests and different grade levels introduces some additional uncertainty about how to interpret the results. The meaning of "proficient" performance differs across states and even across grade levels within a state, and the content of the state tests used to measure reading and mathematics achievement varies substantially. Moreover, the focus on changes in percent proficient, while consistent with the accountability rules under which schools are currently operating, masks changes that occur at other points in the test-score distribution and therefore might not provide a completely accurate indication of how much learning has occurred. Our findings provide a reasonable but rough indication of achievement changes in Edison schools; a more complete understanding of student learning would require the use of a common test and an effort to track changes using a test-score scale that can be used to measure growth.

It is also possible that Edison schools differ from other schools in their ability to maximize performance on the state accountability tests without necessarily attaining commensurate increases in the underlying achievement those tests were designed to measure, a phenomenon known as "score inflation" (Koretz, 2003). For example, to the extent that the benchmark assessments are closely aligned in item format and style (in addition to content) with the state tests, Edison students might be better prepared than other students to perform well on the state tests. On the other hand, Edison's efforts to ensure fidelity of curriculum implementation and attention to nontested subjects might result in a smaller degree of score inflation among Edison schools when compared with conventional schools, where reallocation of effort to tested subjects and topics is common (Hamilton, 2003; Koretz et al., 1996; Pedulla et al., 2003). Again, we do not have enough information to determine whether difference in emphasis on tested material exists or whether Edison would be advantaged or disadvantaged by such a difference.

Finally, we do not have any information about what features of Edison schools are responsible for the relative advantage seen in Y4 and beyond. We explore some sources of variation among Edison schools in the next two chapters, but we do not have the necessary data to examine sources of differences between Edison and comparison schools.

The next chapter presents the main results of our school-level analyses that address the causal question about Edison's effects on achievement.

CHAPTER SIX

Time: Effects of Edison Management on Academic Achievement

Laura S. Hamilton, J. R. Lockwood, Brian P. Gill, and Ron W. Zimmer

In this chapter, we present the results of the analyses that are designed to examine average academic achievement effects in Edison schools. We report analyses addressing three different questions about Edison schools' performance:

1. What are the recent trends in rates of student proficiency in reading and math in currently operating Edison schools? How do those trends compare to those of schools serving similar populations?
2. How do achievement trends from the beginning of Edison management (Y1) in each school compare to achievement trends in non-Edison schools serving similar populations?
3. For schools existing prior to the initiation of Edison management, how do achievement trends from pre-Edison baselines (Y0) compare to achievement trends in non-Edison schools serving similar populations?

The recent trends analysis has the virtue of exploring Edison's overall gains according to the standards that are of greatest interest under NCLB and state accountability regimes: the proportion of children achieving proficiency in reading and math. It is possible to measure changes in proficiency in the recent trends analysis because few states made changes to their testing systems in recent years. By contrast, both the Y0 and Y1 analyses must rely on z-scores to account for changes in state tests, but both attempt to assess the complete Edison effect by examining Edison schools' performance starting with a pretreatment (or close to pretreatment) baseline. The analysis using the Y1 baseline provides information about how Edison schools have performed, relative to comparison schools, from late in the first year of Edison management. The Y0 analysis provides information about how Edison schools have performed, relative to comparison schools, from the spring prior to Edison's management.

In this chapter, we present the results of all three analyses. We also attempt to help the reader understand the extent to which these three sets of descriptive results can be used to make inferences about Edison's causal effect on student achievement. Although we cannot answer the causal question definitively, we can explore the extent to which our descriptive results are likely to provide information relevant to this question.

Recent Achievement Trends in Edison Schools

The set of analyses described in this section of the chapter is similar to that presented in Edison's sixth and seventh annual reports, focusing on the most recent years for which we have data, the 2002–2003 and 2003–2004 school years. We present two sets of results: one showing average one-year achievement trends for the most recent school year (2003–2004), and another showing average two-year trends from 2002 through 2004. Within each of these sets, we report results separately for reading and math. In contrast to the longer-term trends described later in the chapter, for the recent gains, we are able to report changes in the percent of students achieving proficiency on the state test, because few states experienced a test change during the period between 2002 and 2004.

Table 6.1
Recent Changes in Percent of Students Achieving Proficiency in Edison Schools

	Change in Percent Proficient, 2003–2004	Change in Percent Proficient, 2002–2004
Reading	6.85 (n=88)	11.27 (n=58)
Mathematics	9.26 (n=86)	17.26 (n=59)

Table 6.1 reports average gains in achievement for Edison schools from 2003 to 2004 and from 2002 to 2004, in terms of the percent of students achieving proficiency in reading and math. These results show that currently operating Edison schools are making substantial gains in the proportion of students achieving proficiency in reading and math, with especially large gains in math. As noted in Chapter Five, these gains might be viewed as causal effects of Edison management for the period examined, if it is assumed that the schools would have made no gains in the absence of Edison management.

Recent Trends Relative to Comparison Schools

An alternate assumption is that, if Edison were not managing them, the schools would have made gains approximately equivalent to the gains made by schools serving similar populations of students. Table 6.2 presents the average one- and two-year changes in percent proficient and in z-score differences in reading and mathematics performance for Edison schools and comparison schools selected according to the criteria described in Chapter Five. The entries in the first column are the changes in percent proficient for Edison schools; in the second column are analogous numbers for the comparison schools. The third column shows the difference between these two numbers, with a positive number indicating that Edison schools on average achieved a higher test-score gain than their comparison schools. In the fourth column are the differences in z-score changes for Edison schools and their comparison schools. We calculated t-statistics to test whether

Table 6.2
Recent Trends in Proficiency Rates Relative to State Comparison Schools

	Change in Percent Proficient, Edison Schools	Change in Percent Proficient, Comparison Schools	Difference in Change in Percent Proficient	Difference in Z-Score Changes
Reading 2003–2004	6.85	5.74	1.11	0.07 (n=88)
Mathematics 2003–2004	9.26	6.38	2.88*	0.13* (n=86)
Reading 2002–2004	11.27	9.49	1.78	0.12 (n=58)
Mathematics 2002–2004	17.26	12.73	4.53*	0.22* (n=59)

NOTE: * indicates statistical significance at $p < 0.05$.

each difference was statistically significantly different from zero, and indicate with asterisks those differences that are statistically significant using a type I error rate of 0.05.

Table 6.2 shows that comparison schools, like Edison schools, achieved progress between 2003 and 2004, but Edison schools posted statistically significantly higher average gains in mathematics. The gaps in performance gains between Edison schools and comparison schools are larger for 2002–2004 than for the one-year analysis, with a difference in reading of approximately 1.8 using the percent-proficient metric, and a difference in mathematics of approximately 4.5. Again, only the mathematics differential achieves statistical significance.[1]

Academic Achievement in Edison Schools from Y1

The primary limitation of the recent gains analyses is their temporal incompleteness: Except for schools in which Edison has operated for one or two years, the recent change analyses include only a portion of

[1] The two-year advantage for Edison is larger when within-district comparison schools are used rather than statewide comparison schools, as shown in Appendix I.

the total Edison treatment and therefore do not permit valid inferences about the total causal effect of Edison management. The remaining analyses presented in this chapter attempt to measure Edison's effect by including all years in which Edison schools operate.[2]

In this section, we present the differences in z-score changes between Edison schools and comparison schools[3] beginning with the first Edison management year. Figure 6.1 shows the z-score changes in reading achieved by Edison schools and comparison schools in each operation year, and Figure 6.2 presents a comparable set of changes for mathematics. As operation year increases, the number of Edison schools with data decreases; the number of Edison schools included in each estimate is provided above each bar. In both subjects, Edison's gains during the early years are similar to those of the comparison schools, but beginning in Y4 the Edison schools achieve larger gains than comparison schools, especially in mathematics. It is important to note that the estimates for both Edison schools and comparison schools are based on different schools in each operation year, so these results should not be interpreted as trends for a consistent set of Edison schools; we discuss this further below.

---

[2] In any longitudinal analysis in which assignment to the program is nonrandom and in which the selection mechanism for assignment is imperfectly observed—and which therefore depends on the comparison of changes over time—a baseline measure that can be plausibly viewed as an accurate indicator of a pretreatment outcome is essential for capturing the total effect of treatment. This is particularly important if treatment effects are nonlinear over time: If effects in the early years of Edison management of a school differ from effects in later years, then a recent gains analysis that ignores early years will produce biased results.

[3] These analyses use statewide comparison schools. See Appendix J for a comparison of results obtained using state versus district comparison schools.

Figure 6.1
Z-Score Changes in Reading from Y1 Baseline, Edison Schools and State Comparison Schools

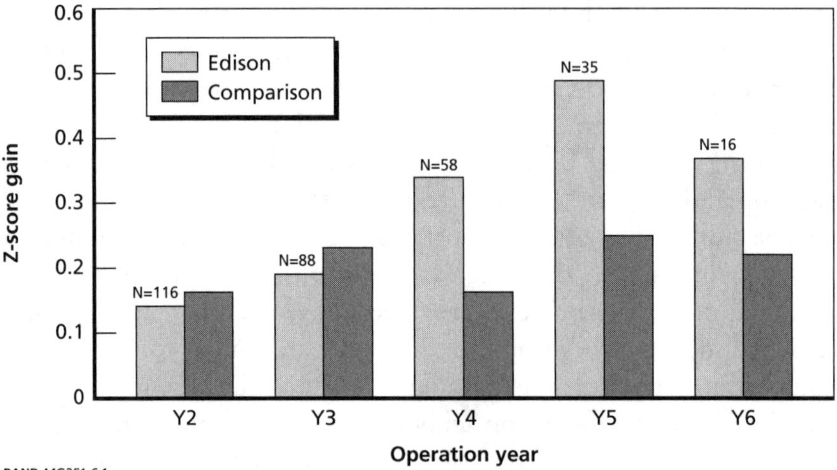

RAND *MG351-6.1*

Figure 6.2
Z-Score Changes in Mathematics from Y1 Baseline, Edison Schools and State Comparison Schools

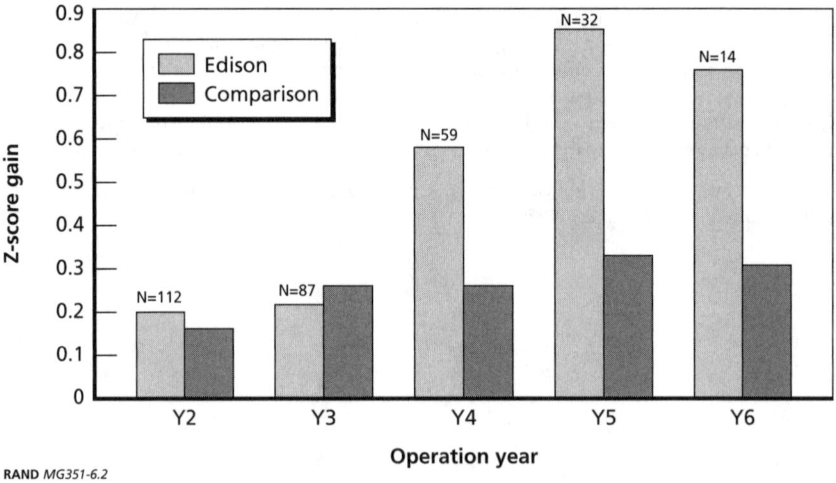

RAND *MG351-6.2*

Table 6.3
Differences in Z-Score Changes in Reading and Mathematics from Y1 Baseline, Edison Schools and State Comparison Schools

	Y2	Y3	Y4	Y5	Y6
Reading	–0.02 (N=116)	–0.04 (N=88)	0.17* (N=58)	0.25* (N=35)	0.15 (N=16)
Mathematics	0.04 (N=112)	–0.04 (N=87)	0.32* (N=59)	0.53* (N=32)	0.45* (N=14)

NOTE: *indicates statistical significance at $p < 0.05$.

The differences between the z-score changes for Edison schools and comparison schools are provided in Table 6.3. For this and subsequent analyses, the table entries for each operation year represent differences between Edison schools and comparison schools in their cumulative z-score gains from Y1. For example, the estimate under "Y3" is the difference in z-score gain between Y1 and Y3. We calculated t-statistics to test whether each difference was statistically significantly different from zero, and indicate with asterisks those estimates that are statistically significant using a type I error rate of 0.05.

The near-zero estimates for Y2 and Y3 are consistent with the similarity in gains between Edison schools and comparison schools shown in Figures 6.1 and 6.2. Average state test scores have been increasing across the board in many states, and Edison schools in their early years of operation have posted similar increases as other schools with comparable prior achievement and student demographics.

By Y4, however, Edison schools had achieved larger average gains than comparison schools by a statistically significant margin, and they maintained that difference through later operation years. The differences in reading are smaller than the differences in mathematics, and the reading difference fails to reach statistical significance in Y6, probably because of the small number of schools included.

Another way to examine these trends is to consider the percentages of schools for which the z-score differences are positive—in other words, the percentages of schools that achieved larger test-score gains than their comparison schools in each year of Edison operation. Figures 6.3 and 6.4 show these percentages (with corresponding sample sizes [N] included in the charts) and indicate that in general, as operation year increases, so does the proportion of Edison schools posting positive trends. The figures also make clear, however, that for both subjects and in every operation year, some Edison schools are achieving larger gains than their comparison schools and others are falling behind. We explore this variability in trends in greater detail in Chapter Seven.

Figure 6.3
Proportion of Edison Schools with Gains That Exceed the Gains of Comparison Schools, from Y1 Baseline, State Comparison Schools (Reading)

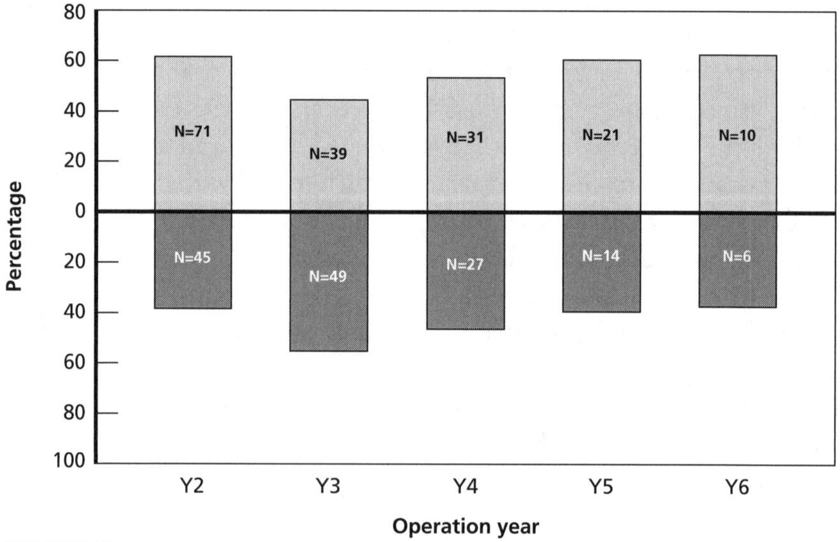

RAND *MG351-6.3*

Figure 6.4
Proportion of Edison Schools with Gains That Exceed the Gains of Comparison Schools, from Y1 Baseline, State Comparison Schools (Math)

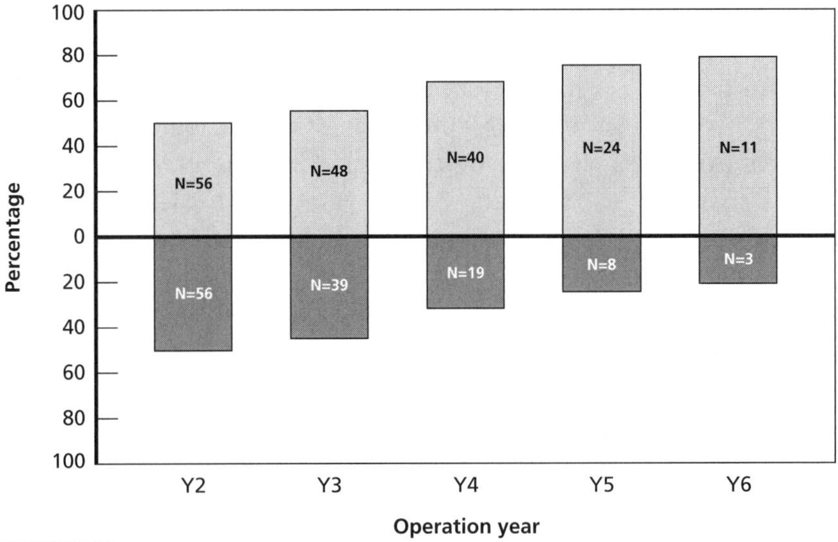

RAND *MG351-6.4*

Understanding the Effects of Attrition

It is possible that the trends shown are due to differences in the Edison schools included in each estimate rather than to changes in schools' performance. One way to address this concern is to examine trends for a set of schools that remains in the sample for the full number of years being examined. We calculated z-score differences for the set of Edison schools that was managed by Edison for at least four years; these results are shown in Appendix M and demonstrate that the overall trends shown in Table 6.3 are not due to the different schools included in each operation-year estimate.

In addition, however, it is important to understand whether attrition from the Edison sample is affecting the results for the later operation years. Between one operation year and the next, schools are eliminated for one of two reasons: Either they are no longer under Edison management, or they are still under Edison management but have not been managed by Edison for the number of years being examined. The former set of schools is of primary concern: If unsuccessful schools are less likely to remain under Edison's management than successful schools, the estimates for the later years could be inflated as a result of selection effects. The latter group of schools, those that are too new to have reached Y4, might be of concern if there were reason to believe Edison's effectiveness at managing schools had changed over time; we address this issue in Chapter Seven.

To explore the possibility that the schools that reached Y4 differ from those that did not, we examined the test-score trajectories for schools that opened in 2000–2001 or earlier. These schools have been open long enough that they could have been included in the Y4 estimate if they had remained under Edison's management for at least four years. All but one school lasted at least three years with Edison, so attrition is not a serious concern prior to Y4. Of the 75 schools that opened in 2000–2001 or earlier and for which we have adequate data in at least one subject, 61, or 81 percent of these schools, were still under Edison's management in Y4.

Table 6.4 compares results for schools that remained under Edison management with those that ended Edison management prior to Y4. Relative to comparison schools, the latter schools achieved lower test-score trajectories between years one and three than those whose contracts remained in place.

Table 6.4
Differences in Z-Score Changes in Reading and Mathematics from Y1 Baseline for Schools That Opened in 2000–2001 or Earlier and That Were or Were Not Managed by Edison Through Y4

	Y2	Y3
Reading: managed by Edison through Y4	–0.09 (N=61)	0.00 (N=61)
Reading: contract ended before Y4	–0.30 (N=14)	–0.22 (N=13)
Mathematics: managed by Edison through Y4	–0.08 (N=57)	–0.03 (N=57)
Mathematics: contract ended before Y4	–0.20 (N=14)	–0.46 (N=13)

We conducted a similar analysis using schools that opened in 1999–2000 or earlier and comparing those that were or were not under Edison's management in operation Y5; the results are similar to those presented in Table 6.4. The difference in trends for schools that did and did not remain under Edison's management suggests the possibility that the positive results we observed for Y4 and later are due, at least in part, to the fact that lower-performing schools are removed from Edison's management before they reach Y4. We have no information that would help us understand how these schools would have done if they had remained under Edison's management, and therefore cannot be certain that the positive Y4 results shown in Table 6.3 generalize to all Edison schools.

One way to address the problem of attrition in later-year results is to shift the focus from examining how schools perform while under Edison's management to examining what happens to schools that are placed under Edison's management, regardless of how long they remain Edison schools. This type of analysis would examine the trends for all schools that are ever Edison schools; schools would remain in the sample even after their contracts have ended. This is analogous to an intent-to-treat study in medicine: The purpose is to understand the effects of hiring Edison to manage a school, regardless of how long the contract lasts.

To be sure, effects in post-Edison years may not be directly attributable to Edison's educational program. Even so, Edison's prospective clients and other policymakers need to know the overall, long-term effect on all schools they initially give to Edison to manage. The initial decision to give management authority to Edison may well have effects that outlast the period of direct Edison operation. From a policy perspective, such effects are worthy of consideration.

Table 6.5 presents the results of this policy-impact analysis. The estimates in each table cell are analogous to those presented in Table 6.3, with one exception: If a school's contract with Edison was severed, but test-score data were available for that school after the end of the contract, those data were included. For example, if a school's contract ended in spring 2002 after Y4, but we could obtain the school's spring 2003 scores, those scores were included in the Y5 estimate.

Table 6.5
Policy Impact from Y1: Differences in Z-Score Changes for Schools Ever Managed by Edison

	Y2	Y3	Y4	Y5
Reading	–0.04 (N=117)	–0.05 (N=89)	0.08 (N=72)	0.15 (N=47)
Mathematics	0.04 (N=113)	–0.05 (N=88)	0.22* (N=73)	0.37* (N=42)

NOTE: * indicates statistical significance at $p < 0.05$.

The results in Table 6.4 show a trend similar to that depicted in Table 6.3: The estimates are close to zero through the third operation year but become positive in Y4. We can therefore conclude that the positive results for later years are not solely due to selective attrition of low-performing Edison schools. However, attrition makes a difference: The positive later-year estimates are smaller for this analysis than those in Table 6.3, and the positive reading results are not statistically significant. As a policy matter, these findings indicate that when schools become (or open as) Edison schools, by the fourth year after Edison management begins, they have achieved larger average test-score gains than comparison schools (from a Y1 baseline) in math and (by nonsignificant margins) in reading—even when including schools that were no longer under contract with Edison by Y4.[4]

Together, the results from the Y1 baseline suggest that Edison schools are outscoring comparison schools in both subjects by their fourth year of operation but that there are no substantial differences between Edison schools and comparison schools prior to the fourth year. A portion of the positive later-year results are probably due to selective attrition of low-performing schools from the Edison population, but there is a positive result in mathematics even when selection is addressed through an analysis that retains all schools, whether or not they remained under Edison's management.

[4] There is also some evidence that schools may experience a dip in performance in the year after terminating the relationship with Edison. If so, the policy impact results may slightly underestimate Edison program effects (i.e., the effects that would have occurred if all the schools had stayed with Edison).

Academic Achievement in Edison Schools from Y0

Next, we present a set of analyses parallel to the set described in the previous section, but starting from a pre-Edison baseline (Y0). The Y1 results provide information on Edison schools' progress starting from the spring of their first year as Edison schools, whereas the results presented in this section indicate what happens to schools' score trajectories after they convert to Edison management. Any effect of Edison during the first year is excluded from the Y1 results, so it is necessary to examine progress from Y0 to understand the full effect.

Before presenting the Y0 results, several limitations of this analysis must be acknowledged. The primary one is that because new start-up schools did not exist prior to Edison's management, they do not have a Y0 score and cannot be included in any of the analyses presented in this section. Therefore, none of the results discussed in this section can be generalized to start-up schools—these results apply to Edison's conversion schools only. A second limitation is that using a Y0 baseline results in including a short period in the Edison effect in the pre-Edison year. A third is that Edison school student populations sometimes change substantially at the time of Edison's takeover, which may undermine the comparability of the school's test scores before and after Edison's entry into the school (Appendix K provides analyses that examine the extent of these problems, including a comparison of results from Y1 for start-up and conversion schools).

An additional problem with the Y0 analyses is that the Edison schools with Y0 baselines are few for most operation years, and because they include relatively large numbers of schools from a few districts that experienced significant turmoil during their conversion to Edison status (Chester, Pennsylvania; Philadelphia; and Dallas), they do not adequately represent the universe of Edison clients. Moreover, the schools Edison managed for at least four or five years experienced different early-year achievement trajectories than other schools included in the Y0 baseline analysis. Specifically, the schools included in the Y4 and Y5 estimates experienced a much larger first-year decline than the other schools, both in absolute terms and relative to comparison schools. Therefore, although our estimates for Y4 and Y5 are representative of all Edison conversion schools that Edison managed for at least four or five years, these results should not be generalized to other, newer Edison conversion schools, which might see better results than these if current trends continue.

As we discussed in Chapter Five, these analyses exclude schools that experienced particularly large changes in enrollment or demographics between the year immediately prior to Edison's management and the first year of Edison's management. We also exclude a small number of schools where the validity of the Y0 scores might have been compromised as a result of testing irregularities (such as the use of nonstandard test administration procedures). As noted earlier, Appendix B provides a complete list of all Edison schools and the analyses in which each is included.

Figure 6.5
Z-Score Changes in Reading from Y0 Baseline, Edison Conversion Schools and State Comparison Schools

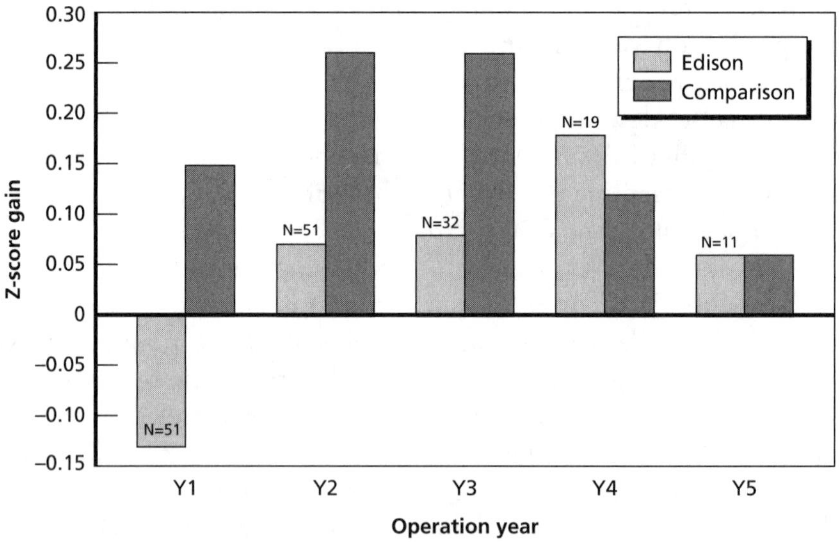

RAND *MG351-6.5*

Figure 6.6
Z-Score Changes in Mathematics from Y0 Baseline, Edison Conversion Schools and State Comparison Schools

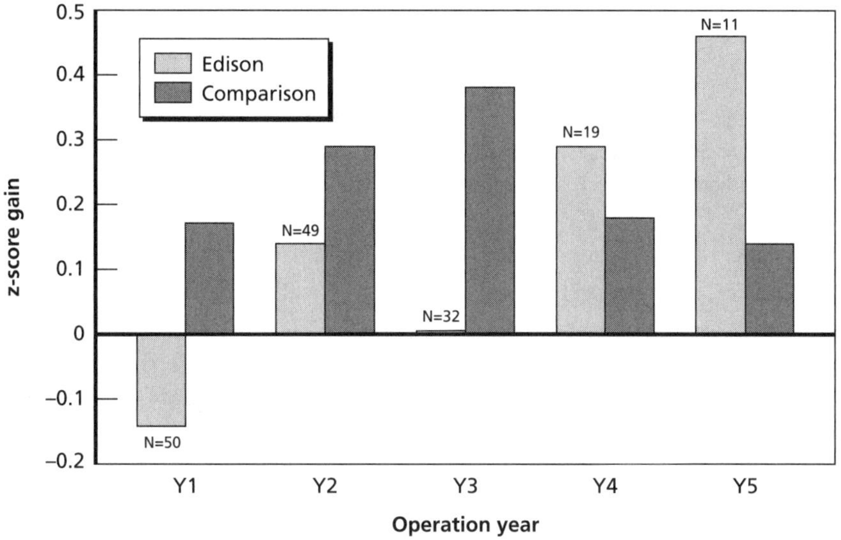

RAND *MG351-6.6*

Figure 6.5 presents the z-score changes in reading for Edison schools and comparison schools using all Edison schools for which Y0 scores were available. Figure 6.6 presents a similar set of results for mathematics. Both figures show that on average, Edison conversion schools experience a slight decline in performance between the spring prior to Edison's management and the spring of the first year under Edison's management.

The differences in z-score gains are shown in Table 6.6. (Appendix J provides a comparison of results obtained using statewide versus within-district comparison schools). We include results only through Y5 because only a handful of schools with Y0 baselines have been under Edison's management for six years or more.

Table 6.6
Differences in Z-Score Changes in Reading and Mathematics from Y0 Baseline, Edison Conversion Schools and State Comparison Schools

	Y1	Y2	Y3	Y4	Y5
Reading	-0.29* (N=51)	-0.18 (N=51)	-0.17 (N=32)	0.06 (N=19)	0.00 (N=11)
Mathematics	-0.31* (N=50)	-0.15 (N=49)	-0.36* (N=32)	0.11 (N=19)	0.32 (N=11)

NOTE: * indicates statistical significance at $p < 0.05$.

The negative entries for the first three operation years indicate that when measured from a pre-Edison baseline, Edison conversion schools' average achievement changes are less favorable than achievement changes among comparison schools through Y3.[5] By years four and five, the differences in z-score gains become slightly positive for Edison schools in mathematics, indicating that Edison conversion schools have achieved more growth (relative to the Y0 baseline) than their comparison schools. The positive math effects for years four and five are not statistically different from zero, but this lack of significance may be due in large part to the small numbers of schools included in these analyses. The reading estimates likewise improve in later years, but only enough to catch up to the comparison schools.

Figures 6.7 and 6.8 indicate the percentages of Edison conversion schools for which the z-score differences are positive each operation year. Although majorities of Edison conversion schools are achieving smaller test-score gains relative to comparison schools in the earlier years in both subjects, majorities of them have surpassed their comparison schools in both subjects by years four and five. Moreover, these results again demonstrate that average estimates mask considerable variability among Edison schools: in every operation year, some Edison conversion schools are surpassing their comparison schools while others are falling behind.

[5] In the first year, Edison conversion schools show a slight decline in absolute test scores, with a decline of 0.13 standard deviation in reading and 0.14 standard deviation in math between Y0 and Y1. By Y2 and in subsequent years, these schools' scores are higher than their Y0 scores, but the average gains from Y0 are smaller than those of comparison schools.

Figure 6.7
Proportion of Edison Conversion Schools with Reading Gains Exceeding the Gains of Statewide Comparison Schools, from Y0 Baseline

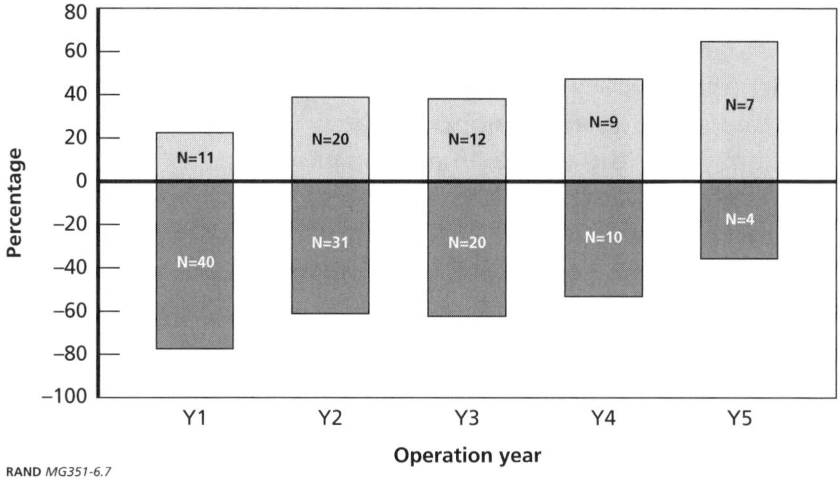

RAND *MG351-6.7*

Figure 6.8
Proportion of Edison Conversion Schools with Math Gains Exceeding the Gains of Statewide Comparison Schools, from Y0 Baseline

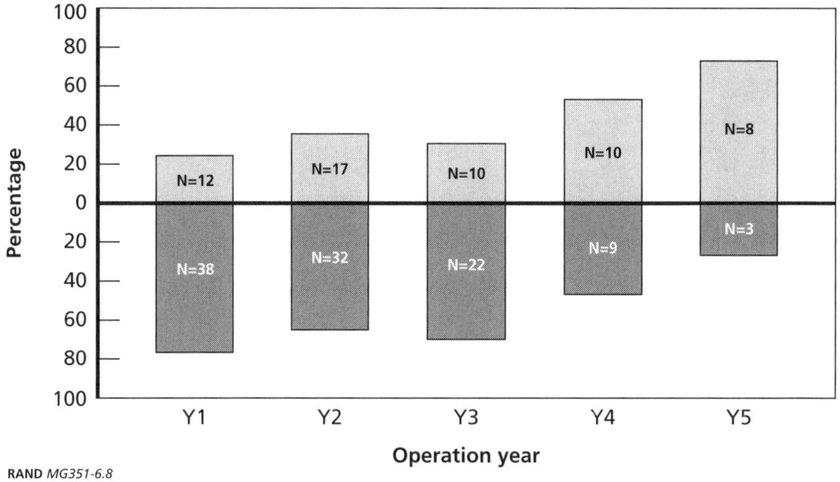

RAND *MG351-6.8*

Understanding the Effects of Attrition

As with the Y1 baseline analysis, the different numbers of schools included in the estimates for each operation year raise concerns about the extent to which the more positive results observed in later years are due to selective attrition from Edison management. Again, we examined trends for schools that were managed by Edison for at least four years. These appear in Appendix M and, as with the Y1 analysis, demonstrate that the changes in performance shown in Table 6.6 are not entirely attributable to differences in the schools included in each operation year estimated.

We also address concerns about attrition by conducting a policy-impact analysis, examining trends from Y0 for all conversion schools ever managed by Edison (with the exceptions noted above), including those in which Edison management ended after three or four years. The results appear in Table 6.7. The trends are similar to those shown in Table 6.6 using only the schools that remained under Edison's management, but the estimates for years four and five are less positive for math and nonpositive for reading. In both cases the estimates for years four and five fail to reach statistical significance.

In sum, judged from a pre-Edison baseline, Edison conversion schools' test-score trends are less favorable than those of comparison schools in the first three years of Edison management. In years four and five, conversion schools that remain under Edison's management appear to catch up to comparison schools in reading, and possibly exceed the gains of comparison schools in math. The policy-impact analysis likewise suggests some improvement in the relative gains of conversion schools ever managed by Edison (including those that concluded relationships with Edison after three or four years), but differences in both reading and math remain close to zero in years four and five.

Table 6.7
Policy Impact from Y0: Differences in Z-Score Changes for Conversion Schools Ever Managed by Edison

	Y1	Y2	Y3	Y4	Y5
Reading	-0.29* (N=51)	-0.18 (N=51)	-0.17 (N=32)	-0.03 (N=29)	-0.16 (N=17)
Mathematics	-0.31* (N=50)	-0.15 (N=49)	-0.36* (N=32)	0.03 (N=29)	0.11 (N=17)

NOTE: * indicates statistical significance at $p < 0.05$.

Performance of Start-Up Schools

Given the difficulty in interpreting trends in the start-up schools—where no pre-Edison scores exist—we supplement the trend analysis with a cross-sectional analysis that focuses exclusively on start-up schools that are in Y4 or beyond in 2004. If the full, net effect of Edison's start-up schools is in fact similar to that of Edison's conversion schools, and if the students in Edison's start-up schools are well-matched to those in demographically similar comparison schools (admittedly a strong assumption, given that most of Edison's start-up schools are charter schools that are chosen by their families), then we might expect to see positive results in Y4 and beyond. A cross-sectional analysis is far from definitive, because differences in student populations that are not captured in race or ethnicity and poverty measures could bias the results either up or down. Nevertheless, such an analysis might provide useful contextual information on the start-up schools. Table 6.8 shows the results of the analysis.

Table 6.8
2004 Cross-Sectional Advantage for Edison Start-Up Schools in Y4 and Beyond, Relative to Within-District Comparison Schools

		Edison Percent Proficient Advantage vs. Comparison Schools	Edison Z-Score Advantage vs. Comparison Schools
Reading	Start-up	2.7% (n=22)	0.11 (n=26)
Mathematics	Start-up	2.3% (n=22)	0.13 (n=26)

For the cross-sectional analysis, we rely on within-district comparison schools, because district context appears to have an important effect on score levels (even though it does not notably affect score gains when controlling for baseline scores). Although the results are not statistically significant, they suggest the possibility of a slight advantage for the Edison schools. Such an advantage would be consistent with the explanation that Edison's start-up schools, like its conversion schools, begin to outperform comparison schools around Y4. It should be noted, however, that other interpretations of the results are also possible. In particular, Edison's start-up schools might be doing better only because they are serving a more advantaged population of students. Again, in the absence of longitudinal data at the student level, considerable caution in interpretation is warranted.

Evidence from Case Studies

As noted in Chapter Four, the case studies provide considerable evidence that both start-up and conversion schools face significant challenges during the first year. These challenges could explain the first-year achievement decline observed in the Y0 analysis. For example, in many of the schools we visited, teachers told us that in the first year, students often had trouble making the transition to the new curricula due to lack of exposure to these programs in earlier grades. Moreover, teachers reported some difficulty in implementing new curriculum programs. Many of our study participants said that learning how to teach using the new programs was difficult—particularly given that curricula in every subject were being changed simultaneously. This challenge undoubtedly affected the quality of curriculum implementation. Indeed, a recognition of the challenges of instituting a comprehensive school design all at once is implicit in Edison's own view of implementation, which assumes that schools generally progress through several levels of implementation and should perform at a proficient level of implementation by the end of their third year (Edison Schools, 2004b; see also Chapter Three of this monograph).

In a few conversion schools, these challenges, along with a general mistrust of Edison, led to outright resistance among some teachers during the first year. Start-up schools were less likely than conversion schools to experience active resistance, but many of them had additional challenges. In particular, Edison's start-up charter schools, like other start-up charter schools across the country, often had to struggle with facilities problems in their first year. Edison and its local staff in new charter schools frequently needed to work with buildings that had either gone unused for extended periods of time or had been originally constructed for a purpose quite different than kindergarten through grade 12 schooling. Nevertheless, first-year charter schools often opened their doors before their facilities were fully retrofitted to be modern schools. Such problems are common among start-up charter schools more generally.

In start-up schools and conversion schools alike, school staff also reported first-year problems resulting from inadequate curriculum materials and technology resources, lack of participation in summer professional development (e.g., when teachers were hired late in the summer), and vacant leadership positions within the schools. Moreover, Edison schools begin operating with a longer school year only in the second year of operation. Indeed, case study schools that we visited during their first year of operation had notably lower levels of implementation of reading and math, of other (nontested) curricula, and of the Edison professional environment, as compared with schools that had longer experience with Edison. And teachers and principals in schools that were well beyond the first year of operation consistently remembered and reported similar challenges with which they had struggled during the first year.

In sum, the observations and interviews conducted in the case study schools provide evidence that the first year of Edison operation is especially challenging, for both conversion schools and start-up schools. This evidence could well explain the observed first-year dip in achievement in the Y0 analysis, and suggests the possibility that such a dip might occur in start-up schools as well as in conversion schools.

Evidence from Other Literature

A pattern of slow early progress followed by gains after several years has been observed in studies of a variety of different education initiatives. Most directly relevant to the Edison context are several studies that used student-level data to examine charter school performance, finding that student achievement often drops during the first year of a charter school's operation, but gradually improves over time (Bifulco and Ladd, 2003; Booker et al., 2004; Hanushek, Kain, and Rivkin, 2002; Solmon, Paark, and Garcia, 2001). Research on comprehensive school reform has also demonstrated a positive relationship between length of implementation and student achievement (Slavin et al., 1994; Ross, Nunnery, and Smith, 1996; Catterall, 1995). Zhang, Shkolnik, and Fashola (2005), for example, found that schools in their third through fifth years of comprehensive school-reform-model implementation achieved higher test-score gains than schools with either more or less experience implementing the models. Ross et al. (2001, p. 327) note that "leading scholars of educational change have hypothesized that finding measurable results will, at best, take between 3 and 10 years" (Fullan and Stiegelbauer, 1991; Fullan, 1999; Fullan and Miles, 1992). Similarly, researchers and comprehensive school-reform-model developers have pointed out that it may take more than five years to accomplish meaningful schoolwide change (Sizer, 1992; Hess, 1995; Darling-Hammond, 1988, 1995, 1997).

The fact that other studies of Edison schools have generally not found positive effects for Edison (see Chapter Two) might reflect the fact that most of the Edison schools examined in earlier studies did not have sufficient time to implement their school design. In fact, the AFT and Miami-Dade school district studies found some evidence consistent with the interpretation that Edison schools' performance improves over time (Nelson and Van Meter, 2003; Gomez and Shay, 2000). Our results provide additional support for the belief, expressed by many education scholars and reformers, that significant change takes time to accomplish.

Summary: The Importance of Time

This chapter presents a variety of analyses that aim to address Edison's causal effect on student achievement. None of the analyses should be viewed as definitive—each depends on a variety of assumptions related to the measurement of the counterfactual, and there are additional limitations that were discussed in Chapter Five. But by making the assumptions and limitations explicit and examining all of the empirical evidence, it is possible to reach some tentative conclusions about Edison's average effect on student achievement.

Most of the analyses presented in this chapter examined changes in the performance of Edison schools over time. It is important to keep in mind that (as noted earlier) different operation-year estimates are based on different sets of Edison schools, so the test-score changes we report should not be interpreted as indicating trends in a common set of Edison schools. We discussed this problem explicitly with respect to the Y0 analysis, but it is relevant to the Y1 and even the recent change analyses as well. The specific schools that are included, and their characteristics, vary across analyses but also across years within analyses. Estimates for later operation years do not include newer Edison schools, and therefore the extent to which the later operation-year results can be generalized to all Edison schools is limited. Whether the Y4 or Y5 estimates that are shown in this chapter would be replicated with newer or future Edison Schools is yet to be seen.

The first analysis presented in the chapter demonstrates that currently operating Edison schools are, on average, increasing the proportion of students achieving proficiency in both reading and mathematics over the last two years. This fact in itself might be viewed as evidence of a positive Edison effect if we believe that the schools would not have made gains in the absence of Edison management. Such an assumption, however, is cast into doubt by the evidence on matched comparison schools that serve similar student populations. Matched non-Edison schools are also showing proficiency gains. Although it is possible that the Edison schools are truly unique—i.e., that poverty, ethnicity, and baseline scores do not fully capture the challenges they face—we believe that the matched comparison is more likely to provide an appropriate counterfactual estimate than are raw gains by the Edison schools.

Over the last two years, average gains of currently operating Edison schools have been larger than those of comparison schools in both reading and math (although the difference was statistically significant only in math). But a full estimate of Edison's effect requires an examination of the total gains of each Edison school (relative to comparison schools) from the beginning of Edison's management. Results from Y1 and Y0 baselines diverge in some respects, but they are consistent in some elements:

- In the first three years of Edison management, average gains for Edison schools in both subjects are, at best, similar to the gains of matched comparison schools.
- Year of operation matters: All estimates indicate improvement in average results for Edison schools over time with Edison.
- Attrition of schools from Edison management plays a small role in the improving trend in years four and five, but the improving trend remains evident even in "policy impact" estimates that include post-termination years for schools that ended Edison management prior to Y5.

Although these results do not provide all of the answers, they provide considerable guidance about the range of possible effects. The results from Y1 suggest that the long-term average effects may be positive, but these results exclude the first year under Edison's management. The results from Y0 reveal a drop in first-year achievement for conversion schools and suggest that Edison conversion schools are generally keeping up with, but not surpassing, comparison schools by years four and five.[6] Either way, results for Edison schools clearly improve over time. This is consistent with what might be expected, based on both case study findings and other literature on school reform. As John Chubb noted recently, "It takes years to affect student achievement in major and lasting ways" (Chubb, 2004, p. 491).

Nevertheless, the differences in results for different analyses of conversion schools and the lack of information about the first year of

---

[6] Because we lack data about first-year changes in start-up schools, it is impossible to determine how well these schools are performing relative to comparison schools from a pre-Edison baseline.

performance for start-up schools leave us with some uncertainty about whether Edison's net, average achievement effects are ultimately superior to those of comparison schools. Moreover, the extent to which these results can be used to predict future Edison effects is limited: Predicting future trends involves assumptions about the stability of Edison's management approach as well as about the kinds of schools and districts with which Edison is likely to work in the future. As we noted earlier, the positive Y4 and Y5 estimates are based on schools that opened in 2000 or earlier, and we have no information on which to base an assumption that schools that opened after that date will perform similarly.

In the context of such uncertainty, it is worth pointing out that test-score trajectories among individual Edison schools vary substantially, and the average effects presented in this chapter mask this variability. None of these effects should be interpreted as applying to any particular currently operating or prospective Edison school. Prospective Edison clients should recognize that a range of outcomes is possible, and those outcomes will ultimately depend on a number of contextual and implementation factors. In the next chapter, we move beyond systemwide averages and explore some of the ways in which test-score trends differ across Edison schools.

CHAPTER SEVEN

Inside the Black Box: Differences in Achievement Among Edison Schools

Brian P. Gill, Laura S. Hamilton, J. R. Lockwood, and Ron W. Zimmer

The results presented in Chapter Six focus on the average performance of all Edison schools across Edison's ten-year history of managing schools. Those results also reveal, however, that regardless of which comparison group, baseline score, and operation year is examined, some Edison schools achieve larger gains than comparison schools, whereas others post smaller gains. In this chapter, we present results of analyses that are designed to identify factors related to the different levels of success across Edison schools.

Some of the variation in performance among Edison schools was discussed in Chapter Six, where we presented the percentages of schools whose z-score gains were larger than their comparison schools for the Y0 and Y1 analyses. An examination of the range of differences in z-score gains between Edison schools and comparable schools provides further illustration of this variability. Table 7.1 provides the same information that appeared in Table 6.3 in Chapter Six (table entries from Table 6.3 are highlighted in Table 7.1), but in addition to the average differences in z-score changes, we have indicated the maximum and minimum values, as well as the values that correspond to the 25th percentile (called "quartile 1," or Q1) and the 75th percentile ("quartile 3," or Q3) in the distribution of z-score change differences for each subject and operation year. For the Y1 analysis, for example, the average difference in z-score change in year two was close to zero for both subjects, but the differences for individual schools and their comparison schools ranged from approximately −2 standard deviation units to approximately two standard deviation units in reading and from approximately −2 to approximately three standard deviation units in mathematics. Similar variability is observed for other operation years.

This represents a very wide range of performance. On the high end, a school that is achieving at a level two standard deviations ahead of its comparison group has an advantage on the order of 25–40 percentage points in proficiency; by the same token, a school that has fallen two standard deviations behind its comparison group has a deficit on the order of 25–40 percentage points in proficiency.

The results from the Y0 baseline are also characterized by extensive variability among test-score trends each operation year. The descriptive statistics in Table 7.2 show that although the change between Y0 and Y1 was on average negative in both subjects, some schools increased their performance relative to comparison schools.

Table 7.1
Descriptive Statistics for Differences in Z-Score Changes in Reading and Mathematics for Y1 Baseline

	Descriptive Statistics for Differences in Z-Score Changes	Y2	Y3	Y4	Y5	Y6
Reading	Minimum	-2.13	-2.46	-1.50	-2.39	-0.75
	Q1	-0.25	-0.45	-0.26	-0.17	-0.08
	Mean	-0.02	-0.04	0.17	0.25	0.15
	Q3	0.25	0.33	0.64	0.74	0.46
	Maximum	2.09	2.77	1.87	3.74	0.94
	N	116	88	58	35	16
Mathematics	Minimum	-2.01	-2.33	-1.38	-1.36	-0.19
	Q1	-0.30	-0.45	-0.13	0.01	0.07
	Mean	0.04	-0.04	0.32	0.53	0.45
	Q3	0.36	0.42	0.71	1.14	0.77
	Maximum	3.16	1.97	2.34	3.01	1.22
	N	112	87	59	32	14

Table 7.2
Descriptive Statistics for Differences in Z-Score Changes in Reading and Mathematics from Y0 Baseline

	Descriptive Statistics for Differences in Z-Score Changes	Y1	Y2	Y3	Y4	Y5
Reading	Minimum	-1.89	-2.08	-1.80	-0.98	-1.20
	Q1	-0.46	-0.52	-0.32	-0.37	-0.28
	Mean	-0.29	-0.18	-0.17	0.06	0.00
	Q3	-0.03	0.16	0.11	0.31	0.28
	Maximum	1.89	1.85	1.33	1.86	0.77
	N	51	51	32	19	11
Mathematics	Minimum	-2.51	-1.63	-1.93	-0.97	-0.62
	Q1	-0.55	-0.43	-0.58	-0.42	0.06
	Mean	-0.31	-0.15	-0.36	0.11	0.32
	Q3	-0.02	0.18	0.17	0.54	0.63
	Maximum	1.16	2.77	1.19	1.84	1.01
	N	50	49	32	19	11

Given this range of variation, understanding differences in achievement among Edison schools may be as important as estimating an average effect. An investigation of differences in design implementation and contextual factors would undoubtedly help to explain many of the differences in achievement trajectories across Edison schools. This type of analysis, which seeks to peer into the "black box" and understand the specific factors that influence achievement, might help policymakers and educators understand the conditions under which positive effects of Edison might be expected. Though a comprehensive analysis of implementation across all Edison schools is beyond the scope of our study, we are able to investigate differences in achievement trends among some categories of Edison schools, providing some information about factors related to academic progress in these schools. In this chapter, we address three possible sources of variation in achievement trends, specifically asking these questions:

1. Are Edison schools in recent years demonstrating better test-score trajectories, relative to comparison schools, than Edison schools in the early years of Edison's history?
2. Are the test-score trajectories for Edison's charter schools different from those of Edison's district contract schools?
3. Are Edison elementary schools performing differently than secondary (middle and high) schools?

In addition to these comparisons that examine the entire population of Edison schools, we report exploratory analyses of achievement results for our case study schools, for which we have richer measures of design implementation and contextual factors than are available for the full population of Edison schools. Because of the small number of schools in this analysis and the fact that they were not sampled to represent all Edison schools, these findings should be interpreted as suggestive rather than conclusive.

How Has Achievement in Edison Schools Changed in Recent Years, Relative to Similar Schools?

The first section of this chapter asks whether Edison schools have achieved greater success in the recent past than in the company's early years. As discussed in Chapters Two and Three, Edison as a system has experienced a number of changes and has modified its design as its leaders have become more knowledgeable about the challenges of managing public schools. As a result of these modifications, we might expect to see improvements in Edison's effectiveness over time. If so, information on Edison's performance in recent years is likely to be of interest to policymakers, parents, and others who are involved with Edison or are considering becoming involved. Here, we examine Edison's own performance and also compare it to the performance of similar schools.

The fact that Edison's performance appears relatively strong in the recent-gains analysis presented in Chapter Six could result from one or both of two factors. First, the Y0 and Y1 analyses described in

Chapter Six revealed that achievement results improve as schools are under Edison's management for several years. The positive recent gains could reflect the fact that many of the Edison schools that are operating today have been under Edison's management for a few years and are reaching the point at which Edison schools' achievement starts to increase (around Y4). Indeed, the trends from both Y1 and Y0 suggest that an analysis that truncates the early years of operation will necessarily show larger average gains (by removing from the analysis the years with smaller gains).

In addition to removing low-gaining years for many schools, the recent gains results might also be favorable because Edison may have improved over time in its systemwide ability to manage schools effectively. To examine this latter hypothesis, it is necessary to compare recent performance with earlier performance, and to control for operation year.

The results by operation year from the Y0 and Y1 baselines, presented in Chapter Six, included schools that opened during any year since 1995 and that were operated by Edison for at least one year. In Chapters Two and Three, we discussed the ways in which Edison's approach to managing and supporting schools has changed over time. For example, improvements in technology accompanied by a strong professional development effort have led to substantial improvements in the implementation and use of Edison's benchmark assessment system. To the extent that this change or others have improved Edison's ability to manage schools effectively or have improved school staff capacity to promote student learning, estimates of student achievement effects would be expected to be higher if calculated using newer rather than older Edison schools. Ideally, our analyses of achievement trends would control for the calendar year as well as operation year so that we could take into account changes in Edison's approach to managing schools. Although the size of our sample does not allow us to examine calendar year and operation year simultaneously, we can examine operation-year trends for different sets of calendar years. We conduct two sets of analyses: one that replicates the Y1 analysis for older and newer schools, and another that examines the first-year results for Edison conversion schools as a function of conversion year.

Year-One Analysis for Older and Newer Edison Schools

We conducted the Y1 baseline analysis presented in Chapter Six for two separate groups of schools: those that opened before the year 2000 (i.e., before the 2000–2001 school year), and those that opened in 2000 (i.e., the 2000–2001 school year) or later. Conversations with Edison staff suggested that 2000 was an appropriate year to use for splitting the sample.[1] A comparison of results for these two groups provides some information about how Edison's effectiveness might have changed over time. By examining the same set of operation years, we can compare Edison's overall effectiveness at managing schools, which the recent gains analysis did not allow us to do (because, as we discussed earlier, it omits part of the Edison effect for schools that had been open longer than one or two years).

Table 7.3 presents the results for both subjects. We conducted statistical tests of the difference between the older and newer schools for each subject and operation year. Because we have a maximum of four years of data for schools that opened in 2000 or later, the tables only include entries for years two through four. In mathematics, the results are consistently more positive for the post-2000 schools than for the pre-2000 schools, although only the Y2 difference is statistically significant. By Y4, the z-score difference between Edison schools that opened in 2000 or later and their comparison schools is 0.49, compared with a difference of 0.24 for schools that opened before 2000. In reading, however, there is no evidence that the Edison system has become more effective over time.

As with the other analyses that use a Y1 baseline, it is important to keep in mind that these results omit some of the Edison effect; a

---

[1] Moreover, splitting the sample in 2000 results in approximately equal numbers of schools on each side, maximizing statistical power to detect differences in effects.

Table 7.3
Differences in Z-Score Changes in Reading and Mathematics from Y1 Baseline for Schools That Opened Before 2000 and Those That Opened in 2000 or Later, Using State Comparison Schools

		Y2	Y3	Y4
Reading	Before 2000	-0.02 (N=51)	0.02 (N=49)	0.16 (N=41)
	2000 or later	-0.03 (N=65)	-0.12 (N=39)	0.19 (N=17)
Mathematics	Before 2000	-0.13* (N=46)	-0.09 (N=46)	0.24 (N=41)
	2000 or later	0.17* (N=66)	0.02 (N=41)	0.49 (N=18)

NOTE: * indicates the difference between schools that opened before 2000 and schools that opened in 2000 or later is significantly different from zero at $p < 0.05$.

larger number of schools with pre-Edison baseline scores would be needed to determine whether Edison's effectiveness during the first year has improved. It is also important to acknowledge that only one of the differences is statistically significant, though the lack of significance for the Y4 difference in math is probably due in part to the relatively small numbers of Edison schools used to calculate each estimate. An examination of policy impact results from Y1, similarly split into pre- and post-2000 schools, suggests similar results: no notable time trends in reading, but an apparent improvement in math trends. For the Y0 analysis, cell sizes are smaller, but separating results into pre- and post-2000 cohorts likewise suggests some evidence of improvement in Edison's recent performance in math, and possible improvement in reading as well. It is important to note, however, that differences in trends for older and newer schools are not only a result of changes in Edison management but also reflect differences in the sets of schools included in each group, so inferences about changes in the effectiveness of Edison over time should be made with caution.

Trends in First-Year Results for Edison Conversion Schools

In light of the evidence of a first-year deficit presented in Chapter Six, one key question is whether Edison's first-year performance has improved. We examined the change between Y0 and Y1 for Edison conversion schools to explore whether the first-year relative decline observed in the analyses presented in Chapter Six varies as a function of the year in which the school converts. Specifically, this involved an examination of the achievement gains of newly opened Edison Schools in their first year of operation for each cohort of Edison conversion schools opening from 1997 through 2002. Sample sizes in all years were small, and we do not present the results here, but they showed little evidence of systematic improvement. Edison's best first-year results were seen in schools opening in 1998. Results for 2002 openings are among Edison's better first-year results, but we do not believe that one year of smaller first-year deficits is sufficient to merit a conclusion that Edison has eliminated such deficits (particularly given that all of the conversion schools opening in 2002 were in Philadelphia, among schools with extraordinarily low pre-Edison baseline scores that gave them little room to decline).[2] Moreover, despite their smaller first-year declines, the conversion schools opening in 2002 had not, on average, surpassed their comparison schools by spring 2004.

Taken together, the results presented in this section suggest that Edison's performance relative to comparison schools may have improved somewhat (evidence is strongest in math), but that operation

[2] Examination of Edison conversion schools' absolute performance (i.e., not relative to comparison schools) in the first year shows an improving trend, with more recently opened schools showing no average first-year decline. There is a straightforward explanation for why Edison's first-year results would improve in absolute terms while Edison schools continue to have a deficit relative to matched comparison schools. In recent years, the conversion schools that have been given to Edison to manage have increasingly been schools with very low pre-Edison achievement levels. The scores for newer schools (those opening in 2000–2002) are statistically significantly lower than the scores for older Edison schools, and as we have noted elsewhere, schools with lower average scores typically achieve larger gains than schools with higher scores.

year—i.e., the length of an individual school's experience with Edison—remains an important influence on student achievement, and the first year continues to present significant challenges.

Achievement Trends for Charter Versus Contract Schools

Table 7.4 examines differences in achievement gains between charter schools and contract schools from a Y1 baseline. There is extensive overlap between this distinction and the one examined in Chapter Six—many charter schools open as new start-ups, and many of the schools operating under contract were converted from pre-existing public schools. The overlap is not complete, however, and it is possible that implementation of the Edison design differs as a function of charter or contract status.[3] Given the overlap between this distinction and the start-up/conversion distinction, it is not surprising that in mathematics, the differences in z-score gains for contract schools are slightly larger than those for charter schools each operation year,

Table 7.4
Differences in Z-Score Changes in Reading and Mathematics from Y1 Baseline for Charter and District Schools

		Y2	Y3	Y4	Y5
Reading	Charter	-0.10 (N=45)	0.04 (N=42)	0.15 (N=34)	0.37 (N=23)
	District	0.00 (N=68)	-0.14 (N=43)	0.13 (N=21)	0.00 (N=12)
Mathematics	Charter	-0.10 (N=45)	-0.05 (N=42)	0.19 (N=37)	0.50 (N=22)
	District	0.10 (N=64)	-0.03 (N=42)	0.44 (N=19)	0.59 (N=10)

NOTE: * indicates that the difference between charter and district schools is significantly different from zero at $p < 0.05$.

[3] Edison's three state partnership schools were excluded from this analysis because they did not fit neatly into either category.

though in some cases the differences are quite small and none of the differences is statistically significant. In reading, most of the differences are small except in Y5, where charter schools show a large and statistically significant advantage over contract schools.

It is difficult to interpret these results given the small sample sizes in the later operation years, but they suggest that there might be an interaction between school type and subject (reading or mathematics). Without more information about curriculum implementation in the two types of schools, however, it is impossible to determine what accounts for this interaction or how robust it would be for a larger sample of schools. Moreover, like the comparison of start-up versus conversion schools, this comparison is potentially undermined by the absence of information about first-year effects. If first-year effects differ systematically in charter schools and contract schools, then comparisons of later years from a Y1 baseline will be biased. Unfortunately, there are too few Edison charter schools with Y0 data to examine this issue.

Achievement Trends for Elementary Versus Secondary Schools

Next, we examine differences between elementary schools and secondary (middle and high) schools. Although many of the core elements of Edison's design are the same for both types of school, the details of implementation, such as the specific curriculum programs used and the allocation of time across subjects, differ. Therefore it is possible that the effects of Edison's management might be different in elementary than in secondary schools.

Recall that we used a set of rules to split schools that had nontraditional grade configurations, so in some cases a single school building is represented in both conditions (e.g., for a kindergarten through grade eight school, the elementary grades would count as an elementary school, and grades six through eight would count as a middle school). We focus on the Y1 baseline results because the sample sizes for secondary schools become quite small in the later operation years using a Y0 baseline. The most notable finding depicted in Table 7.5 is that the score trajectories of elementary and secondary schools relative to comparison schools look quite different in mathematics, though none of the differences reached statistical significance. The overall Y1 results (see Table 6.3) show near-zero effects for operation Y2 and Y3, but Table 7.5 suggests that those results might not be generalizable to Edison's secondary schools, which achieved positive trajectories starting in Y2. The results are difficult to interpret because of the small sample numbers of Edison secondary schools, but the early operation-year results suggest that Edison's secondary schools began outgaining their comparison schools in mathematics from the second year of Edison management, as measured against a Y1 baseline. As in Chapter Six, it is important to keep in mind that the estimates from the Y1 baseline likely represent an upper bound on Edison's causal effect.

It is impossible to tell from the results in Table 7.5 whether the larger secondary school gain in mathematics occurs in the context of a larger or smaller first-year drop (relative to comparison schools), so

Table 7.5
Differences in Z-Score Changes in Reading and Mathematics from Y1 Baseline for Elementary and Secondary Schools

		Y2	Y3	Y4	Y5
Reading	Elementary	-0.07 (N=85)	0.04 (N=71)	0.17 (N=48)	0.27 (N=29)
	Secondary	0.11 (N=31)	-0.05 (N=17)	0.19 (N=10)	0.15 (N=6)
Mathematics	Elementary	-0.02 (N=84)	-0.09 (N=70)	0.28 (N=46)	0.49 (N=27)
	Secondary	0.24 (N=28)	0.17 (N=17)	0.47 (N=13)	0.71 (N=5)

NOTE: * indicates that the difference between elementary and secondary schools is significantly different from zero at $p < 0.05$.

Table 7.6
Differences in Z-Score Changes in Reading and Mathematics Between Y0 and Y1 for Elementary and Secondary Schools

		Y1 Difference in Z-Score Gain (from Y0)
Reading	Elementary	-0.28 (N=34)
	Secondary	-0.29 (N=17)
Mathematics	Elementary	-0.41* (N=34)
	Secondary	-0.11* (N=16)

NOTE: * indicates that the difference between elementary and secondary schools is significantly different from zero at $p < 0.05$.

the relative net effect of Edison management on elementary and secondary schools is not immediately evident. Although the secondary schools with Y0 scores are few, we looked at the differences in z-score changes between Y0 and Y1 for the elementary and secondary schools for which we had Y0 data, and found that secondary schools' achievement trends looked better than elementary schools' trends even from Y0 in mathematics. Table 7.6 presents these first-year effects. Scores in both sets of schools dropped relative to comparison schools in the first year, but in mathematics the decline was smaller for secondary than for elementary schools. The relative decline in reading was similar in both types of schools.

Achievement Trends in Case Study Schools

As noted in Chapter Four, the Edison elementary schools that we examined as case studies were somewhat higher performing than Edison averages. Nevertheless, they represent a wide range of performance, including all quartiles of the Edison achievement distribution, as represented by their achievement z-scores (from a Y1 baseline) for the operation year in which we visited them (as shown in Table 7.7). This range of performance provides a useful opportunity to examine implementation factors that might be related to achievement—even if only for suggestive purposes, given the small size and lack of representativeness of the sample.

First of all, we examined the relationship between our ratings of curriculum implementation and the school's achievement gain score in the year of the visit. Schools that do better implementing the Edison curriculum in reading and math also post larger gains in those subjects, on the order of 0.3 to 0.5 on the achievement z-score scale, as indicated in Table 7.8.[4] Given the small sample sizes involved, the differences are not statistically significant.

Interestingly, however, in the case study schools, reading scores are also predicted by math implementation, and both reading and math scores are predicted by an index of the implementation of nontested aspects of the curriculum, including science, social studies, core values, and specials. Effect sizes for nontested curriculum on math and reading scores are on the order of half a standard deviation, which is at least moderate in size, and pretty substantial by the standards of education research.[5] To be sure, with simple cross-sectional correlations such as these, we cannot conclude that the relationship is

Table 7.7
Achievement Distribution of Case Study Schools in Year of Visit Relative to Total Distribution of Edison Schools

	Math	Reading
Lowest quartile	3	2
Middle quartiles	5	7
Highest quartile	6	5
N	14	14

[4] Similarly, Zhang, Shkolnik, and Fashola (2005) found that schools that had been implementing a comprehensive reform model for three to five years and that were rated as strong implementers achieved larger test-score gains than schools of similar vintage that were judged to be low-implementing.

[5] Note that this effect size cannot be directly compared to the achievement z-score scale, which is standardized relative to a different distribution.

causal. The correlations among the different subjects may simply result from the fact that high-performing schools do many things better than low-performing schools. Nevertheless, these results suggest the intriguing possibility that Edison schools may do better in reading and math achievement if they implement the full Edison curriculum in all of its breadth. At minimum, the results indicate that schools do not need to narrow the curriculum in order to promote strong achievement in math and reading.

An additional finding of the case study analysis is that the quality of the principal's instructional leadership appears to be strongly related to achievement in both reading (where schools of strong principals score higher by about 0.7 on the z-score scale) and math (where schools of strong principals score higher by about 0.6 on the z-score scale), as indicated in Table 7.9.[6] Again, this is a result that might be expected (in Edison schools and non-Edison schools alike), and it is difficult to make a causal attribution. Still, the apparent magnitude of the effect is impressive, suggesting that Edison is right to put substantial effort into identifying, recruiting, and training principals to be effective instructional leaders.

Table 7.8
Mean Achievement Z-Scores in Reading and Math by Level of Implementation of Tested Subject, Case Study Schools

	Strong Implementers in Tested Subject	Others
Reading	0.28 (n=12)	-0.25 (n=3)
Math	0.59 (n=9)	0.28 (n=5)

[6] We examined the relationship between instructional leadership and achievement both for the year of the visit and across all operation years (controlling for Edison-wide operation year trends), on the rationale that a principal's instructional leadership might affect both the current level of the school's achievement and its deviation from general Edison trends in all operation years. Apparent effects on overall trends controlling for operation year are comparable to apparent effects in the operation year of the visit. Sample sizes in Table 7.9 are somewhat smaller than in other case study analyses because we lack instructional leadership ratings for a few principals (as well as lacking achievement results for some schools).

Table 7.9
Mean Achievement Z-Scores by Principal Instructional Leadership, Case Study Schools

	Strong Instructional Leaders	Others
Reading	0.44 (n=6)	-0.23 (n=4)
Math	0.70 (n=5)	0.09 (n=4)

The implementation of the Edison professional environment—including the use of houses, the availability of planning time, and the prevalence of site-based professional development—is also related positively to achievement in the case study schools, with a correlation of about 0.5 in both reading and math. Schools that are following Edison's design for school organization are seeing greater student achievement gains. Again, although we cannot determine that the relationship is causal, the finding provides encouraging support for the importance of the professional environment as an integral part of Edison's school design.

We also examine the relationships between two structural or contextual characteristics of the Edison case study schools and our student-achievement effect estimates. Because these are characteristics that tend not to change over time, we would not necessarily expect to observe an effect on achievement in the particular year of our site visit, but we might expect to observe an effect on achievement across all operation years, controlling for Edison-wide operation year trends. The first contextual variable of interest is the extent to which Edison schools operate under local contractual constraints. Edison schools that operate with more local constraints on the implementation of the Edison model have slightly worse achievement outcomes in reading trends (about 0.3 lower on the z-score scale, on average) and in math trends (about 0.2 lower on the z-score scale, on average). The second variable of interest is the principal's authority over staffing. Schools in which the principal has full authority to hire and fire teachers (as desired by Edison) have slightly better achievement trends in reading (0.4 on the z-score scale) and in math (0.1 on the z-score scale). All of these differences are small (and short of statistical significance), so they should be viewed only as suggestive, but all are consistent with the view that Edison can achieve better results in schools where it can fully implement its design.

Summary

In mathematics, variation in Edison school achievement trajectories is explained to a limited extent by Edison's operational history: Schools opened more recently are doing a bit better than schools opened in Edison's first five years. Reading results show no difference between newer and older Edison schools.

Variation in test-score trends is not primarily attributable to whether the school is a charter or contract school or whether it serves students in elementary or secondary grades. There is some evidence that conversion schools and contract schools (categories that often, but not always, overlap) exhibit stronger achievement gains in mathematics from Y1 than start-up and charter schools, respectively, but most of the differences are not statistically significant. Without a pre-Edison baseline, however, it is impossible to determine whether the total Edison effect differs among these different categories of schools. Student-level data linked over time would be needed to understand the Edison effect, particularly in start-up schools that lack a Y0 score. Edison's secondary schools performed slightly better than elementary schools during their early operation years in mathematics. In this case as well as the charter/contract and start-up/conversion comparisons, we lack the detailed information on implementation to understand these trends, which are worthy of more detailed investigation by Edison and its clients.

The rich implementation data from our case studies provides some evidence that variation in test-score trends in Edison schools is related to specific features of design implementation. In particular, curriculum implementation, full implementation of the Edison professional environment, and principal instructional leadership are associated with higher achievement in both subjects. Moreover, implementation of the Edison curriculum in subjects other than reading and math (i.e., science, social studies, and specials) is correlated with stronger achievement results in reading and math, suggesting that schools need not neglect the broader aspects of the "world-class" curriculum in order to achieve gains in basic skills. Finally, there is limited evidence that Edison schools that operate with fewer local constraints on the model, and where principals have full authority over hiring and firing teachers, may have better achievement trends.

Taken together, the set of analyses discussed in this chapter indicate that information about average test-score trends should be interpreted cautiously and with the knowledge that results vary substantially across Edison schools. They also begin to point toward recommendations for Edison and its clients about ways to get the best possible results from Edison schools—a topic to which we turn in the next (and final) chapter.

CHAPTER EIGHT

Conclusions and Implications

Laura S. Hamilton and Brian P. Gill

Edison-managed schools served approximately 65,000 students in the 2004–2005 school year, more than most school systems in the United States. Edison students, their parents, educators, and policymakers have a clear stake in how well Edison achieves its goals. Moreover, there is growing interest in the broader topic of school privatization, in part as a result of the No Child Left Behind Act (NCLB), which includes provisions to turn unsuccessful schools over to outside management companies. As the nation's largest private operator of public schools, Edison's experiences are relevant to this broader debate about private management.

The objectives of this monograph are to provide Edison with information to help it improve its systems, and to inform clients and prospective clients about Edison's progress to help them make decisions about whether or how to engage Edison in their efforts to improve education. The analyses presented in this monograph provide the most comprehensive assessment of the performance of Edison schools to date, but they also leave some questions unanswered. In this chapter, we briefly summarize the findings from the analyses of implementation and achievement, and we present some recommendations for Edison and for policymakers.

Summary of Findings

We examined Edison's strategies for promoting student achievement, the implementation of those strategies in schools, and the achievement outcomes of schools under Edison's management. In this section, we revisit each of our research questions and provide brief summaries of our findings relevant to each.

Inspiration: What Are Edison's Strategies for Promoting Student Achievement in the Schools It Manages?

The resources and accountability systems that together constitute Edison's strategies for promoting student achievement are impressively comprehensive in addressing all elements relevant to high-quality delivery of instruction, including capacities, motivation, and opportunities for school staff. Edison is distinct from other comprehensive reform models in having operational authority over the schools. At the same time, Edison is distinct from conventional school districts in its favored modes of accountability, relying more extensively on outcomes-based and market-based systems, and less on political and bureaucratic accountability. Indeed, Edison's well-developed information systems and focus on achievement-based accountability should make it especially well suited to the high-stakes testing environment of NCLB. At the same time that it focuses on improving proficiency in reading and mathematics, Edison offers a broad curriculum that includes science, social studies, foreign language, art, and music, with the stated aim of providing a "world-class" education to all students. By focusing on both resources and accountability systems, Edison's strategies address all of the key elements necessary for promoting school improvement.

Perspiration: How Are Edison's Strategies Implemented in the Schools It Manages?

The breadth and comprehensiveness of Edison's design require significant commitment from its clients and school staff. Our school visits suggest that the best-functioning Edison schools, characterized by high levels of commitment and effort, demonstrate the promise inherent in Edison's model. They are schools with strong instructional leadership, motivated teachers, effective use of achievement data, high-fidelity implementation of the Edison curricula, and high levels of social capital. Although realization of this ideal is not universal across Edison schools, nearly all of the Edison schools we visited across the country showed enough consistency of implementation to be clearly recognizable as Edison schools.

Among the 23 Edison schools we visited, several factors appear to be important in explaining some of the variation in implementation of the Edison model:

- Full implementation of the Edison design takes time. Schools in the first year of operation had frequent challenges implementing various elements of the design—a finding that is not surprising given the complexity and comprehensiveness of Edison's model. Edison has been largely, but not entirely, successful in keeping its contracts long enough to ensure the opportunity for full implementation; its record of maintaining contracts appears more favorable than that of most comprehensive school reform models. Edison's charter schools tend to be more stable contractually than its district schools.
- Strong instructional leadership by the principal is associated with stronger implementation of the curriculum, in both tested and nontested subjects.
- Among the case study schools, strong instructional leadership by principals appeared to be somewhat more prevalent in charter schools than in district schools. But charter status did not appear to affect curriculum implementation directly.
- Local constraints, sometimes resulting from compromises required by Edison's clients, undermine the implementation of Edison's preferred professional environment in some schools.

Together, the findings from our case study visits illustrate the challenges inherent in implementing Edison's comprehensive design, and reveal the importance of high levels of commitment among clients and school staff.

Time: How Does Edison's Management of Schools Affect Student Achievement?

We began the analysis of student achievement by examining test-score trends in Edison schools between 2002 and 2004. Edison schools showed substantial test-score gains in both reading and math over the last two years. Matched comparison schools also showed gains over the period, but Edison's average gains were larger (though the difference between Edison and comparison school trends was statistically significant only in mathematics).

The results for 2002–2004 provide incomplete information about Edison's effects because they do not include the full period of Edison management for most schools. We conducted analyses from the beginning of Edison's management of each school in attempt to capture Edison's full effect over time. Using the first year under Edison management as a baseline for examining achievement trends, both Edison schools and comparison schools showed positive test-score gains. Edison schools' test-score trajectories were similar to those of comparison schools until the Edison schools' fourth year of operation, at which point they had achieved larger test-score gains relative to comparison schools in both reading and math. A portion of the Edison advantage in the later years is probably due to selective attrition of low-performing schools from the Edison population, but there is an Edison advantage in mathematics (and a nonsignificant advantage in reading) even in a policy impact analysis that includes post-termination results for schools that ended their relationships with Edison prior to Y5.

Edison schools' performance appears weaker when measured from a pre-Edison baseline (Y0, or spring of the year before Edison began managing the school) than from a Y1 baseline, though caution is warranted when interpreting these pre-Edison baseline results because they only apply to a subset of Edison schools. In particular, the Y0 baseline analysis includes only conversion schools because start-up schools did not exist prior to Edison's management. Moreover, in years one through three, the results are dominated heavily by schools from three districts (Chester, Pennsylvania; Philadelphia; and Dallas) and do not represent the full range of Edison's clients. The test-score trends for Edison's conversion schools are less favorable than those of comparison schools in the first three years of Edison management, whereas by years four and five, conversion schools that remain under Edison's management appear to catch up to comparison schools in reading, and possibly exceed the gains of comparison schools in math. As with the Y1 baseline analysis, the results for the later years might be affected by differences in the schools included in the estimates for the later operation years, and in particular by the loss of lower-performing Edison schools from the estimates. The policy impact analysis suggests improvement over time in the relative gains of conversion schools ever managed by Edison, but differences in both reading and mathematics for these schools do not significantly exceed zero in years four and five.

Although these results are not always consistent, they provide considerable guidance about the range of possible effects. In absolute terms, Edison schools are improving their proficiency rates over time. In their first three years of Edison management, the gains of Edison schools do not exceed those of comparison schools on average. In years four and five, Edison schools show better results relative to comparison schools than in earlier years of operation.

The key question is whether the relative gains shown by Edison schools produce a net positive average effect over the long term. Both the Y1 and Y0 analyses attempt to address this question, but both are incomplete: The Y1 analysis is nearly comprehensive in its coverage of Edison schools, but it omits the first year of Edison management of each school, while the Y0 analysis is comprehensive in including the full period of Edison management, but includes only Edison conversion schools. The results from a Y1 baseline suggest that the long-term effects of Edison management are positive in math and perhaps in reading. The results for Edison conversion schools from Y0 suggest that the improving trends may be only enough to compensate for first-year declines, leaving the Edison conversion schools approximately on par with comparison schools after four or five years. We are left with some uncertainty about whether gains of Edison schools after four or five years are comparable to or superior to those of matched comparison schools.

What Factors Explain Differences in Achievement Trends Among Edison Schools?

Estimates of average performance across all Edison schools mask substantial variation in the achievement trajectories of individual Edison schools. We examined several factors that might be related to the variation in performance among Edison schools. First, to assess whether Edison's effects are different for newer schools than for older ones, we compared test-score changes between Edison schools and comparison schools from the first year of Edison operation through the fourth year of operation for schools that opened before 2000 and those that opened in 2000 or later. Schools that opened in 2000 or later showed slightly larger relative gains in mathematics than those that opened earlier, but no difference in relative gains between newer and older Edison schools was observed for reading. Thus, there is some weak evidence that Edison's effectiveness as an organization might have improved over time.

We also compared achievement results for Edison's charter schools versus district schools, and elementary versus secondary schools. We observed some small differences in a few cases, but trends were generally consistent across these categories of Edison schools.

Finally, we used findings from the case study schools to shed light on differences in achievement trajectories among Edison schools. Case study findings are not definitive, because the sample is small and relationships can be measured only in simple, correlational terms, but they are nevertheless suggestive. Among Edison case study schools, several features of program implementation predicted achievement in both subjects. These features included strong curriculum implementation, good principal instructional leadership, and the implementation of the Edison professional environment. These analyses indicate the importance of local context and Edison design implementation in trying to understand achievement trends in Edison schools.

Recommendations

This monograph aims not only to describe Edison's historical record in managing schools, but also to provide guidance to policymakers, clients, prospective clients, parents, and Edison staff about what to expect in the future and how to promote favorable outcomes in the future. The historical record provides considerable evidence that Edison's existing schools, on average, are likely to continue to improve, both in absolute terms (as measured by proficiency levels on state high-stakes tests) and relative to matched comparison schools. Most Edison schools have raised their students' achievement results as they have gained experience with Edison, and there is evidence that Edison's systemwide achievement trends have also improved in recent years.

Unfortunately, the data limitations described above render the historical evidence on Edison's net long-term effects equivocal. Predicting future long-term effects for new or prospective Edison schools is therefore doubly challenging, subject not only to the inherent uncertainty of anticipating Edison's systemic performance over the next four to five years, but also to the ambiguity in Edison's historical long-term effects. In consequence, we cannot make strong predictions for prospective clients about whether they will achieve better long-term results with Edison or with an alternate approach. Nevertheless, Edison's improving trends are encouraging.

Moreover, some schools have clearly done well under Edison management, making it clear that Edison is capable of producing favorable results, with satisfied teachers, well-organized schools, and large achievement gains relative to comparison schools. Implementation challenges, weak achievement trends, or both, however, have characterized other schools' experiences. Although our analyses do not permit us to make strong claims about the effectiveness of a particular approach to implementing Edison's design, we are able to draw some conclusions about factors that are likely to promote successful implementation. We present two sets of recommendations: one for Edison, and another for Edison's current and prospective clients.

Recommendations for Edison

Provide improved support and oversight during the first year. In Edison conversion schools with available data, achievement analyses that examined performance between a pre-Edison baseline and schools' initial year of Edison management suggested that achievement often falls behind relative to comparison schools. At the same time, a substantial minority of schools showed positive trends during this period. Although we cannot conclusively determine what factors accounted for these differences in trends, it is clear from our discussions with teachers and principals that Edison educators need a great deal of support during the initial year. Edison does in fact provide extensive professional development, but our interview participants told us they would benefit from additional, ongoing support throughout the year. The challenges of the first year were apparent in start-up schools (typically charter schools) and conversion schools (typically district contract schools) alike. One promising approach might be to build and strengthen interactions between staff at new schools and staff at existing, successful schools by facilitating mentoring relationships, arranging for instructional leaders in new schools to spend time in existing schools prior to the first year, and encouraging a small, select group of educators from existing schools to transfer to new schools. All of these efforts should be monitored so that any problems that arise are quickly addressed.

Apply value-added assessment methods to benchmark data. One of the strengths of Edison's design, according to our interview participants, is its high-quality assessment system for helping principals and teachers track student progress. The benchmark assessments are used not only as a tool to help school staff improve their instruction, but as a monitoring device to help Edison improve its oversight of and services to schools. To improve the utility of the benchmarks for this latter purpose, Edison should consider applying value-added assessment (VAA) methods to identify which schools and teachers have been most successful at improving the performance of individual students, and which appear to need more assistance in this regard. VAA involves using longitudinally linked student-level data to estimate the effects of teachers and schools (Sanders and Horn, 1998).

Although there are unresolved statistical and measurement issues with respect to VAA, and the application of this approach to the benchmark data presents some unique challenges, it has the potential to be a useful diagnostic tool (see McCaffrey et al., 2004, for a review of the strengths and limitations of VAA) and can provide estimates that are less error-prone than the more commonly used school-level averages. It is critical, however, that the results not carry consequences for individual teachers or principals because such consequences would undoubtedly lead to some corruption of scores and a reduction in the utility of the benchmarks for both instructional guidance and monitoring purposes.

Continue to promote a comprehensive vision of the curriculum. Although the achievement measures that are typically used to evaluate public schools focus heavily on mathematics and reading, our case study visits provide evidence that schools need not neglect other subjects in order to improve achievement in math and reading. The schools that had the best achievement results typically had strong implementation of the full range of Edison's broad curriculum.

Take further steps to ensure the development of principals' instructional leadership skills. We have good evidence in our Edison case study schools that principals' instructional leadership is directly related not only to effective implementation of Edison curricula but also to student achievement. Edison's efforts to identify, recruit, and train effective instructional leaders in the principalship are well founded—but these efforts have not yet led to uniformly high levels of instructional leadership and student achievement throughout the Edison system. Edison should also carefully consider whether to accept contracts from clients that do not allow Edison to choose its own principals.

Avoid compromises to the design that may undermine the professional environment in the schools. The relationship between professional environment and achievement outcomes that we found in the case study schools is a tentative one, but it is consistent with emerging views of the importance of "professional learning communities" (e.g., Coburn, 2001; McLaughlin and Mitra, 2001). The professional environment appears to be an important component of Edison's school design.

Recommendations for Clients and Prospective Clients

Manage the transition with care. The first year often presents challenges that hinder effective implementation of Edison's design, in conversion schools and start-up schools alike, and Edison's achievement trajectories from pre-Edison baselines suggest that these challenges reduce early levels of student achievement (although the results from Y0 are subject to other possible interpretations as well). In some conversion schools, the first-year challenges appear to be at least partly attributable to local opposition. District staff (or chartering authority staff, in the cases where Edison schools are chartered by organizations other than the local district) should work closely with Edison before and during the first year of Edison operation to reduce problems associated with the transition (or start-up), and should seek opportunities to facilitate interactions between their staff and staff at Edison schools that have demonstrated success. A successful first year may increase the buy-in of school staff and lead to more successful implementation in future years.

Give Edison full authority to implement its design. The quality of implementation varies across Edison schools. This variation results from several factors, including differences in the extent to which districts permit Edison to implement all of the components of its design. Moreover, Edison schools operating under more local constraints appear to have lower achievement gains. Edison's comprehensive approach to school management is designed on the assumption that all aspects of schooling need to be addressed to promote real reform. The decision to hire Edison to manage a school should reflect the belief that this comprehensive approach is needed. Those responsible for hiring Edison should work to ensure that the design can be implemented as intended, and that Edison's management does not merely create an additional accountability system that that competes with existing state or district accountability requirements.

Ensure that teachers and principals support the model. Committed principals and teachers are critical for the effective implementation of the Edison design, and Edison schools should be staffed only with those educators who believe in the approach and want to work toward the goal of fully implementing the model. Educators who do not support Edison's approach or who do not want to work in an Edison school for some other reason (e.g., because of the longer hours) should be given options to transfer to other schools. In the case of conversion schools, existing school staff should be involved in the decision to transfer management to Edison, and any concerns they express should be given serious consideration as the decision is made. Attaining educator support is likely to require providing extensive education and training on the design and its benefits to overcome pre-existing concerns and stereotypes that many teachers hold. District and chartering authority staff need to work to build support whenever they can, and to provide alternatives for school staff who are unwilling to support the model.

Do not expect instant improvement. In today's high-stakes accountability environment, district and school staff typically face pressure to demonstrate immediate gains in student achievement. This pressure is likely to be especially intense for schools that have failed to demonstrate adequate achievement gains in the past, and these are often the schools that are turned over to an outside management company such as Edison. This need for quick fixes conflicts with the well-known finding that reforming schools takes time. Although local educators and administrators have limited authority to challenge state and federal accountability policies, it is important that everyone involved in the decision to bring in a school management company understand that the desired results might not materialize for a few years.

Develop data systems that facilitate following individual students. The most significant limitation of our study is our inability to follow individual students over time. The questions that remain regarding the source of the differences between our results using the Y0 and Y1 baselines, for example, could have been resolved if we had been able to examine the achievement trajectories of individual students as they enter and exit Edison schools. Our limited set of student-level analyses demonstrated the advantages of being able to follow students over time, whether or not they remain in the same school. Such data are not only useful for evaluations of large-scale programs like Edison, but would also be invaluable for districts that want to evaluate their own local initiatives. In addition to promoting better research and evaluation, this type of data system could be used as a resource for teachers and principals who want to use data to inform decisions about curriculum and instruction.

Carefully consider the incentives created by state and local accountability systems. All public schools are currently facing pressure under NCLB to increase proficiency levels on state achievement tests, and districts often impose their own accountability systems to supplement the state rules. Edison's accountability system creates additional incentives to raise test scores, but includes other elements of accountability as well. District staff need to understand the pressures facing schools and the extent to which the goals imposed on schools by the state, the district, and Edison are compatible with one another. For example, we heard from some Edison staff that the professional development workshops the district required them to attend often emphasized topics and goals that conflicted with what Edison expected them to do. Even when it comes to achievement goals, the district's expectations can deviate from Edison's, particularly with respect to the relative emphasis placed on status versus growth measures. Districts need to examine whether undesirable incentives are created by these multiple accountability systems and whether these incentives work to undermine the implementation of Edison's design. If undesirable incentives are identified, districts can work to address them through training or through modification of their own approaches for motivating and rewarding school staff.

Conclusion

Edison is the largest private manager of public schools, and its experiences provide a model to help policymakers and the public understand the benefits and limitations of nontraditional forms of school management. Interest in alternative management is likely to increase under No Child Left Behind as schools and districts that fail to meet their annual targets face some of the more severe sanctions of the law.

The results provided by this study should serve as a catalyst for additional research on Edison and other approaches to school reform. In particular, it is important to understand Edison's test-score trajectories in the context of other efforts to fix schools facing long-term problems. These include comprehensive school reform models, other education management organizations, and district and state reconstitution policies. Our analysis examined a set of matched comparison schools, but we lack information on what kinds of reform efforts were being undertaken in those schools. There is little information yet available on whether any of these alternate approaches leads to short-term or long-term gains, or how the time period required for Edison to surpass other schools' performance compares with the time trajectories of other approaches.

Our analyses provide evidence regarding what can be expected when schools are turned over to Edison management, both in terms of how the program is implemented in schools and what happens to student achievement over time. Edison has a comprehensive and ambitious set of strategies for school improvement, encompassing both resources and accountability systems. Successful implementation of the Edison model requires a sustained commitment from clients and hard work from Edison's school staff, but there is evidence of an eventual benefit: Given sufficient time, achievement trends in Edison schools generally move upward, particularly when the model is faithfully implemented. Whether Edison's average achievement effects ultimately exceed those of comparison schools is not certain, but the Edison model is capable of producing positive effects: Our case study sample suggests that schools that effectively implement the wide-ranging Edison curriculum, that establish Edison's professional environment, and that operate with strong instructional leaders under limited constraints have positive achievement results. Given that Edison's results have not been uniformly positive, the findings of this monograph suggest some actions that Edison and its current and future clients can take to promote greater consistency of results, in terms of both implementation and student achievement.

APPENDIX A

Causal Inference in the Analysis of Academic Achievement in Edison Schools

J. R. Lockwood

The goal of our first achievement-related research question is to estimate the causal effect of Edison management on individual student achievement. Making causal inference with observational data is a perennial challenge in social science research. We make use the of the Rubin (1974) potential outcomes framework to motivate our approach. In this appendix, we describe our application of this framework to the analysis of achievement in Edison schools.

It is important to emphasize at the outset that we cannot directly estimate a causal effect of Edison management on individual student achievement using the school-level aggregate data from successive cohorts at our disposal. School-level aggregate data do not provide information about individual students, and the estimands and estimators that we derive from these data are at best an imperfect structure by which to address the causal question of interest. Some headway can be made by switching the relevant unit of analysis to the school rather than the student. That is, rather than contemplating how individual students would have performed with and without Edison education, we contemplate how schools would have performed, in the aggregate, with and without Edison management.

The potential outcomes framework assumes that for every school n in the universe of schools under consideration, in each year t, that school has two potential outcomes: $Y_{n,t}(1)$, the score that would be obtained for that school and year under Edison management, and $Y_{n,t}(0)$, the score that would be obtained for that school and year without Edison management. The fundamental problem of causal inference is that for each school, Edison and non-Edison, we observe a noisy estimate of one of these two potential outcomes, but not both. We assume without loss of generality that the noise is mean zero and refer only to the measured achievement, rather than true achievement, henceforth. The achievement measure typically is the percentage of students in the school achieving proficiency on whatever is the state accountability test, but could also refer to other metrics such as normal curve equivalent (NCE) or percentile rank of mean NCE. In addition, for many of the analyses that we present, we standardize the scores to facilitate combining the results across states with different tests and performing longitudinal analyses in the face of changing tests over time. The fact that our standardizations depend on observed outcomes for all of the non-Edison schools makes the discussion approximate rather than exact, but for clarity we do not address this issue in the notation.

Acting as if the school, rather than the student, is the relevant unit of treatment mitigates but does not entirely eliminate challenging conceptual questions. First, we assume that $Y_{n,t}(0)$ is the score that would be obtained in a given year had the school never been managed by Edison, rather than simply not managed by Edison this year but possibly managed by Edison in other years.

Second, there are two broad classes of Edison schools: conversions and new start-ups. For conversions, $Y_{n,t}(0)$ is well defined because the school existed prior to Edison takeover, and thus it is reasonable to contemplate how the school would have performed had Edison not taken over. The situation with new start-ups is conceptually more difficult, because it is not clear what should constitute $Y_{n,t}(0)$. In principle, it should be the aggregate outcome that would have been realized with the set of students in the Edison school, had Edison not opened the school. However, these students would likely not have been grouped together had Edison not opened the school. Because we lack student-level data in most places, we have no information about the students who ended up attending the new Edison school; in particular, we have no information about how these students were performing prior to attending the new Edison school. This makes our inferences about new start-up schools extremely sensitive to the assumptions we make about the compositions of these schools and their potential outcomes under non-Edison management.

There is a similar situation with conversion schools for which we have no pre-Edison performance data. We know that serious selection bias exists for conversion schools in that Edison generally takes over singularly challenged schools. Thus we have reason to believe that Edison schools were, and may still be, facing a more challenging student and institutional situation than other schools that might otherwise be used to estimate a non-Edison potential outcome. But we cannot estimate to what extent this is true without pre-Edison data. As shown below, it would be inappropriate to compare such schools cross-sectionally to other schools that appear similar based on the coarse school-level demographic measures at our disposal. Thus, like new start-up schools, inferences about conversion schools that lack pre-Edison data will be entirely reliant on our assumptions.

To summarize, we can classify the Edison schools into three broad categories: conversion schools where pre-Edison data are available, conversion schools where pre-Edison data are not available, and new start-up schools. The first of these three provide the strongest evidence, given the available data, for estimating a causal effect on school outcomes of Edison management. Causal inferences from the schools in the other two categories are necessarily more tenuous.

We define the estimands of interest, using the school as the unit of analysis, as

$$B(t) = E[Y_{e,t}(1) - Y_{e,t}(0) \mid T = 1]$$

where T is an indicator of Edison treatment, taking the value $T = 1$ for schools that Edison manages. That is, for each year t (which for different analyses will be variously contemplated as an operation year or a calendar year), we would like to estimate the average causal effect of Edison management for the schools managed by Edison. The quantity is commonly called the population average treatment effect for the treated (Imbens, 2003; Rubin, 1977). If we observed $Y_{e,t}(0)$ for every Edison school under consideration, $B(t)$ would be straightforwardly estimated by the simple sample average of $Y_{e,t}(1)-Y_{e,t}(0)$ across $e=1,\ldots,N$ Edison schools.

Of course, the challenge of the analysis is that we do not observe $Y_{e,t}(0)$ for any Edison school. As such, through the discussion, we occasionally refer to $Y_{e,t}(0)$ as a counterfactual outcome. Most of the details of our analysis focuses on how to estimate $Y_{e,t}(0)$ using outcomes from non-Edison schools, and the sensitivity of the findings to different assumptions about how to obtain the counterfactuals. In the remainder of this appendix, we discuss various estimation strategies, and how these strategies help to deal with potential biases.

Potential Methods for Counterfactual Estimation

Let x refer to school-level covariates; in practice as described later we use the school-level demographic variables of percentage minority students and percentage of students receiving free or reduced-price lunch (FRL), but for this discussion x could be more general. Under the assumptions of unconfoundedness (the Edison and non-Edison outcomes are conditionally independent of assignment to Edison treatment given x) and overlap (every school, regardless of its x, has some probability strictly between zero and one of having become an Edison school) (Imbens, 2003), the average treatment effect of interest is identifiable. We could estimate it by taking, for each Edison school, a set of non-Edison comparison schools whose x values are sufficiently similar to the Edison school x value. We would then estimate $Y_{e,t}(0)$ by the average of $Y_{c,t}(0)$ over a set M_e of comparison schools for Edison school e. Under the assumption that this average is unbiased for $Y_{e,t}(0)$ given x, we could produce an unbiased estimate of $B(t)$.

However, this approach is largely threatened by pretreatment selection bias of both schools and students. For start-up schools, where an unknown degree and direction of student self-selection occurs, the unbiasedness assumption is tenuous and untestable. For conversion schools, we have evidence that the unbiasedness assumption is violated because Edison takes over schools whose scores tend to be lower than non-Edison schools that share the same x. Thus, purely cross-sectional approaches to estimating the counterfactual are not likely to provide a credible method for estimating the effects of interest.

A potential solution is to use longitudinal information to derive a better counterfactual estimator, as we discuss in Chapter Five. It is important to note that while the estimators that we discuss use gain scores, gain scores are not necessary to defining the causal effect of interest. However, they may be incidentally useful to estimate these causal effects because they protect against time-invariant effects of selection bias. To present the assumptions underlying our use of longitudinal information to estimate the causal effects of interest, we make use of the following alternative expression for $B(t)$, for any year b such that $b < t$:

$$\begin{aligned} B(t) &= E[Y_{e,t}(1) - Y_{e,t}(0) \mid T = 1] \\ &= E[(Y_{e,t}(1) - Y_{e,b}(1)) - (Y_{e,t}(0) - Y_{e,b}(0)) + (Y_{e,b}(1) - Y_{e,b}(0)) \mid T = 1] \\ &= E[(Y_{e,t}(1) - Y_{e,b}(1)) - (Y_{e,t}(0) - Y_{e,b}(0)) \mid T = 1] + B(b) \end{aligned}$$

That is, $B(t)$ can be expressed as the expected value, given $T = 1$, of the observed Edison gain from b to t minus the counterfactual Edison gain from b to t, plus the causal effect at year b. Expressing $B(t)$ in this manner makes clear the different assumptions underlying the various analysis that we perform using gain scores from different baselines.

Assumptions of Y0 Analysis

For conversion schools for which we have observed pre-Edison scores, we can use $b = 0$ (in terms of operation years) as a baseline. We compare the observed Edison gain to the average gain over the same time span as a set of comparison schools. The latter is intended to provide an unbiased estimate of the counterfactual gain. If we condition only on *x*, there is some concern that because Edison schools tend to have lower pre-Edison scores, this estimator will be negatively biased (that is, the comparison schools will tend to show smaller gains). This could be due to both mean reversion bias and the possibility that schools are more likely to make larger true gains when starting from lower true scores. Forcing schools to have $Y_{c,0}(0)$ near $Y_{e,0}(1)$, in addition to similar *x*, to be eligible as a comparison school is likely to mitigate much of this anticipated bias. A complementary concern is that $(Y_{e,t}(1) - Y_{e,0}(1))$, while it is the observed Edison gain score, might be of suspect validity because of particular changes in the student population that occur from $b = 0$ to $b = 1$ for the Edison school. We present evidence examining the legitimacy of this concern elsewhere in the monograph.

The primary advantage of taking $b = 0$ is that, notwithstanding the concerns in the previous paragraph and other potential biases such as student selection to be discussed elsewhere, producing an unbiased estimate of $B(t)$ requires only the assumption that $B(0) = 0$. That is, that the score in the school immediately preceding Edison conversion is unaffected by the fact that Edison will take over the next year. While there is some concern that this assumption might be violated, as we discuss in Chapter Five, it is probably the most reasonable assumption among the class of similar assumptions that have to be made in order to interpret the results from other baselines as estimates of the causal effect of interest.

Assumptions of Y1 Analysis

Taking $b = 1$ (in terms of operation years) as a baseline eliminates the concern of a population change in the Edison school specific to the first year, allowing $(Y_{e,t}(1) - Y_{e,1}(1))$ to be a reasonable quantity to consider. Provided that we also match on baseline scores as discussed above, the average of the 1 to t gains of the comparison schools can plausibly be assumed to provide an unbiased estimate of the counterfactual gain. The primary conceptual difficulty of taking $b = 1$ as a baseline is that it requires the assumption that $B(1) = 0$ to produce an unbiased estimate of $B(t)$. This assumption may or may not be met; we argue in a later section that all of our supporting evidence suggests that $B(1)$ is not likely to be positive, implying that our estimates from this analysis provide an upper-bound estimate for $B(t)$.

Assumptions of Recent Score Change Analyses

These analyses take b to be a calendar year of 2002 or 2003, which correspond to different operation years for different Edison schools. In order to provide an unbiased estimate of $B(t)$ for $t = 2004$, it is necessary to assume that $B(b) = 0$. This assumption is unreasonable because for many of the Edison schools, $b = 2002$ or 2003 corresponds to operation years far beyond Y0 or Y1. At best we can assume that the recent gains analyses provide unbiased estimates of $B(2004) - B(2003)$ and $B(2004) - B(2002)$, the difference in the average causal effect across Edison schools in calendar year 2004 and the average causal effect in a prior calendar year. Thus, these analyses are not useful for addressing the questions regarding Edison's total causal effect.

An Alternative Method for Counterfactual Estimation

All longitudinal methods for estimating $B(t)$ thus far discussed used gain scores. These analyses rely on untestable assumptions about average observed gain scores providing unbiased estimates of counterfactual gain scores. An alternative longitudinal approach making different assumptions is the following. For all demographically similar comparison schools to each Edison school, we estimate a flexible nonparametric nonlinear regression of $Y_{c,t}(0)$ on $Y_{c,b}(0)$, for $b = 0$ or 1. That is, we estimate a function that provides a prediction of the year *t* performance as a function of the year *b* performance for schools with similar *x* to the Edison school. Evaluating the estimated function at the observed Edison value of $Y_{e,b}(0)$ provides an estimate of $Y_{e,t}(0)$. Subtracting this value from $Y_{e,t}(1)$ provides an estimator of the desired counterfactual. The primary advantage of this method relative to the gain score method is that by fitting a regression function, it automatically corrects for mean reversion bias. Matching on baseline scores in the gain score method also corrects for mean reversion bias, but does not do so perfectly because the practicality of finding comparison schools necessitates using a score window for matching rather than exact score matching. Fortunately, the two approaches produced results that were not materially different; Appendix E reports results.

Finally, it is important to note that the all of the aforementioned methods are susceptible to other potential biases in addition to those discussed above. These include, for example, sorting of students into Edison schools in later operation years and potential competitive effects that Edison might have on local comparison schools. These issues are addressed elsewhere in the monograph.

APPENDIX B

Analyses in Which Each Edison School Was Included

Table B.1 summarizes the inclusion status of each Edison school for each of the primary analyses (Y1 baseline, Y0 baseline, 2003–2004 recent gains, and 2002–2004 recent gains). Some schools were ineligible for certain analyses (e.g., schools with no pre-Edison score could not be included in the Y0 analysis). Other schools were eligible but were not included in certain analyses for various reasons, including lack of comparable schools or large enrollment changes.

There are some specific issues with regard to eligibility for individual schools that should be mentioned. The Learn Now schools of Community Academy in the District of Columbia, Hope Community Charter and the William E. McGee Institute of Technology (MIT) in Minnesota, Smedley Middle School, Stetser Elementary School, and Chester High School in Pennsylvania were not included in any analysis. However, three Learn Now schools (Southeast in the District of Columbia, Marianna Bracetti Academy in Pennsylvania, and Harriet Tubman School in New York) were included in some analyses, using where possible spring 2001 as a Y0 baseline and spring 2002 as a Y1 baseline, because these schools had come completely under Edison management by that time. Schools in the District of Columbia do not contribute to the recent gains results that use percent-proficient outcomes, because our available data did not include this metric. However, they do contribute to the z-score results for the recent gains analyses. Jefferson Edison Elementary School in Davenport, Iowa, was not included in any analysis because of lack of available data. None of the Wichita schools were included in any analysis because the available historical data is from Kansas state assessment, while Edison was contractually accountable for a different test for which we did not have data. Michigan high schools were not included in any analysis because the school-level data are based on aggregate results of juniors and seniors across two years; thus, we could not tie these school-level results to school performance in a single year. Meek-Milton Primary Academy in Michigan, Wetherill School and William Penn Elementary in Pennsylvania, and Charles West Middle School in Nevada are not included in any analysis because they serve no tested grades on the state accountability test. Granville junior and senior academies in New Jersey were not included in any analysis because of lack of reliable data. Renaissance Academy of Pittsburgh Alternative of Hope (RAPAH) in Pennsylvania and Confluence Academy in Missouri were not included in any analysis because they opened too recently (they have only baseline 2003–2004 data). Recent gains analyses apply only to schools whose Y1 was spring 2002 or later, and whose contracts were not terminated prior to spring 2004. Five of the six elementary schools in Nevada were not included in the recent gains analysis because they followed year-round schedules. The testing schedule changed in 2003–2004, and for these year-round schools, the test administered in spring 2004 failed to capture a year's worth of growth.

Table B.1
Schools Included in Each Analysis

			Status in Analysis			
School Name	**District Name**	**State**	**2-Yr Gain**	**1-Yr Gain**	**Y0**	**Y1**
Edison Brentwood Acad.	Ravenswood City Elem.	Calif.	I	I	I	I
Edison Charter Acad.	San Francisco Unified	Calif.	I	I	I	I
Edison McNair Acad. (grades 4–5)	Ravenswood City Elem.	Calif.	I	I	I	I

Table B.1—continued

			Status in Analysis			
School Name	District Name	State	2-Yr Gain	1-Yr Gain	Y0	Y1
Edison McNair Acad. (grades 6–8)	Ravenswood City Elem.	Calif.	I	I	I	I
Edison-Bethune Charter Acad.	Fresno Co. Unified	Calif.	I	I	I	I
Feaster-Edison Charter Sch.	Chula Vista Elem.	Calif.	I	I	NB	I
Phillips-Edison Partnership Sch.	Napa Valley	Calif.	I	I	I	I
San Jose-Edison Acad. (grades 2–6)	West Covina Unified	Calif.	I	I	U	I
San Jose-Edison Acad. (grades 7–8)	West Covina Unified	Calif.	I	I	NB	NB
Starr King-Edison Acad.	Long Beach Unified	Calif.	I	I	I	I
Academy-Edison Elem. Sch.	Academy 20	Colo.	I	I	U	I**
Emerson-Edison Partnership Sch.	Colorado Springs 11	Colo.	I	I	NB	NB
Roosevelt-Edison Charter Sch.	Colorado Springs 11	Colo.	I	I	NB	I**
Timberview-Edison Jr. Acad.	Academy 20	Colo.	E	E	NB	NB
Wyatt-Edison Charter Sch. (grades 3–5)	Denver Co. 1	Colo.	I	I	NB	I**
Wyatt-Edison Charter Sch. (grades 6–8)	Denver Co. 1	Colo.	I	I***	U	NB
Wintergreen Interdistrict Magnet Sch. (grade 4)	Hamden Public	Conn.	E	E	U	I
Wintergreen Interdistrict Magnet Sch. (grades 6–8)	Hamden Public	Conn.	E	E	U	NB
Community Academy Public Charter Sch.—Learn Now	D.C. Public	D.C.	E	E	E	E
Friendship Edison—Blow Pierce Campus	D.C. Public	D.C.	I	I	U	I
Friendship Edison—Carter G. Woodson Campus	D.C. Public	D.C.	I***	I	U	I*
Friendship Edison—Chamberlain Campus	D.C. Public	D.C.	I	I	U	I
Friendship Edison —Woodridge Campus	D.C. Public	D.C.	I	I	U	I

Table B.1—continued

			Status in Analysis			
School Name	District Name	State	2-Yr Gain	1-Yr Gain	Y0	Y1
Southeast Acad. of Scholastic Excellence—Learn Now (grades 1–5)	D.C. Public	D.C.	I	I	NB	I
Southeast Acad. of Scholastic Excellence—Learn Now (grades 6–8)	D.C. Public	D.C.	I***	I*	NB	I***
Thomas A. Edison Charter Sch. (grades 3–5)	Colonial Sch. District	Del.	I	I***	U	I
Thomas A. Edison Charter Sch. (grade 8)	Colonial Sch. District	Del.	NC	NC	U	NB
Henry S. Reeves Elem. Sch.	Miami-Dade	Fla.	I	I	U	NB
Charles R. Drew Charter Sch. (grades 3–5)	Atlanta Public	Ga.	I	I	U	I
Charles R. Drew Charter Sch. (grade 6)	Atlanta Public	Ga.	I	I	U	NB
Martin Luther King, Jr.-Edison Elem.	Bibb Co.	Ga.	E	E	O Y0	I
Riley-Edison Elem.	Bibb Co.	Ga.	E	E	I	I
Jefferson-Edison Elem. Sch.	Davenport Community SD	Ia.	E	E	E	E
Chicago Int'l Charter—Longwood campus (grades 3–5)	Chicago Public	Ill.	I	I	NB	I
Chicago Int'l Charter—Longwood Campus (grade 5)	Chicago Public	Ill.	I	I	NB	I
Feitshans-Edison Sch.	Springfield SD 186	Ill.	I	I	LDC	I
Franklin-Edison Sch.	Peoria SD 150	Ill.	I	I	I	I
Loucks Edison Jr. Acad. (grade 5)	Peoria SD 150	Ill.	I	I	LEC	I
Loucks Edison Jr. Acad. (grade 8)	Peoria SD 150	Ill.	I	I	LEC	I
Northmoor-Edison Sch.	Peoria SD 150	Ill.	I	I	I	I
Rolling Acres Edison (grade 5)	Peoria SD 150	Ill.	I	I	LEC	I
Rolling Acres Edison (grade 8)	Peoria SD 150	Ill.	I	I	LEC	I
Jeremiah Gray-Edison Elem. Sch.	Perry Township	Ind.	I	I	E	I

Table B.1—continued

			Status in Analysis			
School Name	District Name	State	2-Yr Gain	1-Yr Gain	Y0	Y1
Rosa Parks-Edison	Perry Township	Ind.	E	I	E	I
Dodge-Edison Elem. Sch.	Wichita	Kan.	E	E	E	E
Edison-Ingalls Elem.	Wichita	Kan.	E	E	E	E
Edison-Isley Elem.	Wichita	Kan.	E	E	E	E
Jardine-Edison Jr. Acad.	Wichita	Kan.	E	E	E	E
Boston Renaissance Charter Sch.	Boston Public	Mass.	E	E	U	NB
Seven Hills Charter Sch. (grades 3–4)	Worcester Public	Mass.	I	I	U	NB
Seven Hills Charter Sch. (grades 6–8)	Worcester Public	Mass.	I	I*	U	NB
Furman Templeton Elem.	Baltimore City	Md.	I	I	I	I
Gilmor-Edison Elem. Sch.	Baltimore City	Md.	I	I	I	I
Montebello-Edison Elem. Sch.	Baltimore City	Md.	I	I	I	I
Baylor Woodson Elem. Sch.	Inkster-Edison PS	Mich.	I	I	O Y0	I
Blanchette Middle Sch.	Inkster-Edison PS	Mich.	I	I	O Y0	I**
Detroit Academy of Arts and Sciences—Jefferson Campus	Detroit City	Mich.	E	E	U	I
Detroit Academy of Arts and Sciences—Medbury Campus	Detroit City	Mich.	E	E	U	I
Detroit-Edison Public Sch. Acad. (grade 4)	Detroit City	Mich.	E	E	U	I
Detroit-Edison Public Sch. Acad. (grade 7–8)	Detroit City	Mich.	E	E	U	I
Dr. Martin Luther King-Edison Elem.-Part 1	Mount Clemens	Mich.	E	E	NB	I
Edison-Oakland Public Sch. Acad. (grade 4)	Ferndale Public	Mich.	I	I	U	I
Edison-Oakland Public Sch. Acad. (grade 7)	Ferndale Public	Mich.	NC	NB	U	I****
Edison-Perdue Acad. (grade 4)	Pontiac City	Mich.	E	E	U	I
Edison-Perdue Acad. (grades 7–8)	Pontiac City	Mich.	E	E	U	NB
Flint Northwestern Community HS Edison Partnership	Flint City	Mich.	I	I	U	I

Table B.1—continued

			Status in Analysis			
School Name	District Name	State	2-Yr Gain	1-Yr Gain	Y0	Y1
Garfield-Edison Partnership Sch.	Flint City	Mich.	I	I	I	I
Inkster High Sch.	Inkster-Edison PS	Mich.	E	E	E	E
Meek-Milton Primary Acad.	Inkster-Edison PS	Mich.	E	E	E	E
Mid-Michigan Public Sch. Acad. (grade 4)	Lansing Public	Mich.	E	E	U	I
Mid-Michigan Public Sch. Acad. (grade 7)	Lansing Public	Mich.	E	E	U	NB
Mount Clemens Jr. Acad.	Mount Clemens	Mich.	E	E	NB	I
Mount Clemens Sr. Acad.	Mount Clemens	Mich.	E	E	E	E
Southwestern Edison Jr. Acad.	Battle Creek PS	Mich.	E	E	I	I
Washington-Edison Partnership Sch.	Battle Creek PS	Mich.	E	E	I	I
Williams-Edison Partnership Sch.	Flint City	Mich.	I	I	I	I
Wilson-Edison Partnership Sch.	Battle Creek PS	Mich.	E	E	O Y0	I
YMCA Service Learning Acad. (grade 4)	Detroit City	Mich.	I	I	U	I
YMCA Service Learning Acad. (grades 7–8)	Detroit City	Mich.	I	I	U	NB
Edison/PPL Charter Sch.	Minneapolis Public	Minn.	E	E	U	I
Hope Community Acad. Charter Sch.	St. Paul	Minn.	E	E	E	E
Kenwood-Edison Charter Sch.	Duluth Public	Minn.	I	I	U	I
MIT—Learn Now	St. Paul	Minn.	E	E	E	E
Raleigh-Edison Acad.	Duluth Public	Minn.	I	I*	U	NB
Washburn-Edison Jr. Acad.	Duluth Public	Minn.	I	I	U	I*
Allen-Edison Village Sch. (grades 3–4)	Kansas City 33	Mo.	I	NC	U	I
Allen-Edison Village Sch. (grades 7–8)	Kansas City 33	Mo.	I*	NC	U	I***

Table B.1—continued

			Status in Analysis			
School Name	District Name	State	2-Yr Gain	1-Yr Gain	Y0	Y1
Confluence Acad.	Kansas City 33	Mo.	E	E	E	E
Derrick Thomas Acad.	Kansas City 33	Mo.	E	I	E	I
Westport Edison Middle and Sr. Acad. (grades 7–8)	Kansas City 33	Mo.	E	E	NB	I
Westport Edison Middle and Sr. Acad (grades 10–11)	Kansas City 33	Mo.	E	E	NB	I
Woodland-Edison Classical Acad.	Kansas City 33	Mo.	E	E	I	I
Carver Heights-Edison Elem. Sch.	Wayne County PS	N.C.	E	E	I	I
Dillard Middle Sch.	Wayne County PS	N.C.	E	E	E	E
Swift Creek-Edison Elem.	Nash-Rocky Mount	N.C.	E	E	LEC	I
Granville Elem. Sch.	Trenton City	N.J.	E	E	U	I
Granville Jr. Acad.	Trenton City	N.J.	E	E	E	E
Granville Sr. Acad.	Trenton City	N.J.	E	E	E	E
Schomburg Charter Sch.	Jersey City	N.J.	E	E	U	I
Ann Lynch Elem.	Clark Co.	Nev.	E	E	NB	I
Cahlan Elem.	Clark Co.	Nev.	E	E	NB	I
Charles I. West Middle Sch.	Clark Co.	Nev.	E	E	E	E
Crestwood Elem. Sch.	Clark Co.	Nev.	E	E	NB	I
John S. Park Elem.	Clark Co.	Nev.	I	I	NB	I
Lincoln Elem.	Clark Co.	Nev.	E	E	NB	I
Ronnow Elem.	Clark Co.	Nev.	E	E	NB	I
Charter School for Applied Technologies	Buffalo City SD	N.Y.	I	I	U	I
Harriet Tubman Charter Sch.—Learn Now	New York City PS	N.Y.	NB	I	NB	NB
New Covenant Charter Sch. (grade 4)	Albany City Public	N.Y.	I	I	NB	I
New Covenant Charter Sch. (grade 8)	Albany City Public	N.Y.	NB	I***	NB	NB
Stepping Stone Acad. Charter Sch.	Buffalo City SD	N.Y.	I	I	U	I
The Charter Sch. of Science and Technology (grade 4)	Rochester City SD	N.Y.	I	I	U	I

Table B.1—continued

			Status in Analysis			
School Name	District Name	State	2-Yr Gain	1-Yr Gain	Y0	Y1
The Charter Sch. of Science and Technology (grade 8)	Rochester City SD	N.Y.	I	I	U	NB
The Riverhead Charter Sch.	Riverhead Central SD	N.Y.	I	I	U	I
Dayton View Acad. (grade 4)	Dayton City SD	Ohio	I	I	U	I
Dayton View Acad. (grade 6)	Dayton City SD	Ohio	I	I	U	NB
The Dayton Acad. (grade 4)	Dayton City SD	Ohio	I	I	U	I
The Dayton Acad. (grade 6)	Dayton City SD	Ohio	I	I	U	NB
Alcorn Elem. Sch.	Philadelphia City SD	Pa.	E	I***	I	I***
Anderson Elem. Sch.	Philadelphia City SD	Pa.	E	I	I	I
Barratt Middle Sch.	Philadelphia City SD	Pa.	E	I	I	I
Chester High Sch.	Chester-Upland	Pa.	E	E	E	E
Columbus Elem.	Chester-Upland	Pa.	I	I	I	I
Comegys Elem. Sch.	Philadelphia City SD	Pa.	E	I	I	I
Gillespie Middle Sch.	Philadelphia City SD	Pa.	E	I	I	I
Harrity Elem. Sch.	Philadelphia City SD	Pa.	E	I	I	I
Kelley Elem. Sch.	Philadelphia City SD	Pa.	E	I	I	I
Kenderton Elem. Sch.	Philadelphia City SD	Pa.	E	I	I	I
Lincoln-Edison Charter Sch.	York City SD	Pa.	I	I	I	I
Locke Elem. Sch.	Philadelphia City SD	Pa.	E	I	I	I
Ludlow Elem. Sch.	Philadelphia City SD	Pa.	E	I	I***	I
Main Street Elem./Middle (grade 5)	Chester-Upland	Pa.	I	I	I	I
Main Street Elem./Middle (grade 8)	Chester-Upland	Pa.	I	I	I	I
Mariana Bracetti Acad. Charter Sch.—Learn Now	Philadelphia City SD	Pa.	I	I	NB	I

Table B.1—continued

			Status in Analysis			
School Name	District Name	State	2-Yr Gain	1-Yr Gain	Y0	Y1
Morton-McMichael Elem. Sch.	Philadelphia City SD	Pa.	E	I	I	I
Munoz-Marin Elem. Sch.	Philadelphia City SD	Pa.	E	I	I	I
Penn Treaty Middle Sch.	Philadelphia City SD	Pa.	E	NC	NC	NC
Potter-Thomas Elem. Sch.	Philadelphia City SD	Pa.	E	I	I	I
Pulaski Middle (Parry Acad.)	Chester-Upland	Pa.	I	I	LDC	I
Renaissance Acad., Alternative of Hope	Pittsburgh	Pa.	E	E	E	E
Shaw Middle Sch.	Philadelphia City SD	Pa.	E	I	I	I
Showalter Middle	Chester-Upland	Pa.	I*	I***	O Y0	I*
Smedley Middle Sch.	Chester-Upland	Pa.	E	E	E	E
Stetser Elem. Sch.	Chester-Upland	Pa.	E	E	E	E
Stetson Middle Sch.	Philadelphia City SD	Pa.	E	I	I	I
Stoddart-Fleisher Middle Sch.	Philadelphia City SD	Pa.	E	I	I	I
Sulzberger Middle Sch.	Philadelphia City SD	Pa.	E	I	I	I
The Renaissance Academy-Edison Charter Sch. (grade 5)	Phoenixville Area SD	Pa.	I	I	U	I
The Renaissance Academy-Edison Charter Sch. (grade 8)	Phoenixville Area SD	Pa.	I	I	U	I*
Tilden Middle Sch.	Philadelphia City SD	Pa.	E	I	I	I
Waring Elem. Sch.	Philadelphia City SD	Pa.	E	I	I	I
Wetherill Elem.	Chester-Upland	Pa.	E	E	E	E
William Penn Elem.	Chester-Upland	Pa.	E	E	E	E
Dillingham Intermediate Sch.	Sherman Independent	Tex.	E	E	NB	NB
Edison-Blair Acad.	Dallas Independent	Tex.	E	E	I	I

Table B.1—continued

			Status in Analysis			
School Name	District Name	State	2-Yr Gain	1-Yr Gain	Y0	Y1
Edison-Henderson Acad.	Dallas Independent	Tex.	E	E	I	I
Edison-Hernandez Elem. Acad.	Dallas Independent	Tex.	E	E	I	I
Edison-Maple Lawn Acad.	Dallas Independent	Tex.	E	E	I	I
Edison-Medrano Acad.	Dallas Independent	Tex.	E	E	I	I
Edison-Runyon Acad.	Dallas Independent	Tex.	E	E	I	I
Edison-Titche Acad.	Dallas Independent	Tex.	E	E	I	I
Elm Creek-Edison Elem. Sch.	Southwest Independent	Tex.	E	E	U	I
Kriewald Road-Edison Elem. Sch.	Southwest Independent	Tex.	E	E	U	I
McNair-Edison Jr. Acad.	Southwest Independent	Tex.	E	E	I	I
Scobee-Edison Jr. Acad.	Southwest Independent	Tex.	E	E	NB	NB
Stewart-Edison Jr. Acad.	Tyler ISD	Tex.	E	E	I	I
Washington Elem. Sch.	Sherman Independent	Tex.	E	E	NB	NB
Milwaukee Acad. of Science (grade 4)	Milwaukee Public	Wisc.	I	I	U	I
Milwaukee Acad. of Science (grade 8)	Milwaukee Public	Wisc.	I	I	U	NB
Mul Acad. of Business and Economics	Milwaukee Public	Wisc.	I*	I*	U	I*

SOURCE: Edison Schools, Inc.

NOTES: I = school included in analysis for both subjects, except where noted. NB = no baseline; school excluded because baseline score was missing. U = undefined; school did not exist in Y0 (start-up school). NC = no comparisons; school excluded because comparison schools could not be identified. LDC = school excluded because of large demographic changes from Y0 to Y1. LEC = school excluded because of large enrollment changes from Y0 to Y1. O Y0 = outlier Y0; school excluded because of large Y0 score relative to other years. E = school excluded for other reasons (typically because it did not exist in years covered by analysis). * no comparisons in reading, so school included in math analysis only. ** no baseline for math, so school included in reading analysis only. *** no comparisons in math, so school included in reading analysis only. **** indicates no math scores available, so school included in reading analysis only.

APPENDIX C

Calculating Standard Errors for Estimated Effects

As discussed elsewhere (e.g., Appendix A), the estimators we use to compare Edison school outcomes to those from comparison schools share a common form. For a collection of N Edison schools (labeled $\mathcal{E}$) and for a particular point in time (as measured by either operation years or calendar years), we compare the gains of the Edison schools relative to some baseline to the analogous gains of comparison schools. Specifically, let $\mathcal{M}$ be the set of all comparison schools for the Edison schools in $\mathcal{E}$ obtained under a particular matching rule (matching variables, bandwidth choices, and location of matches). For $n \in \mathcal{E}$, let $\mathcal{M}_n$ be the subset of schools in $\mathcal{M}$ that serve as comparison schools to Edison school n. Let $|\mathcal{M}_n|$ be the number of comparison schools in $\mathcal{M}_n$. Note that $\cup_{n\in\mathcal{E}} \mathcal{M}_n = \mathcal{M}$, and the intersections of pairs of the $\mathcal{M}_n$ are not necessarily empty because a single school can serve as a comparison for more than one Edison school.

Define

$$U_n = (Y_n^{(edison)} - \frac{1}{|\mathcal{M}_n|} \sum_{m\in\mathcal{M}_n} Y_m^{(not)}) \qquad \text{(C.1)}$$

where $Y_n^{(edison)}$ is the relevant gain score for the Edison school as discussed above, and $Y_m^{(not)}$ are the analogous quantities for the comparison schools. We use the superscripts (*edison*) and (*not*) to make explicit the notion that in the potential outcomes framework, every school has two outcomes. For the Edison school n, we observe the Edison potential outcome, and for the comparison schools, we observe the non-Edison potential outcome. Letting $U^T = (U_1,...,U_N)$, our estimators are of the form $w^T U$. Moreover, because we wish to weight Edison schools equally, we take $w^T = (1/N,...,1/N)$ for all of our estimators.

Variance Calculation

To carry out tests of hypotheses, we need to estimate the variance of $w^T U$. If Σ is the $(N \times N)$ variance-covariance matrix of U, then from the standard formula of the variance of a linear combination of random variables,

$$V(w^T U) = w^T \Sigma w = \frac{1}{N^2}(1^T \Sigma 1).$$

The purpose of the remainder of this appendix is to describe how we derived an estimator $\widehat{\Sigma}$ for Σ.

Variances in the Rubin causal model framework are calculated with respect to the assignment mechanism, which is assumed to be probabilistic. That is not the situation for the data at hand, but we need to act as if it is to derive a meaningful variance estimator. We assume that for "cluster" n consisting of $|\mathcal{M}_n| + 1$ schools (the comparison schools plus Edison school n), one was randomly picked to be an Edison school, for which we observe the Edison outcome. For the remaining schools, we observe the non-Edison outcome. We assume that for each school in each cluster, $Y^{(edison)} = \beta + Y^{(not)}$, whether or not it is an actual Edison school. β can vary across clusters but must be constant within a cluster. Under this model, the within-cluster variance σ_n^2 of the Edison potential outcomes is the same as that of the non-Edison potential outcomes, and the sample variance of the observed non-Edison outcomes within the cluster is unbiased for σ_n^2. If each cluster contained a large number of comparison schools, we could reasonably estimate σ_n^2 for each cluster and do our analyses with these cluster-specific variances. However, most clusters are rather small, and some contain only a single comparison school. Thus, for the purposes of our standard error calculation, we assume $\sigma_n^2 \equiv \sigma^2$, which is estimated as a weighted average of the within-cluster sample variances of the comparison outcomes. In practice, this estimate of σ^2 differed negligibly from that obtained with a standard ordinary least squares (OLS) regression model with fixed effects for districts in which Edison operates.

From these considerations and Equation C.1,

$$VAR(U_n) = \sigma^2(1 + \frac{1}{|\mathcal{M}_n|}). \tag{C.2}$$

The covariance of any two U_n for different Edison schools is zero if the schools share no comparison schools, and more generally for Edison schools i and j

$$COV(U_i, U_j) = \frac{\sigma^2 |\mathcal{M}_i \cap \mathcal{M}_j|}{|\mathcal{M}_i||\mathcal{M}_j|} \tag{C.3}$$

where the numerator is the number of shared comparison schools. The covariance is always nonnegative, and is larger when there are more shared schools. The result is that we have parameterized the full covariance matrix Σ of $U = (U_1, \ldots, U_N)$ with a single unknown parameter σ^2, which is straightforwardly estimated from the data. The other parameters of the covariance structure—the numbers of comparison schools for each Edison school and the sizes of all of the pairwise intersections of the sets of comparison schools—are known.

Complications

The variance calculation above assumes that the only source of covariance between U_i and U_j from different clusters are shared comparison schools, and that such shared schools are perfectly correlated. This is not always the case, for several reasons. The first is that as noted elsewhere, single Edison schools are subject to a set of school-splitting rules that are designed to make it easier to find comparison schools. For example, a K–8 Edison school is treated as two schools—one K–5 and one 6–8, so that traditional elementary and middle schools can serve as comparisons for the two derived schools. The above variance calculation assumes that all Edison schools are distinct and uncorrelated. This assumption is questionable when the two schools are actually disjoint grade ranges of the same school.

Similar difficulties arise among the comparison schools. One is a direct result of splitting Edison schools. If a K–8 Edison school has been split, then any other K–8 school eligible for matching will be split as well and treated as two separate comparison schools for the two derived Edison schools. A similar but more challenging problem can arise if the same comparison school is a comparison for two different Edison schools, but provides different comparison outcomes resulting from the two Edison schools having different sets of tested grades. In addition, even if the two Edison schools have the same sets of tested grades, the same comparison schools can provide different outcomes if the two Edison schools opened in different years.

All of these difficulties share the property that a single entity with a single school label can contribute two or more distinct outcomes to the overall calculation. Acting as if all such quantities have zero covariance is likely to result in improper standard errors of the estimates. To deal with this problem, we take a bounding approach. We calculate two estimates of the covariance matrix Σ. The first, Σ_{lower}, assumes that split Edison schools are independent, and assumes that the covariance of any two comparison outcomes sharing a school label is zero unless those outcomes are identical. That is, Σ_{lower} results from the simplified assumptions of the previous section. We label this covariance matrix "lower" because it acts as if there is more independent information than is actually available, and thus is likely to result in standard errors that are too small. The other side of the bound is Σ_{upper}, which assumes that any two outcomes sharing a school label are perfectly correlated. Thus, the covariance of two outcomes U_i and U_j from the same split Edison school has a leading term of σ^2. We label this covariance matrix "upper" because it conservatively assumes that any quantities that might be positively correlated for the reasons stated earlier are perfectly positively correlated. This is likely to result in an upper bound for the standard error.[1]

Fortunately, the differences between two resulting standard errors are extremely small. By construction, the standard errors based on assuming that Σ_{upper} is the correct covariance matrix are always at least as large as those based on assuming Σ_{lower}. However, those based on Σ_{upper} are on average only about four percent larger, and are at most nine percent larger, across different comparisons using different baseline years, different operation years, different sets of calendar years, different subjects, and different sets of comparison schools. Thus, in keeping with standard practice that seeks to minimize type I error (erroneous rejection of the null hypothesis), all of our reported results use the conservative standard errors based on Σ_{upper}.

[1] The above bounding assumes that correlation between outcomes that share a school label are positive or zero. This is consistent with a model stating that there are school-level effects (deriving from either the school itself, the population of students, or some other factor shared by all students in the school) that affect all outcomes for the school in the same direction. A different model would assume negative correlation between outcomes that share a school label, perhaps due to competing resources where improvements in one set of grades might co-occur with declines in a different set of grades. We tested this model and it led to standard errors that were approximately 10 percent smaller than those obtained with Σ_{upper}.

APPENDIX D

Comparison of Traditional and Rank-Based Z-Scores

J. R. Lockwood

In addition to the traditional z-scores (z_{trad}) reported throughout the achievement analysis chapters, we explored the use of a rank-based z-score, which is calculated as follows: $z_{perc} = \Phi^{-1}(F(Y))$ where F is the empirical cumulative distribution function (CDF) of the scores in the state for all non-Edison schools with observed scores that year, and Φ^{-1} is the inverse standard normal CDF. That is, $F(Y)$ is the percentile ranging from 0 to 1 of Y in the distribution of scores, and Φ^{-1} maps that percentile to a standardized normal (z) score. This method is described in detail in Kirby et al. (2002). These rank-based z-scores are also known as "rankits."

If the underlying distribution of Y is normal or approximately so, then F is approximately a normal CDF and z_{trad} approximately equals z_{perc}. In general, z_{trad} and z_{perc} have a monotone increasing though not necessarily linear relationship; the deviation from linearity increases as the underlying distribution of Y deviates from normal.

We calculate the rank-based z-score primarily as a sensitivity test to determine whether violations of assumptions underlying the traditional z-score approach contributed to the results. In particular, when a test changes over time, the gains of the traditional z-scores can be distorted (i.e., show spurious gains depending on where the school is located in the distribution) unless the true scores on the new test are a linear transformation of the true scores on the old test. The rank-based z-score method is robust to all monotone increasing nonlinear relationships between the new test and the old test and thus requires fewer assumptions to obtain valid gain scores. Our sensitivity tests appear in Tables D.1 and D.2 and suggest that the results using both methods were similar in most cases. The rank-based z-scores tend to be somewhat more favorable to Edison during the early years in the Y1 analysis, but most of the differences are diminished or reverse direction by Y4. In the Y0 analysis, the direction of the differences varies, but most are quite small.

Table D.1
Comparison of Results Using Traditional and Rank-Based Z-Scores (Y1 Baseline, State Comparisons)

		Y2	Y3	Y4	Y5	Y6
Reading	Traditional	-0.03 (n=116)	-0.04 (n=88)	0.17* (n=58)	0.25* (n=35)	0.15 (n=16)
	Rank-based	0.05 (n=116)	0.06 (n=88)	0.18* (n=58)	0.25* (n=35)	0.22 (n=16)
Mathematics	Traditional	0.04 (n=112)	-0.04 (n=87)	0.32* (n=59)	0.53* (n=32)	0.45* (n=14)
	Rank-based	0.10 (n=112)	0.02 (n=87)	0.29* (n=59)	0.44* (n=32)	0.48* (n=14)

NOTE: * indicates statistical significance at $p < 0.05$.

Table D.2
Comparison of Results Using Traditional and Rank-Based Z-Scores (Y0 Baseline, State Comparisons)

		Y1	Y2	Y3	Y4	Y5
Reading	Traditional	-0.29* (n=51)	-0.18 (n=51)	-0.17 (n=32)	0.06 (n=19)	-0.01 (n=11)
	Rank-based	-0.35* (n=51)	-0.16 (n=51)	-0.12 (n=32)	0.06 (n=19)	-0.03 (n=11)
Mathematics	Traditional	-0.31* (n=50)	-0.15 (n=49)	-0.37* (n=32)	0.11 (n=19)	0.32 (n=11)
	Rank-based	-0.30* (n=50)	-0.08 (n=49)	-0.28* (n=32)	0.11 (n=19)	0.31 (n=11)

NOTE: * indicates statistical significance at $p < 0.05$.

APPENDIX E

Comparison of Gain Score Method to an Alternative Approach Using Predicted Level Scores

J. R. Lockwood

As discussed in Appendix A, in addition to considering various gain score methods for counterfactual estimation, we also considered an approach that used a direct estimate of the counterfactual level scores for Edison schools. The purpose of exploring this alternative method was to examine the robustness of our findings to different plausible assumptions about how to estimate the counterfactuals of interest. The method involved predicting a school's score in a given year based on a regression as a function of its baseline score. Both this approach and the gain score approach are intended to estimate the same causal effect. The prediction method produced results that were quite similar to those of the z-score gain method, as shown in Tables E.1 and E.2. Because the regression-based prediction method can be used only in cases with a substantial number of comparison schools, and therefore results in a loss of some Edison schools from the analysis, we rely on the gain score approach for presenting the results in the body of the monograph.

Table E.1
Comparison of Results Using Gain Scores and Regression Prediction (Y1 Baseline, State Comparisons)

		Y2	Y3	Y4	Y5
Reading	Gain scores	-0.14 (n=80)	-0.08 (n=67)	0.11 (n=45)	0.09 (n=25)
	Regression	-0.15 (n=80)	-0.12 (n=67)	0.14 (n=45)	0.14 (n=25)
Mathematics	Gain scores	-0.02 (n=74)	-0.14 (n=62)	0.28 (n=42)	0.44 (n=23)
	Regression	-0.02 (n=74)	-0.16 (n=62)	0.26 (n=42)	0.38 (n=23)

NOTE: We were unable to test the significance of the estimates derived through the regression approach because this would require the standard error of the predicted value, which does not follow easily from the estimation, and because it would require making some untestable assumptions.

Table E.2
Comparison of Results Using Gain Scores and Regression Prediction (Y0 Baseline, State Comparisons)

		Y1	Y2	Y3	Y4	Y5
Reading	Gain scores	-0.36 (n=36)	-0.20 (n=36)	-0.24 (n=28)	0.02 (n=18)	-0.01 (n=11)
	Regression	-0.36 (n=36)	-0.22 (n=36)	-0.23 (n=28)	0.01 (n=18)	0.00 (n=11)
Mathematics	Gain scores	-0.41 (n=36)	-0.16 (n=36)	-0.42 (n=29)	0.11 (n=19)	0.32 (n=11)
	Regression	-0.41 (n=36)	-0.16 (n=36)	-0.41 (n=29)	0.13 (n=19)	0.29 (n=11)

NOTE: We were unable to test the significance of the estimates derived through the regression approach because this would require the standard error of the predicted value, which does not follow easily from the estimation, and because it would require making some untestable assumptions.

APPENDIX F

Comparison of Schools with Large and Small Enrollment Change Between Y0 and Y1

As discussed in Chapter Six, we compared achievement results for Edison schools that experienced less than 15 percent enrollment change between Y0 and Y1 to the results for schools that experienced greater than 15 percent change. The results, in Table F.1, show that relatively large enrollment change was not associated with weaker achievement outcomes. If anything, schools that experienced more than 15 percent enrollment change performed slightly better than other schools, though the sample sizes are quite small for this group.

Table F.1
Comparison of Y0 Baseline Results for Edison Schools That Experienced Less Than 15 Percent Enrollment Change and Those That Experienced Greater Than 15 Percent Enrollment Change Between Y0 and Y1

		Y1	Y2	Y3	Y4	Y5
Reading	Less than 15% change	-0.30* (n=36)	-0.20 (n=36)	-0.28 (n=21)	-0.18 (n=10)	-0.06 (n=6)
	Greater than 15% change	-0.27* (n=13)	-0.18 (n=13)	0.06 (n=9)	0.34 (n=7)	0.04 (n=4)
Mathematics	Less than 15% change	-0.37* (n=36)	-0.21 (n=35)	-0.55* (n=21)	-0.04 (n=10)	0.33 (n=6)
	Greater than 15% change	-0.15 (n=12)	0.05 (n=12)	0.07 (n=9)	0.37 (n=7)	0.04 (n=4)

NOTE: * indicates statistical significance at $p < 0.05$.

APPENDIX G

Changes in Demographic Characteristics of Edison Students Through Years Four and Five

Table G.1
Changes in Percent Minority for Edison Schools and Comparison Schools

Baseline	Final Year	Change in Edison Schools	Change in Comparison Schools	Difference	Number of Edison Schools
Y0	Y4	7.1	3.0	4.1	13
Y0	Y5	5.1	3.5	1.6	7
Y1	Y4	4.6	2.8	1.8	38
Y1	Y5	5.8	3.5	2.3	22

Table G.2
Changes in Percent Free or Reduced-Price Lunch for Edison Schools and Comparison Schools

Baseline	Final Year	Change in Edison Schools	Change in Comparison Schools	Difference	Number of Edison Schools
Y0	Y4	-0.1	0.2	-0.3	12
Y0	Y5	0.9	-0.4	1.3	7
Y1	Y4	-0.1	2.2	-2.3	33
Y1	Y5	-0.5	1.8	-2.3	20

APPENDIX H

Comparison of Results for Philadelphia Schools and Other Schools

We examine Edison-wide achievement trends separately for Philadelphia because there is reason to believe that the implementation of Edison's design was compromised, at least initially. Philadelphia schools were in their second year of operation in 2003–2004, and all of them were preexisting public schools that were turned over to Edison management. Therefore, we are able to examine test-score trends in Philadelphia from both the Y1 and Y0 baselines. These are presented in Tables H.1 and H.2, respectively. The results suggest that Philadelphia's Edison schools did at least as well as other schools on average and that their achievement was not unduly hindered by any implementation problems that might have occurred in Philadelphia.

Table H.1
Differences in Z-Score Changes in Reading and Mathematics from Y1 Baseline for Philadelphia Schools and Other Schools

		Y2
Reading	Philadelphia schools	0.17 (n=19)
	All other schools	-0.06 (n=97)
Mathematics	Philadelphia schools	0.17 (n=18)
	All other schools	0.02 (n=94)

Table H.2
Differences in Z-Score Changes in Reading and Mathematics from Y0 Baseline for Philadelphia Schools and Other Schools

		Y1	Y2
Reading	Philadelphia schools	-0.22 (n=19)	-0.10 (n=19)
	All other schools	-0.33 (n=32)	-0.23 (n=32)
Mathematics	Philadelphia schools	-0.05 (n=18)	-0.08 (n=18)
	All other schools	-0.46 (n=32)	-0.19 (n=31)

APPENDIX I

Comparison of Recent Change Analyses Using District Versus State Comparison Schools

Table I.1 shows the results of the one- and two-year change analyses using state and district comparison schools. Only those Edison schools that could be included in both analyses (i.e., those for which both state and district comparison schools could be identified) are included here, so any difference in results for state versus district comparison schools is a result of differences in achievement trends among the comparison schools and is not due to differences in the Edison schools included in each analysis. In the one-year change analysis, the state comparison schools favored Edison for mathematics and the district comparison schools favored Edison for reading, but the differences were small in all cases. In the two-year analysis, by contrast, the district comparison schools consistently produced results more favorable to Edison.

Table I.1
One- and Two-Year Changes in Reading and Mathematics, 2003–2004, for State vs. District Comparison Schools Using a Common Set of Edison Schools

	Difference in Percent Proficient Changes, One-Year Analysis (2003–2004)		Difference in Percent Proficient Changes, Two-Year Analysis (2002–2004)	
Reading: State	2.48	(n=58)	2.77	(n=29)
Reading: District	3.10	(n=58)	5.97*	(n=29)
Mathematics: State	4.68*	(n=55)	3.13	(n=29)
Mathematics: District	3.76*	(n=55)	5.43	(n=29)

NOTE: * indicates statistical significance at $p < 0.05$.

APPENDIX J

Comparison of Y1 and Y0 Results Using District Versus State Comparison Schools

Table J.1 shows the Y1 results obtained with district and state comparison schools, using a common set of Edison schools for both conditions. In other words, this analysis includes only those Edison schools for which both state and district comparison schools could be identified, which means many Edison schools in small districts are excluded. Its purpose is to illustrate how the choice of comparison schools affects the Edison achievement effects estimates while holding constant the specific Edison schools included in each condition. From a Y1 baseline, the choice of state versus district comparison schools has virtually no effect on the reading estimates. For mathematics, the district comparison schools are slightly more favorable to Edison than the state comparison schools.

Table J.1
Differences in Z-Score Changes in Reading and Mathematics from Y1 Baseline, District and State Comparison Schools Using a Common Set of Edison Schools

	Y2	Y3	Y4	Y5	Y6
Reading: State comps	-0.01 (n=80)	0.07 (n=52)	0.23* (n=35)	0.58* (n=19)	0.15 (n=12)
Reading: District comps	-0.05 (n=80)	0.09 (n=52)	0.29* (n=35)	0.57* (n=19)	0.09 (n=12)
Mathematics: State comps	-0.03 (n=78)	-0.09 (n=54)	0.29* (n=38)	0.63* (n=18)	0.39 (n=10)
Mathematics: District comps	-0.07 (n=78)	0.04 (n=54)	0.29 (n=38)	0.70* (n=18)	0.63* (n=10)

NOTE: * indicates statistical significance at $p < 0.05$.

Table J.2 provides the Y0 results using a common set of Edison schools for the state and district comparison schools analyses. In some cases, the use of district comparison schools favors Edison, whereas in other cases the state comparisons do. Again, most of the differences are small.

Table J.2
Differences in Z-Score Changes in Reading and Mathematics from Y0 Baseline, District and State Comparison Schools Using a Common Set of Edison Schools

	Y2	Y3	Y4	Y5	Y6
Reading: State comps	-0.25* (n=44)	-0.17 (n=44)	-0.10 (n=25)	0.18 (n=15)	0.16 (n=9)
Reading: District comps	-0.22* (n=44)	-0.20 (n=44)	0.11 (n=25)	0.17 (n=15)	0.09 (n=9)
Mathematics: State comps	-0.31* (n=43)	-0.16 (n=43)	-0.38* (n=25)	0.06 (n=16)	0.28 (n=9)
Mathematics: District comps	-0.33* (n=43)	-0.23* (n=43)	-0.19 (n=25)	-0.25 (n=16)	0.37 (n=9)

NOTE: * indicates statistical significance at $p < 0.05$.

APPENDIX K

Supplemental Analyses to Explore the Y0 Results

As noted in Chapter Six, there are several concerns about the analyses that use a Y0 baseline:

1. Student populations in Edison schools sometimes change substantially at the time of Edison's takeover, which may undermine the comparability of the school's test scores before and after Edison's entry into the school. The students who enter the Edison school might be either more or less disadvantaged than those who leave it, depending on local circumstances and the other options available to students.
2. Edison begins operating a school in the fall, and any changes in school performance that occur after the spring test but prior to Edison's management will be attributed to Edison. Moreover, a few schools saw unusually large spikes in achievement in Y0, and there may have been test irregularities that inflated scores that year.
3. A substantial minority of Edison schools, typically charter schools, initially opened as Edison schools. For those schools, no scores exist for Y0. Their performance can be examined only from Y1 forward.

We address each of these points below. We find no evidence that the population change creates a bias in results, though we cannot prove definitively that there is no such bias. The second issue can be addressed with a careful definition of the Edison effect and exclusion of a small number of cases with implausible score fluctuations. The third point cannot be definitively addressed, and describes a problem that is inherent in all studies of new start-up schools. It does not affect the validity of inferences about performance in schools that convert to Edison status, but does undermine generalization of Y0 results to start-up schools. Nevertheless, other studies of charter schools suggest that a first-year dip in performance is a common phenomenon (Sass, undated; Bifulco and Ladd, 2003; Booker et al., 2004; Hanushek, Kain, and Rivkin, 2002; Solmon, Paark, and Garcia, 2001). Finally, qualitative evidence from our case studies is consistent with the expectation of lower performance in the first year, followed by improvement.

Population Comparability in Y0 and Y1

Results relying on school-level trends from a Y0 baseline would be deceptive if the characteristics of students enrolled in the school after it shifts to Edison management differ in systematic ways from the characteristics of students who were enrolled in the school before the management change.[1] Edison might end up with harder-to-educate students as a result of enrollment decisions made by parents or district staff at the time of the Edison takeover. For example, according to our conversations with Edison staff, at the time of takeover, some schools faced parental resistance resulting in a loss of some students, and others were impeded by district personnel who did not effectively manage applications to the school. If such events occur systematically at the time Edison begins operating schools, then the apparent first-year decline could merely reflect a change in the population of students in the schools rather than a decline in the school's performance.

Alternately, Edison schools might experience the opposite effect—attracting high-performing students and their parents, while

[1] Of course, population changes in subsequent years also undermine the comparability of results over time, but as we discuss later, changes in the first year seem to be more widespread than in later years.

lower-performing students may be reluctant to accept the demands of the program or may even be discouraged from remaining in or entering the Edison school. This type of cream skimming is a concern expressed by many analysts seeking to understand the effects of school choice (see, e.g., Lee and Croninger, 1994; Lacireno-Paquet et al., 2002). If cream skimming were occurring in Edison schools, our estimates of first-year changes relative to comparison schools would be too favorable toward Edison.

Unfortunately, except in a small subset of Edison schools, we lack the student-level data necessary to determine definitively whether the apparent first-year decline in the scores is the result of student population change rather than school performance. Nevertheless, we examine a variety of circumstantial evidence that might provide indications of whether population change is especially likely to undermine the validity of the Y0 baseline. Because the first-year estimates are negative, we focus on exploring the possibility that first-year changes result in estimates that are biased against Edison rather than on the possibility of cream skimming. Together, the evidence does not suggest that population changes are the source of the first-year decline, although it cannot definitively rule out the possibility. These analyses are described in detail below; we summarize the results here:

1. Average changes in total enrollment in Edison schools are somewhat larger in the first operation year than in other years, but changes in the demographic composition of the enrollment (as measured by race or ethnicity and poverty) are negligible.
2. Edison schools with larger first-year enrollment changes (i.e., greater than 15 percent) do not have larger declines in achievement than schools with small first-year enrollment changes (less than 15 percent).
3. In most of the 13 schools for which student-level data were available, the population of students who were in the school in Y1 did not have lower average pre-Edison scores than students who were in the school in Y0. In other words, population changes in those schools did not leave Edison with lower-achieving students than were previously enrolled in the schools.

Moreover, Y0 school-level estimates of performance for those schools generally corresponded with student-level estimates of their performance, with no bias in either direction evident.

4. For the 20 Edison schools in Philadelphia, we have baseline scores from both spring of Y0 (on the state exam) and fall of Y1 (on a district-administered Terra Nova exam, a commercially available standardized achievement test). If a population change between Y0 and Y1 is driving results, we would expect Edison's results to be more favorable from fall Y1 than from spring Y0. In fact, Edison's fall-to-spring score changes on the Terra Nova test in its first year in Philadelphia are no better than its spring-Y0-to-spring-Y1 results for the state exam (relative to comparison schools). The use of Y0 test scores therefore does not underestimate Edison's first-year effect in its Philadelphia schools.

Analysis of Aggregate Enrollment and Demographic Changes

First, we examine the demographic and enrollment changes in Edison schools that had existed prior to Edison operation (so the sample excludes all start-up schools). We were particularly interested in understanding the magnitude of enrollment change between Y0 and Y1, whether it was associated with changes in the types of students (as measured by demographics) enrolled in the schools, and whether it appeared to be larger than the change that occurred during a subsequent transition (i.e., between Y1 and Y2).

To answer these questions, we first examine the demographic and enrollment changes of Edison schools that had existed prior to Edison operation, which would exclude all start-up contract and charter schools. In total, we examine the enrollment and demographic changes of 86 Edison schools using Common Core Data (CCD) from the National Center for Education Statistics (NCES). The CCD data include total enrollment and enrollment by race and free

Table K.1
Percent Changes in Demographics and Enrollment in Y1 from Y0 (n=86)

Percent Change in Hispanic and Black Students	Percent Change in Free and Reduced-Price Lunch Students	Percent Absolute Value Change in Enrollment
1.1	-0.6	20.1

and reduced-price lunch status for Edison schools over years. We use these data to calculate the percent change in enrollment, Hispanic and black students, and free and reduced-price lunch students. We should note that the enrollment changes are measured in absolute values, so that large enrollment drops and gains from school to school do not offset each other. Absolute values address the issue with which we are grappling: whether there are large changes in enrollment (in either direction) at Edison schools.

Table K.1 shows the results, and reveal that there is, on average, a substantial change in enrollment for Edison schools in the first year of operation. Moreover, the average 20-percent enrollment change (which most often involves an increase rather than a decline in enrollment) is substantially greater than the average enrollment change in the subsequent year, which is only 11 percent. However, the results do not suggest a substantial change in the types of students Edison schools enroll, as the percent of Hispanic and black students increased by 1.1 percent, and the percent of students that participate in the free and reduced-price lunch program dropped by 0.6. Given the substantial change in enrollment in the transition year for Edison schools, we next turn to the student-level data to see if these data can shed greater light on whether using Y0 may bias our results.

Relationship Between Enrollment Changes and Achievement Changes at the School Level

To explore the extent to which performance changes might be attributable to enrollment changes, we examined whether schools that experienced an enrollment change of 15 percent or more differed in their achievement trends from schools that experienced a change of less than 15 percent. The schools that had been excluded from the earlier analyses as a result of extremely large enrollment changes, large demographic changes, or possible testing irregularities were also excluded from this analysis. We find no evidence that larger enrollment changes are associated with reduced levels of achievement (see Appendix F for details). In particular, the operation Y1 results from the Y0 baseline for reading are essentially equivalent for schools with greater than 15-percent change in enrollment and those with less than 15-percent change in enrollment, regardless of how comparison schools are chosen. For math, schools with less than 15-percent change in enrollment had lower Y1 achievement relative to comparison schools than schools with greater than 15-percent change in enrollment, again regardless of how comparison schools are chosen. This latter pattern is opposite of what would be expected if new Edison students tended to be lower scoring than students already enrolled in the school. Indeed, in both reading and mathematics, Edison schools that had larger test-score gains than their comparison schools had larger enrollment changes on average than Edison schools that did not surpass their comparison schools.

It is possible that shifts in student characteristics that are independent of enrollment changes might be driving the observed first-year declines. This analysis cannot rule out that possibility. Nevertheless, it provides no evidence that population changes are driving the results, and no evidence that results from the Y0 baseline are biased against Edison.

Examination of Population Changes and Achievement Changes Using Student-Level Data

So far, all analyses we have described have used school-level data, which allow us to examine changes in enrollments but not changes in student populations (i.e., we know the number of students enrolled each year but have no way to determine how many of the same students remained enrolled the following year). We conducted a set of analyses using student-level data in a subset of Edison schools for which they are available to understand the likely effects of enrollment changes. These data allow us determine whether the students who were enrolled in the school in the first year of Edison management differ in average pre-Edison achievement from those who were enrolled in the school in Y0, before Edison took over. We describe our student-level data and analytic approach before turning to the results.

Student-level data. As we noted in Chapter Five, we attempted to obtain student-level data for Edison and comparison schools from as many schools and districts as possible, but ultimately were able to secure only a small number of agreements from districts to obtain these data.

We were able to obtain student-level data from nine districts (Chicago; Chula Vista, California; Dallas; Fresno; Long Beach; Napa Valley; West Covina, California; Wichita; and Tyler, Texas) representing 16 separate Edison schools. In all but two of these districts (Dallas and Tyler) the outcome measure of performance was normal curve equivalents (NCEs). The outcome measure in Dallas and Tyler was the Texas Learning Index (TLI), which is a transformation of scores on the state's accountability test. All of these data files included student identifiers that allowed us to track students over time.

The student-level data could be used to examine student achievement in a subset of Edison schools, but because the schools for which we have student-level data are not representative of the entire population of Edison schools, they do not allow us to make inferences about Edison's overall performance. However, they can be used to inform our broader, school-level analysis in two ways. First, they enable us to examine relationships between population changes and achievement changes in these schools. Second, they allow us to examine the correspondence between the school-level and student-level analytic approaches. Below, we briefly describe our approach to analyzing the student-level data. The results are discussed in Chapter Six.

Achievement analyses using student-level data. The student-level analysis provides the best estimates of Edison's performance for the subset of schools with student-level data, because it allows the tracking of individual student performance over time. Utilizing this feature, we estimate a student fixed-effects model, in which each student serves as his or her own control. Effects are identified by students who switched in and out of a school managed by Edison, including students who switched into a school while it was under

Edison management as well as students who remained in the same school and were tracked prior to and during Edison management of the school.[2] Formally, our model is as follows:

$$Y_{it} = \mathcal{M}_{gt} + \alpha_i + \gamma S_{it} + \delta_{e(t)} E_{it} + e_{it}.$$

Y_{it} is the NCE/TLI score for a given student *i* in year *t*. We let *g* index grade level. We need to distinguish grade levels from years because our data contain multiple cohorts.[3]

$\mathcal{M}_{gt}$ is a grade- and year-specific mean (with *g* in this particular case being the grade of student *i* in year *t*).[4] We considered models that allowed each grade and year to have a separate marginal mean, as well as those that allowed only temporal trends, assuming that these trends applied to all grades ($\mathcal{M}_{gt}$ versus $\mathcal{M}_t$). The motivation for this was to explore the sensitivity of our estimated effects to different assumptions about the marginal mean structure. The substantive findings were not affected by this choice.

The term α_i is a fixed student-specific effect that accounts for constant level effects on Y_{it} of all stable student characteristics. We did not have any time-varying student characteristics other than school attendance in our data. Including student fixed effects in the models is a powerful tool for removing potential bias due to unobserved student characteristics, and is a commonly applied analytical

---

[2] In some cases, we were also able to track students after they left an Edison school.

[3] For all models, *g* is allowed to span the minimum and maximum tested grade level ever observed for a student who attended an Edison school at some point. In all cases, this includes at least the tested grade levels spanned by the Edison school, and in general can extend beyond this to allow for observing students prior to, and after, attending an Edison school. In a few cases, we truncated the grade spans to reasonably populated ranges of grade levels; for example, if only a few (less than five) students who ever attended an Edison school were observed in a particularly high or low grade, we did not include these grades in the analysis.

[4] Grade-specific means are necessary when modeling scores on a vertically equated scale. Although in our case we modeled NCEs and TLIs, which do not necessarily grow across grades, it is still potentially useful to include the terms to capture any cohort or test variations. Similarly, including means that vary with time can also help to capture cohort differences as well as systematic changes over time (e.g., students learning how to take exams).

approach for estimating school effects with longitudinal student achievement data (Solmon, Paark, and Garcia, 2001; Hanushek, Kain, and Rivkin, 2002; Bifulco and Ladd, 2003; Zimmer et al., 2003; Booker et al., 2004). The result of including such effects in the models is that the other terms in the model are estimated relative to each individual student's average performance in terms of the outcomes Y_{it}. For example, the performance of a student while under Edison management is compared to that same student's performance while not under Edison management.

The term S_{it} is an indicator of school switching, taking on the value 1 if the student switched schools from year $t-1$ to year t and 0 otherwise, with fixed effect γ.[5] The term is included to control for any systematic changes in performance related to school switching.[6] In some instances, it has been demonstrated that switching schools may affect achievement during the year switched (Hanushek, Kain, and Rivkin, 2004).

The term of greatest interest is E_{it}, which is an indicator of Edison attendance in time t, with associated effects $\delta_{e(t)}$. The index $e(t)$ takes on the value 1 for the first school year under Edison management, 2 for the second school year under Edison management, and so on. That is, we let the Edison effects vary as a function of the number of years that the school has been operated by Edison.[7]

---

[5] There are some imperfections with this variable, most notably the fact that we cannot observe $S_{it} = 1$ for the earliest record available for each student in our dataset. More specifically, we can observe school switching only within the district; if a student appears in the middle of the data series without being in the prior series, we might assume that $S_{it} = 1$, but we cannot be sure. Because we were concerned that S_{it} cannot be known properly for all students (in that there are almost certainly cases where we assume that $S_{it} = 0$ when indeed $S_{it} = 1$), we wanted to understand how the inclusion or exclusion of this variable affected our inferences. The inferences about the parameters of interest were negligibly impacted by whether or not we controlled for school switching.

[6] Note that students who were in a school prior to it coming under Edison management are not considered to have switched schools when the school came under Edison management.

[7] In the one district of the nine where not all of the Edison schools in the district came under Edison management during the same school year (Wichita), we made sure the effect was defined correctly, with the schools being associated the time-varying effects appropriate to their particular time courses. We also adjusted the Wichita data because the district used a

The final term of the model, e_{it}, is a residual error term assumed to be independent and identically distributed both across and within students, with constant variance.

In addition to the sensitivity tests about how to model the marginal mean structure and whether or not school switching was accounted for, we carried out some additional analyses that explored the sensitivity to the set of students included in the estimation. We fit the model after eliminating all students who only ever attended non-Edison schools with lower percentages of minority students than the Edison school. We also fit the model after eliminating all students who ever attended a non-Edison school with school-level aggregate achievement substantially different than the Edison school. The idea in both of these cases was to eliminate students who ever attended schools that looked nothing like the Edison school in terms of student demographics and achievement. Neither of these restrictions had an appreciable impact on the estimated Edison effects.

Analysis of student population change using student-level data. In addition to using the student-level data to examine achievement trends, we also used them to assess the extent to which the conversion to Edison management was associated with a change in student population with respect to achievement. Our student-level achievement data included at least one year of pre-Edison data for 13 Edison schools (including seven in Dallas; the remaining six were from distinct school districts). These pre-Edison data allowed us to examine whether the population of students who were enrolled in the school during the first year of Edison management were lower achieving or higher achieving on average than the students who were enrolled in the school prior to Edison management. We addressed this as follows. Let the Edison school have grades ranging from g_1 to g_n. We then compared the following two quantities:

---

fall rather than a spring test. Specifically, the outcome measured by the fall test in year T was attributed to the school the student attended in year $T-1$ rather than to the school the student attended in year T.

1. the average Y0 score for students who were in the Edison school during Y0 (i.e., prior to Edison takeover) and in grades g_1 to g_{n-1}
2. the average Y0 score for students who were in the Edison school during Y1 and in grades g_2 to g_n.

We compared these values separately for each school and subject. The two quantities would be exactly equal if there were no student turnover and all students progressed grade levels. Even with student turnover, the two quantities should be approximately equal provided that there was no systematic shift in the school's composition. A large difference in the two quantities is evidence that the conversion of the school to Edison management corresponded with a systematic shift in the population of students served by the school.

Results. In total, we have student-level test score data from Y0 and Y1 for 13 schools. However, we do not have pre-Edison enrollment data for one of these schools. The remaining 12 schools for which we have enrollment data from before their first year of operation, like other Edison schools, showed a substantial first-year enrollment change (17 percent, versus 20 percent among the larger Edison population). Because we have test-score data for all 13 schools, we compare the Y0 and Y1 scores for students enrolled in Y0 and for students enrolled in Y1. In 11 of 13 cases for math and 10 of 13 cases for reading, the population of students who were in the school in Y1 had slightly higher average pre-Edison scores than the students who were in the school in Y0. In other words, to the extent that the student populations changed between Y0 and Y1, in a majority of cases the population of students in the school after Edison entered was higher achieving than the pre-Edison population. In the cases in which the population in the school in Y0 had the higher scores, the differences were on the order of one to two points (on the NCE and TLI scales described earlier) or smaller.

This analysis shows that in most of the Edison schools with student-level data, use of a Y0 baseline in a school-level analysis would actually bias results in favor of Edison, not against Edison. To be sure, these 13 schools may not be representative of the total population of Edison schools. Given the uncertainty about whether the schools are representative, the analysis of their enrollment changes cannot be considered definitive. Nonetheless, it provides no evidence that population changes bias the Y0 baseline results against Edison.

In a related set of analyses, we examine the correspondence between school- and student-level trends in achievement between Y0 and Y1 in the schools with student-level data. In these schools, we can examine score changes for the students who remained in the school over time and compare these with the changes in scores for the total school population. In 18 out of 22 cases (mathematics and reading scores in each of 11 schools), the signs of the score changes correspond. Of the four comparisons in which they do not correspond, Edison fares better using student-level data in two and using school-level data in the other two. We did this comparison using both state and district comparison schools for the school-level analyses, and the results were the same in both cases. Again, the results are not definitive, but again, they provide no evidence that the Y0 analysis is biased against Edison.

Analysis of Fall-to-Spring Score Changes in Philadelphia

Finally, we used Philadelphia data, which include fall-to-spring scores for both Edison schools and comparison schools during Edison's first year in the district, to assess the extent to which our results would change if we used a fall Y1 rather than a spring Y0 baseline in Philadelphia. Although this analysis does not address enrollment changes directly, it provides information about the likelihood of bias resulting from using the spring Y0 scores; this bias might result from enrollment change or from other factors discussed in the next section. Unfortunately we do not have this type of data in other districts and therefore cannot conduct a comprehensive analysis of Edison schools' performance from a fall Y1 baseline. We simply use Philadelphia as one additional source of evidence to assess the likelihood that results from a Y0 baseline are biased against Edison.

Table K.2
Differences in Fall-to-Spring Y1 Changes in Terra Nova Z-Scores Versus Differences in Spring Y0 to Spring Y1 Changes in PSSA Z-Scores for Philadelphia Schools, Against Comparison Schools Within Philadelphia

	Fall-to-Spring Y1 Terra Nova Z-Score Difference	Spring Y0 to Spring Y1 PSSA Z-Score Difference
Mathematics	-0.12	-0.03
Reading	-0.32	-0.20

If the Y0 baseline results are biased against Edison in Philadelphia, then we would expect to see better results for Edison when examining relative gains from fall to spring of the first year, versus examining relative gains from spring Y0 to spring Y1. Table K.2 presents Edison's z-score changes in Terra Nova scores from fall to spring of Y1 relative to within-district comparison schools (selected using the same criteria we use for the main achievement analyses, i.e., matched on demographics and baseline scores),[8] alongside Edison's z-score changes in Pennsylvania System of School Assessment (PSSA) scores from spring Y0 to spring Y1 relative to within-district comparison schools.

As the table indicates, Edison's fall-to-spring Terra Nova results in its first year in Philadelphia are no better than its spring Y0 to spring Y1 results for the state exam. The use of Y0 test scores therefore does not underestimate Edison's first-year effect in its Philadelphia schools. Once again, the results are not definitive because they include only a sample of Edison schools; the Philadelphia schools may well differ from other Edison schools. Once again, however, the analysis provides no evidence that results from a Y0 baseline are biased against Edison.

Together, these various analyses do not provide any evidence that Y0-to-Y1 population changes cause results from a Y0 baseline to be biased against Edison. Each of the analyses provides an incomplete

---

8 The Terra Nova results exclude six Edison schools in Philadelphia because they could not be matched on baseline scores as well as demographics. Matching on demographics only, however, the results are virtually unchanged using 19 Edison schools.

picture of the total population of Edison schools, and none of them provides definitive evidence that the Y0 baseline is not biased against Edison. In particular, the schools for which we have student-level data and the Philadelphia schools may not be representative of the entire population of Edison schools. By presenting this circumstantial evidence, we intend to provide the reader with all of the information available to help determine which baseline is most appropriate, but we do not claim to have resolved this issue definitively.

Performance Changes Prior to Edison's Management

Apart from the possibility of a change in student populations, there are two factors related to changes in school operations in the months preceding Edison's management that could undermine the validity of Y0 scores for baseline purposes. First, it is possible that test irregularities designed to raise scores may have occurred in some schools seeking to avoid being converted to Edison management. As we noted earlier, we identified cases where this appeared to be a possibility, and removed them from the analysis. Although there is no guarantee that we identified every such case, it is unlikely that inappropriate practices in the remaining schools are sufficiently widespread to affect our results in a meaningful way.

A second concern about operational changes in the months prior to Edison's takeover of a school is that testing occurs several months before the initiation of Edison management. Schools remain in session for some time after spring testing. While some schools may respond to the threat of an Edison takeover by taking extraordinary measures to raise test scores, other schools may respond as lame ducks, leading to academic losses after testing that are then unfairly attributed to Edison. The decision to transfer management to Edison may negatively affect staff morale and cause disruptions during the spring prior to Edison's management beginning. In short, it is possible that observed declines from spring of the pre-Edison year to spring of Edison's first year, if not attributable to population change, are attributable to events occurring in the school prior to Edison's arrival. We do not have specific evidence that such disruptions occurred, but it was a concern some Edison staff expressed.

An accurate estimate of the effect that Edison's programs have on a student would take as the starting point the student's achievement level at the time when Edison's management of the school begins (or, for students who enter the school in later years, their achievement levels at the time they enter the Edison school). But beyond the specific program effects, an understanding of how a school's transfer to Edison management affects students should also address any effects of the transition in management. An estimate of the effect of the transfer should include any change in performance that results from this pre-Edison disruption, even though that change was not Edison's fault.[9]

The ideal analysis, therefore, would provide separate estimates of Edison's direct program effects on student achievement and of the larger effect of turning over a school to Edison's management. These distinct effects would involve distinct baselines: Assessing the direct effect of Edison programs would ideally use a baseline score from the beginning of the school's first year under Edison management, while assessing the larger effect of turning over a school to Edison's management would require an earlier baseline that can capture any changes occurring in anticipation of the management change.

Unfortunately, most state tests are given only in the spring, which provides a reasonable baseline for assessing the overall effect of the management change, but leaves us with no way to parse the pre-Edison score changes to determine what portion of them are due to the Edison program and what portion are due to anticipatory changes occurring prior to Edison's arrival.[10]

---

[9] Indeed, from a policy perspective, it is important to understand what is likely to happen to a public school that is turned over to a private manager, even if some of the changes that occur cannot be directly attributed to that manager, but result from other factors associated with the management change. Given the accountability system imposed by NCLB, school boards and superintendents need to be aware of a possible one-year decline in school-level test results, regardless of the cause to which they attribute that decline.

[10] One way to understand the role of pre-Edison events is to examine fall-to-spring test-score changes during Edison's first year. Edison has fall and spring scores in its first year in several

As discussed earlier, in Philadelphia, which is the only district for which fall and spring scores are available for both Edison schools and their comparison schools, we find no evidence that spring-to-spring comparisons are biased against Edison relative to fall-to-spring comparisons.

Unfortunately, Philadelphia is the only Edison site where such an analysis is possible. Nevertheless, even if Philadelphia is unusual, and in other locations the Y0 baseline captures a small amount of pre-Edison effect that is not directly attributable to Edison's programs and operations, for the purposes of estimating a causal effect of the management change it is a useful measure.

Start-Up Schools Lacking Y0 Scores

A third major limitation of the Y0 baseline is the lack of availability of Y0 scores for many schools. The Y1 analysis includes nearly all the Edison schools, while the Y0 analysis necessarily includes only conversion schools, leaving out Edison's new start-up schools (typically charter schools), for which no Y0 scores exist. If Edison's conversion schools are doing dramatically worse than its start-up schools, then the difference in samples could be responsible for the difference between results from Y1 and results from Y0. To determine the extent to which the discrepancy is attributable to the inclusion of different schools, we compare the Y0 and Y1 analyses using only conversion schools that could be included in both analyses. These results appear in Appendix L and indicate that the difference between the results from the Y0 and Y1 baselines remains even when the same schools are included in each analysis. The choice of baseline year, not the difference in samples, is producing the difference in results.

---

schools, most of which show an increase from fall to spring. However, these results are difficult to interpret in the absence of similar data for comparable schools and in light of documented validity problems with fall-to-spring comparisons (including inflation of gains as a result of practice effects, norming problems, and summer achievement losses; see Linn, 2000; Linn et al., 1982; and McCaffrey et al., 2004).

Nevertheless, the difference in samples raises a question about what can be said about the performance of Edison start-up schools, for which no pre-Edison baseline score exists. Indeed, the problem of a missing pretreatment baseline score is inherent in many analyses of charter schools and illustrates why student-level data are critical to understanding the effects of these schools. In this context, although Edison uses the same design in both types of school, the different challenges associated with converting programs and management in an existing school versus creating a new school from scratch might affect the likelihood that schools will be successful at increasing student achievement.

Table K.3 provides the differences in z-score changes for each type of school relative to comparison schools, using the Y1 baseline. In reading, most of the differences between conversion and start-up schools are negligible, with the exception of the third operation year, when start-up schools posted larger (though not statistically significantly so) relative gains than conversion schools. In mathematics, for most operation years, conversion schools achieved larger test-score gains than did start-up schools, relative to comparison schools, though only the Y2 difference is statistically significant.[11]

These results suggest a small advantage for conversion schools in mathematics but not in reading. But interpretation of trends for start-up schools is hindered by the absence of any information on students' achievement changes from a pre-Edison baseline. It is possible that start-up and conversion schools have different first-year effects, and therefore a comparison of these two types of schools from a Y1 baseline is potentially misleading. We lack the information needed to understand any first-year differences, however, so we must rely on the Y1 baseline and use appropriate caution in interpreting the results.

---

[11] We also compared the specific set of schools included in the Y0 analysis with the schools not included in that analysis. These two groups are similar but not identical to the conversion and start-up groups, respectively. We compared the test-score changes between Y1 and each operation year for the two groups and found that, in all cases, the test-score changes from Y1 were similar to or more favorable for the schools included in the Y0 analysis. This pattern was observed both for absolute gains among Edison schools and for gains relative to comparison schools.

Table K.3
Differences in Z-Score Changes in Reading and Mathematics from Y1 Baseline for Conversion and Start-Up Schools

		Y2	Y3	Y4	Y5
Reading	Conversion	0.00 (N=80)	-0.12 (N=56)	0.16 (N=33)	0.27 (N=18)
	Start-up	-0.09 (N=36)	0.11 (N=32)	0.19 (N=25)	0.23 (N=17)
Mathematics	Conversion	0.16* (N=76)	-0.04 (N=54)	0.42 (N=32)	0.67 (N=16)
	Start-up	-0.19* (N=36)	-0.04 (N=33)	0.20 (N=27)	0.39 (N=16)

NOTE: * indicates that the difference between conversion and start-up schools is significantly different from zero at $p < 0.05$.

APPENDIX L

Comparison of Y1 and Y0 Analyses Using a Common Set of Edison Schools

Table L.1 provides a comparison of the Y0 and Y1 results for a common set of schools. The purpose of this comparison was to determine whether the difference we observed between the Y0 and Y1 results could be attributed to the fact that many of the schools included in the Y1 analysis could not be included in the Y0 analysis. As Table L.1 shows, the differences between the two sets of results when a common set of schools is used are large, and only the Y1 baseline shows significant positive effects in years four and five. These findings suggest that something other than the different samples included in the Y0 and Y1 analyses is driving the difference in the results presented in Chapter Six.

Table L.1
Results for Y0 and Y1 Baselines Using a Common Set of Edison Schools

	Y2	Y3	Y4	Y5
Reading: Y0 baseline	-0.18 (n=51)	-0.17 (n=32)	0.06 (n=19)	-0.01 (n=11)
Reading: Y1 baseline	0.04 (n=51)	-0.05 (n=32)	0.24* (n=19)	0.37* (n=11)
Mathematics: Y0 baseline	-0.13 (n=48)	-0.37* (n=32)	0.11 (n=19)	0.32 (n=11)
Mathematics: Y1 baseline	0.17* (n=48)	-0.05 (n=32)	0.39* (n=19)	0.60* (n=11)

NOTE: * indicates statistical significance at $p < 0.05$.

APPENDIX M

Differences in Z-Score Changes for Edison Schools That Were Managed by Edison for at Least Four Years

In the tables that report differences in z-score changes from the Y1 and Y0 baselines, the number of Edison schools varies by operation year (e.g., the number of schools managed for at least one year is larger than the number managed for at least two years). It is possible that the trends shown in these tables are due to differences in the schools included in each estimate rather than to changes in schools' performance. To explore this possibility, we calculated the same estimates using only those schools that have been managed by Edison for at least four years using both the Y1 and the Y0 baselines. These results appear in Tables M.1 and M.2, and show that the trends described in Chapter Six are, by and large, not due to differences in the schools included in each column. We show the results only through Y4 because extending the table to later years would result in an even smaller sample size. However, we examined trends through Y5 and obtained similar results for the schools that were under Edison's management for at least five years.

Table M.1
Differences in Z-Score Changes in Reading and Mathematics from Y1 Baseline for Schools That Were Managed by Edison Through Y4

	Y2	Y3	Y4
Reading	-0.09 (n=58)	0.00 (n=58)	0.17 (n=58)
Mathematics	-0.08 (n=59)	-0.05 (n=59)	0.32 (n=59)

Table M.2
Differences in Z-Score Changes in Reading and Mathematics from Y0 Baseline for Schools That Were Managed by Edison Through Y4

	Y1	Y2	Y3	Y4
Reading	-0.42 (N=19)	-0.25 (N=19)	-0.22 (N=19)	0.06 (N=19)
Mathematics	-0.45 (N=19)	-0.09 (N=19)	-0.35 (N=19)	0.11 (N=19)

References

American Federation of Teachers, *Student Achievement in Edison Schools: Mixed Results in an Ongoing Enterprise*, Washington, D.C.: American Federation of Teachers, 1998.

American Institutes for Research, *An Educators' Guide to Schoolwide Reform*, Arlington, Va.: Educational Research Service, 1999.

Berends, Mark, Sheila Nataraj Kirby, Scott Naftel, and Christopher J. McKelvey, *Implementation and Performance in New American Schools: Three Years into Scale-Up*, Santa Monica, Calif.: RAND Corporation, MR-1145-EDU, 2001. Online at http://www.rand.org/publications/MR/MR1145/ as of June 15, 2005.

Bettinger, Eric P., "The Effect of Charter Schools on Charter Students and Public Schools," *Economics of Education Review*, Vol. 24, No. 2, 2005, pp. 133–147.

Bifulco, Robert, and Helen F. Ladd, *The Impacts of Charter Schools on Student Achievement: Evidence from North Carolina*, Durham, N.C.: Terry Sanford Institute of Public Policy, Duke University, 2003. Online at http://www.pubpol.duke.edu/people/faculty/ladd/san04-01.pdf as of June 17, 2005.

Bodilly, Susan J., *Lessons from New American Schools Development Corporation's Demonstration Phase*, Santa Monica, Calif.: RAND Corporation, MR-729-NASDC, 1996. Online at http://www.rand.org/publications/MR/MR729/ as of June 15, 2005.

———, *Lessons From New American Schools' Scale-Up Phase*, Santa Monica, Calif.: RAND Corporation, MR-942-NAS, 1998. Online at http://www.rand.org/publications/MR/MR942/ as of June 15, 2005.

Bodilly, Susan, and Mark Berends, "Necessary District Support for Comprehensive School Reform," in Gary Orfield and Elizabeth H. DeBray, eds., *Hard Work for Good Schools: Facts Not Fads in Title I Reform*, Cambridge, Mass.: The Civil Rights Project, Harvard University Press, 1999, pp. 111–119.

Booker, Kevin, Scott M. Gilpatric, Timothy Gronberg, and Dennis Jansen, *Charter School Performance in Texas*, College Station, Tex.: Texas A&M University, 2004. Online at http://www.tamu.edu/perc/publication/0410.pdf as of June 17, 2005.

Bryk, Anthony S., and Barbara L. Schneider, *Trust in Schools: A Core Resource for Improvement*, New York, N.Y.: Russell Sage Foundation, 2002.

Bulkley, Katrina, Leah Mundell, and Morgan Riffer, Contracting Out Schools: The First Year of the Philadelphia Diverse Provider Model, Philadelphia, Pa.: Research for Action, 2004. Online at http://www.researchforaction.org/PSR/PublishedWorks/COS051004.pdf as of September 8, 2005.

Catterall, J. S., *Different Ways of Knowing: 1991–94 National Longitudinal Study, Program Effects on Students and Teachers (Final Report)*, Los Angeles, Calif.: University of California at Los Angeles, Graduate School of Education and Information Studies, 1995.

Charter Schools Institute, *Report to the Board of Trustees: Findings and Recommendations of the Charter Schools Institute as to the Application for Charter Renewal of the Charter School of Science and Technology*, Albany, N.Y.: Charter Schools Institute, State University of New York, 2005.

Chubb, John E., "The First Few Years of Edison Schools: Ten Lessons in Getting to Scale," in Thomas K. Glennan, Jr., Susan J. Bodilly, Jolene R. Galegher, and Kerri A. Kerr, eds., *Expanding the Reach of Education Reforms: Perspectives from Leaders in the Scale-Up of Educational Interventions*, Santa Monica, Calif.: RAND Corporation, MG-248-FF, 2004, pp. 487–516.

Chubb, John E., and Terry M. Moe, *Politics, Markets, and America's Schools*, Washington, D.C.: Brookings Institution, 1990.

Coburn, Cynthia E., "Collective Sensemaking About Reading: How Teachers Mediate Reading Policy in Their Professional Communities," *Educational Evaluation and Policy Analysis*, Vol. 23, No. 2, 2001, pp. 145–170.

Cochran, William G., and Donald B. Rubin, "Controlling Bias in Observational Studies," *Sankhya: The Indian Journal of Statistics*, Vol. 35, No. 4, 1973, pp. 417–446.

Cohen, Jacob, *Statistical Power Analysis for the Behavioral Sciences*, New York: Academic Press, 1969.

Cookson, Peter W., Katie Embree, and Scott Fahey, *The Edison Partnership Schools: An Assessment of Academic Climate and Classroom Culture*, New York, N.Y.: Teachers College, Columbia University, 2000.

Darling-Hammond, Linda, "Policy and Professionalism," in Ann Lieberman, ed., *Building a Professional Culture in Schools*, New York, N.Y.: Teachers College Press, 1988, pp. 57–77.

———, "Policy for Restructuring," in Ann Lieberman, *The Work of Restructuring Schools: Building from the Ground Up*, New York, N.Y.: Teachers College Press, 1995, pp. 157–175.

———, *The Right to Learn: A Blueprint for Creating Schools That Work*, San Francisco, Calif.: Jossey Bass, 1997.

Datnow, Amanda, "The Sustainability of Comprehensive School Reform Models in Changing District and State Contexts," *Educational Administration Quarterly*, Vol. 41, No. 1, 2005, pp. 121–153.

Dryden, Michael A., "The Performance of Edison Schools Inc. in the Dallas Schools," presented at the American Education Research Association Annual Conference, San Diego, Calif., 2004.

Edison Schools, "A Better Use of Time," undated Web page (a). Online at http://www.edisonschools.com/design/d02.html as of June 15, 2005.

———, "Edison's Inspiration," undated Web page (b). Online at http://www.edisonschools.com/design/research/d_re05.html as of June 15, 2005.

———, "Four Academic Levels," undated Web page (c). Online at http://www.edisonschools.com/design/curriculum/d_cu02.html as of June 15, 2005.

———, "Technology for an Information Age," undated Web page (d). Online at http://www.edisonschools.com/design/technology/d_te0.html as of June 15, 2005.

———, "The Ten Fundamentals Behind Edison's School Design," undated Web page (e). Online at http://www.edisonschools.com/design/designdefault/d0.html as of June 15, 2005.

———, *Annual Report on School Performance*, New York, N.Y.: Edison Schools, 1997.

———, *Second Annual Report on School Performance*, New York, N.Y.: Edison Schools, 1999.

———, *Third Annual Report on School Performance*, New York, N.Y.: Edison Schools, 2000.

———, *Fourth Annual Report on School Performance*, New York, N.Y.: Edison Schools, 2001a.

———, *Strengthening the Performance of the Philadelphia School District: Report to the Governor of Pennsylvania*, 2001b. Online at http://www.philaedfund.org/pdfs/completereport.pdf as of June 10, 2005.

———, "Assessment and Accountability," *Edison Pages*, New York, N.Y.: Edison Schools, 2002a.

———, "School Organization and Administration," *Edison Pages*, New York, N.Y.: Edison Schools, 2002b.

———, "Student Management," *Edison Pages*, New York, N.Y.: Edison Schools, 2002c.

———, *Fifth Annual Report on School Performance*, New York, N.Y.: Edison Schools, 2003.

———, "Edison Schools Applauds Philadelphia School District's Historic Leap in Student Achievement," New York, N.Y.: Edison Schools, August 24, 2004a.

———, *Sixth Annual Report on School Performance*, New York, N.Y.: Edison Schools, 2004b.

———, *Seventh Annual Report on School Performance*, New York, N.Y.: Edison Schools, 2005. Online at http://www.edisonschools.com/design/d23.html as of June 10, 2005.

Evans, W., C. Baugh, J. Sheffer, G. Martin, and R. Scarentino, "Sustained Effects of CSR Programs and the Relationship to No Child Left Behind Requirements," paper presented at the Annual Meeting of the International Reading Association, Reno, Nev., 2004.

Fullan, Michael, *Change Forces: The Sequel*, London, UK: Falmer Press, 1999.

Fullan, M. G., and M. M. Miles, "Getting Reform Right: What Works and What Doesn't," *Phi Delta Kappan*, Vol. 73, No. 10, 1992, pp. 744–752.

Fullan, Michael, and Suzanne M. Stiegelbauer, *The New Meaning of Educational Change*, 2nd ed., Toronto, Ont.: Ontario Institute for Studies in Education, 1991.

GAO. See Government Accountability Office.

Gewertz, Catherine, "Edison Buffeted by Probe, Loss of Contracts," *Education Week*, Vol. 22, No. 1, 2002, p. 3.

———, "Philadelphia Cheers Better Test Scores," *Education Week*, Vol. 24, No. 1, 2004, p. 6.

Gomez, J. J., and S. A. Shay, *Evaluation of the Edison Project School: Third Interim Report: 1998–99 School Year*, Miami, Fla.: Miami-Dade School District, 2000.

Government Accountability Office, *Public Schools: Insufficient Research to Determine Effectiveness of Selected Private Education Companies, Report to the Ranking Minority Member, Subcommittee on the District of Columbia, Committee on Appropriations, House of Representatives*, Washington, D.C.: United States General Accounting Office, October 2002, GAO-03-11. Online at http://www.gao.gov/cgi-bin/getrpt?GAO-03-11 as of June 13, 2005.

———, *Public Schools: Comparison of Achievement Results for Students Attending Privately Managed and Traditional Schools in Six Cities, Report to the Chairman, Committee on Education and the Workforce, House of Representatives*, Washington, D.C.: United States General Accounting Office, October 2003, GAO-04-62. Online at http://www.gao.gov/cgi-bin/getrpt?GAO-04-62 as of June 13, 2005.

Greene, Jay P., Greg Forster, and Marcus A. Winters, *Apples to Apples: An Evaluation of Charter Schools Serving General Student Populations*, New York, N.Y.: The Manhattan Institute, 2003. Online at http://www.manhattan-institute.org/html/ewp_01.htm as of June 21, 2005.

Greene, Jay P., and Marcus A. Winters, "Competition Passes the Test," *Education Next*, Vol. 4, No. 3, 2004, pp. 66–71. Online at http://www.

educationnext.org/20043/66.html and http://www.educationnext.org/20043/pdf/66.pdf as of June 17, 2005.

Gronberg, Timothy J., and Dennis W. Jansen, *Navigating Newly Chartered Waters: An Analysis of Texas Charter School Performance*, Austin, Tex.: Texas Public Policy Foundation, 2001. Online at http://www.texaspolicy.com/pdf/2001-05-17-educ-newly.pdf as of June 17, 2005.

Hamilton, Laura S., "Assessment as a Policy Tool," *Review of Research in Education*, Vol. 27, 2003, pp. 25–68.

Hanushek, Eric A., "Conceptual and Empirical Issues in the Estimation of Educational Production Functions," *Journal of Human Resources*, Vol. 14, No. 3, 1979, pp. 351–388.

Hanushek, Eric A., John F. Kain, and Steven G. Rivkin, *The Impact of Charter Schools on Academic Achievement*, n.p., 2002.

———, "Disruption Versus Tiebout Improvement: The Costs and Benefits of Switching Schools," *Journal of Public Economics*, Vol. 88, No. 9–10, 2004, pp. 1721–1746.

Haynes, Norris M., "Lessons Learned," *Journal of Education for Students Placed at Risk*, Vol. 3, No. 1, 1998, pp. 87–99.

Henriques, Diana B., "Edison Stays Afloat by Altering Course," *The New York Times*, July 3, 2003, pp. C1, C3.

Hentschke, Guilbert C., Scot Oschman, and Lisa Snell, *Trends and Best Practices for Education Management Organizations*, San Francisco, Calif.: WestEd, 2003. Online at http://www.wested.org/online_pubs/PP-03-02.pdf as of June 10, 2005.

Hess, Frederick M., *Spinning Wheels: The Politics of Urban School Reform*, Washington, D.C.: Brookings Institution Press, 1999. Online at http://brookings.nap.edu/books/0815736355/html/index.html as of June 15, 2005.

Hess, G. Alfred, *Restructuring Urban Schools: A Chicago Perspective*, New York, N.Y.: Teachers College Press, Teachers College, Columbia University, 1995.

Hill, Paul T., "Foreword," in Katrina E. Bulkley and Priscilla Wohlstetter, eds., *Taking Account of Charter Schools: What's Happened and What's Next?* New York, N.Y.: Teachers College Press, 2004.

Hill, Paul Thomas, Lawrence C. Pierce, and James W. Guthrie, *Reinventing Public Education: How Contracting Can Transform America's Schools*, Chicago, Ill.: University of Chicago Press, 1997.

Holmes, George Mark, Jeff DeSimone, and Nicholas G. Rupp, *Does School Choice Increase School Quality?* Cambridge, Mass.: National Bureau of Economic Research, 2003. Online at http://www.nber.org/papers/W9683.pdf as of June 17, 2005.

Horn, Jerry G., and Gary Miron, *An Evaluation of the Michigan Charter School Initiative: Performance, Accountability, and Impact*, Kalamazoo, Mich.: The Evaluation Center, Western Michigan University, 2000.

Hoxby, Caroline M., "How School Choice Affects the Achievement of Public School Students," prepared for the Koret Task Force meeting on September 20–21, 2001, Hoover Institution, Stanford, Calif., Cambridge: Harvard University, 2001. Online at http://post.economics.harvard.edu/faculty/hoxby/papers/choice_sep01.pdf as of June 15, 2005.

———, "School Choice and School Competition: Evidence from the United States," *Swedish Economic Policy Review*, Vol. 10, 2003, pp. 9–65. Online at http://www.ekradet.konj.se/sepr/SEPRvol10Nr2/Hoxsby.pdf as of June 14, 2005.

Hoxby, Caroline M., and Jonah E. Rockoff, *The Impact of Charter Schools on Student Achievement: A Study of Students Who Attend Schools Chartered by the Chicago Charter School Foundation*, Cambridge, Mass.: Harvard University, 2004. Online at http://post.economics.harvard.edu/faculty/hoxby/papers/hoxbyrockoff.pdf as of June 15, 2005.

Imbens, Guido, *Nonparametric Estimation of Average Treatment Effects Under Exogeneity: A Review*, Cambridge, Mass.: National Bureau of Economic Research, 2003. Online at http://www.nber.org/papers/T0294.pdf as of June 21, 2005.

Kirby, Sheila Nataraj, Mark Berends, and Scott Naftel, *Implementation in a Longitudinal Sample of New American Schools: Four Years into Scale-Up*, Santa Monica, Calif.: RAND Corporation, MR-1413-EDU, 2001. Online at http://www.rand.org/publications/MR/MR1413/ as of June 15, 2005.

Kirby, Sheila Nataraj, Daniel F. McCaffrey, J. R. Lockwood, Jennifer Sloan McCombs, Scott Naftel, and Heather Barney, "Using State School Accountability Data to Evaluate Federal Programs: A Long Uphill Road," *Peabody Journal of Education*, Vol. 77, No. 4, 2002, pp. 122–145.

Koretz, Daniel, "Using Multiple Measures to Address Perverse Incentives and Score Inflation," *Educational Measurement: Issues and Practice*, Vol. 22, No. 2, 2003, pp. 18–26.

Koretz, Daniel M., Sheila I. Barron, Karen Janice Mitchell, and Brian M. Stecher, *The Perceived Effects of the Kentucky Instructional Results Information System (KIRIS)*, Santa Monica, Calif.: RAND Corporation, MR-792-PCT/FF, 1996.

Lacireno-Paquet, Natalie, Thomas T. Holyoke, Michele Moser, and Jeffrey R. Henig, "Creaming Versus Cropping: Charter School Enrollment Practices in Response to Market Incentives," *Educational Evaluation and Policy Analysis*, Vol. 24, No. 2, 2002, pp. 145–158.

Lee, Valerie E., and Robert G. Croninger, "Parental Choice of Schools and Social Stratification in Education: The Paradox of Detroit," *Education Evaluation and Policy Analysis*, Vol. 16, No. 4, 1994, pp. 434–457.

Lee, Valerie E., Robert G. Croninger, and Julia B. Smith, "Equity and Choice in Detroit," in Bruce Fuller, Richard F. Elmore, and Gary Orfield, eds., *Who Chooses? Who Loses?* New York, N.Y.: Teachers College Press, 1996, pp. 70–94.

Levin, Henry M., *Potential of For-Profit Schools for Educational Reform*, New York, N.Y.: National Center for the Study of Privatization in Education, Teachers College, Columbia University, Occasional Paper No. 47, 2002.

Linn, Robert L., "Assessments and Accountability," *Educational Researcher*, Vol. 29, No. 2, 2000, pp. 4–16.

Linn, Robert L., Stephen B. Dunbar, Delwyn L. Harnisch, and C. Nicholas Hastings, "The Validity of the Title I Evaluation and Reporting System," in Ernest R. House, Sandra Mathison, James A. Pearsol, and Hallie Preskill, eds., *Evaluation Studies Review Annual, Vol. 7*, Beverly Hills, Calif.: Sage Publications, 1982, pp. 427–442.

McCaffrey, Daniel F., Daniel Koretz, J. R. Lockwood, and Laura S. Hamilton, *Evaluating Value-Added Models for Teacher Accountability*, Santa Monica, Calif.: RAND Corporation, MG-158-EDU, 2004. Online at http://www.rand.org/publications/MG/MG158 as of June 20, 2005.

McLaughlin, Milbrey W., and Dana Mitra, "Theory-Based Change and Change-Based Theory: Going Deeper and Going Broader," *Journal of Educational Change*, Vol. 2, No. 4, 2001, pp. 301–323.

Michigan Education Digest, "Edison Spurs Controversy, Reform for Michigan and United States," *Michigan Education Report: News and Analysis for Parents, Educators, and Policy-Makers*, April 25, 2001. Online at http://www.mackinac.org/pubs/mer/article.asp?ID=3412 as of June 10, 2005.

Minneapolis Public Schools, *Edison Project School Information Report*, Minneapolis: Minneapolis Public Schools, 2000.

Miron, Gary, and Brooks Applegate, *An Evaluation of Student Achievement in Edison Schools Opened in 1995 and 1996*, Kalamazoo, Mich.: The Evaluation Center of Western Michigan University, 2000. Online at http://www.wmich.edu/evalctr/edison/wmu_edison_rpt.pdf as of June 10, 2005.

Miron, Gary, Christopher Nelson, and John Risley, *Strengthening Pennsylvania's Charter School Reform: Findings from the Statewide Evaluation and Discussion of Relevant Policy Issues, Year 5 Report*, Kalamazoo, Mich.: Western Michigan University, 2002. Online at http://www.wmich.edu/evalctr/charter/pa_5year as of June 21, 2005.

Molnar, Alex, "Calculating the Benefits and Costs of For-Profit Public Education," *Education Policy Analysis Archives*, Vol. 9, No. 15, 2001. Online at http://epaa.asu.edu/epaa/v9n15.html as of June 21, 2005.

Molner, Alex, David Garcia, Carolyn Sullivan, Brendan McEvoy, and Jamie Joanou, *Profiles for For-Profit Education Management Organizations: 2004–2005*, Tempe, Ariz.: Commercialism in Education Research Unit, Education Policy Studies Laboratory, Arizona State University, 2005. Online at http://www.asu.edu/educ/epsl/EPRU/epru_2005_Research_Writing.htm as of September 8, 2005.

Molnar, Alex, Glen Wilson, and Daniel Allen, *Profiles of For-Profit Education Management Companies: Sixth Annual Report 2003–2004*, Tempe, Ariz.: Commercialism in Education Research Unit, Education Policy Studies Laboratory, Arizona State University, 2004. Online at http://www.asu.edu/educ/epsl/ceru/documents/epsl-0402-101-ceru.pdf.

Nelson, F. Howard, *Trends in Student Achievement for Edison Schools, Inc.: The Emerging Track Record*, Washington, D.C.: American Federation of Teachers, 2000.

Nelson, F. Howard, and Nancy Van Meter, *Update on Student Achievement for Edison Schools Inc.*, Washington, D.C.: American Federation of Teachers, AFL-CIO, 2003.

Newmann, Fred M., and Gary Wehlage, *Successful School Restructuring: A Report to the Public and Educators by the Center on Organization and Restructuring of Schools*, Madison, Wis.: The Center, 1995.

No Child Left Behind Act of 2001. See Public Law 107-110.

Olson, Lynn, "Quality Counts 2005 Examines Changes in School Finance," *Education Week*, Vol. 24, No. 16, 2005, p. 12.

Pedulla, Joseph J., Lisa M. Abrams, George F. Madaus, Michael K. Russell, Miguel A. Ramos, and Jing Miao, *Perceived Effects of State-Mandated Testing Programs on Teaching and Learning: Findings from a National Survey of Teachers*, Chestnut Hill, Mass.: National Board on Educational Testing and Public Policy, 2003.

Pennsylvania Office of the Auditor General, *A Performance Audit of the Pennsylvania Department of Education's Contract with Edison Schools, Inc., to Analyze the Academic and Financial Problems of the Philadelphia School District*, Harrisburg, Pa.: Pennsylvania Office of the Auditor General, 2002. Online at http:// www.auditorgen.state.pa.us/Department/Info/Performance/EdisonAudit.pdf as of June 21, 2005.

Public Law 107-110, *No Child Left Behind Act of 2001*, January 8, 2002.

"Public Schooling for Profit," editorial, *The New York Times*, May 26, 2002, p. 10.

Rhim, Lauren Morando, "School Privatization by Way of a Comprehensive Management Contract: A Single Case Study of the Extent to Which Privatization Theory Transfers to Practice in a Public Charter School," presented at the Annual Meeting of the American Educational Research Association, New Orleans, April 2002.

Rhim, Lauren Morando, *Restructuring Schools in Chester Upland, Pennsylvania: An Analysis of State Restructuring Efforts*, Denver: Education Commission of the States, 2005. Online at http://www.ecs.org/html/Document.asp?chouseid=5794 as of June 15, 2005.

Rivkin, Steven G., Eric A. Hanushek, and John F. Kain, "Teachers, Schools, and Academic Achievement," *Econometrica*, Vol. 73, No. 2, 2005, pp. 417–458.

Rogosa, David, *Student Progress in California Charter Schools, 1999–2002.* Palo Alto, Calif.: Stanford University, 2003. Online at http://www-stat.stanford.edu/~rag/api/charter9902.pdf as of June 21, 2005.

Ross, S. M., J. Nunnery, and L. J. Smith, *Evaluation of Elementary School-Wide Programs: Clover Park School District Year 1: 1996–97*, Memphis, Tenn.: University of Memphis, Center for Research in Educational Policy, 1996.

Ross, Steven M., William L. Sanders, S. Paul Wright, Sam Stringfield, L. Weiping Wang, and Marty Alberg, "Two- and Three-Year Achievement Results from the Memphis Restructuring Initiative," *School Effectiveness and School Improvement*, Vol. 12, No. 3, 2001, pp. 323–346.

Ross, S. M., A. Troutman, D. Horgan, S. Maxwell, R. Laitinen, and D. Lowther, "The Success of Schools in Implementing Eight Restructuring Programs to Schools: Selection, Negotiation, and Preparation," *School Effectiveness and School Improvement*, Vol. 8, No. 1, 1997, pp. 95–124.

Rubin, "Estimating Causal Effects of Treatments in Randomized and Non-Randomized Studies," *Journal of Educational Psychology*, Vol. 66, 1974, pp. 688–701.

Rubin, Donald B., "Assignment to Treatment Group on the Basis of a Covariate," *Journal of Educational Statistics*, Vol. 2, No. 1, 1977, pp. 1–26.

Rubin, Joel, "Are Schools Cheating Poor Learners? Officials Say Federal Rules Compel Them to Focus on Pupils More Likely to Raise Test Scores," *Los Angeles Times*, November 28, 2004, p. B1.

Sanders, William L., and Sandra P. Horn, "Research Findings from the Tennessee Value-Added Assessment System (TVAAS) Database: Implications for Educational Evaluation and Research," *Journal of Personnel Evaluation in Education*, Vol. 12, No. 3, 1998, pp. 247–256.

Sass, Tim R., *Charter Schools and Student Achievement in Florida*, Tallahassee, Fla.: Florida State University, undated.

Shepard, Lorrie A., and Katherine Cutts Dougherty, *Effects of High-Stakes Testing on Instruction*, Chicago, Ill.: Spencer Foundation, 1991.

Slavin, R. E., N. L. Karweit, B. A. Wasik, N. A. Madden, and L. J. Dolan, "Success for All: A Comprehensive Approach to Prevention and Early Intervention," in R. E. Slavin, N. L. Karweit, and B. A. Wasik, eds., *Preventing Early School Failure: Research on Effective Strategies*, Boston, Mass.: Allyn and Bacon, 1994.

Sizer, Theodore R., *Horace's School: Redesigning the American High School*, Boston, Mass.: Houghton Mifflin Co., 1992.

Smith, Lana J., S. Maxwell, Deborah Lowther, Douglas Hacker, Lind Bol, and John Nunnery, "Activities in Schools and Programs Experiencing the Most, and Least, Early Implementation Successes," *School Effectiveness and School Improvement*, Vol. 8, No. 1, 1997, pp. 125–150.

Snyder, S., "Edison Won Fans, But Doubts Linger, Vallas and Other Officials Are Pleased. Critics Point to Cost and Discipline," *Philadelphia Inquirer*, June 13, 2004, p. B01.

Solmon, Lewis, Kern Paark, and David Garcia, *Does Charter School Attendance Improve Test Scores? The Arizona Results*, Phoenix, Ariz.: Goldwater Institute Center for Market-Based Education, 2001. Online at http://www.goldwaterinstitute.org/article.php/111.html as of June 17, 2005.

Spillane, James P., "School Districts Matter: Local Educational Authorities and State Instructional Policy," *Educational Policy*, Vol. 10, No. 1, 1996, pp. 63–87.

Stecher, Brian M., "Consequences of Large-Scale, High-Stakes Testing on School and Classroom Practices," in Laura S. Hamilton, Brian M. Stecher, and Stephen P. Klein, eds., *Making Sense of Test-Based Accountability in Education*, Santa Monica, Calif.: RAND Corporation, MR-1554-EDU, 2002, pp. 79–100. Online at http://www.rand.org/publications/MR/MR1554 as of June 17, 2005.

Stringfield, Sam, Mary Ann Millsap, Linda Winfield, Nancy Brigham, Nancy Yoder, Marc Moss, Pamela Nesselrodt, Eugene Schaffer, Sam Bedinger, and Beth Garnse, *Special Strategies for Educating Disadvantaged Children: Urban and Suburban/Rural, Second Year Report*, Washington, D.C.: Planning and Evaluation Service, U.S. Department of Education, 1997.

Taylor, James E., *Sustainability: Examining the Survival of Schools' Comprehensive School Reform Efforts*, Washington, D.C.: American Institutes for Research, 2005. Online at http://www.air.org/news/documents/

AERA2005Sustainability%20of%20CSR%20Efforts.pdf as of June 17, 2005.

Timar, Thomas, "The Politics of School Restructuring," *Phi Delta Kappan*, Vol. 71, No. 4, 1989, pp. 165–175.

Title I. See U.S. Congress (2005).

U.S. Congress, 20 U.S. Code 6301, Title I (Improving the Academic Achievement of the Disadvantaged), 2005.

U.S. Department of Education, *National Longitudinal School-Level State Assessment Score Database*. Online at http://208.253.216.16/Assessment as of June 17, 2005.

Venezky, R. L., "An Alternative Perspective on Success for All," in K. Wong, ed., *Advances in Educational Policy: Perspectives on the Social Functions of Schools*, Stamford, Conn.: Jai, 1998, pp. 145–165.

Walsh, Mark, "Edison Outlines Strategies to Reassure Wall Street," *Education Week*, Vol. 21, No. 43, August 7, 2002, p. 19.

Wehlage, Gary, Gregory Smith, and Pauline Lipman, "Restructuring Urban Schools: The New Futures Experience," *American Educational Research Journal*, Vol. 29, No. 1, 1992, pp. 51–93.

Whittle, Christopher, interview during "Public Schools Inc.," *Frontline*, Public Broadcasting Service, original air date July 2, 2003. Online at http://www.pbs.org/wgbh/pages/frontline/shows/edison/ as of June 13, 2005.

———, interview with the authors, Pittsburgh, Pa., October 4, 2004.

Wichita State University, *An Independent Program Evaluation for the Dodge-Edison Partnership School: First Year Interim Report*, Wichita, Kan.: Wichita State University, Department of Education Administration, 1996.

Zhang, Yu, Jamie Shkolnik, and Olatokunbo Fashola, *Evaluating the Implementation of Comprehensive School Reform and Its Impact on Growth in Student Achievement*, Washington, D.C.: American Institutes for Research, 2005. Online at http://www.air.org/news/documents/AERA2005Implementation%20of%20CSR-Impact%20on%20Student%20Achievement.pdf as of June 20, 2005.

Zimmer, Ron W., Richard J. Buddin, Derrick Chau, Brian P. Gill, Cassandra M. Guarino, Laura S. Hamilton, Cathy S. Krop, Daniel McCaffrey,

Melissa Sandler, Dominic J. Brewer, *Charter School Operations and Performance: Evidence from California*, Santa Monica, Calif.: RAND Corporation, MR-1700-EDU, 2003. Online at http://www.rand.org/publications/MR/MR1700 as of June 17, 2005.